Get the eBook FREE!
(PDF, ePub, Kindle, and liveBook all included)

We believe that once you buy a book from us, you should be able to read it in any format we have available. To get electronic versions of this book at no additional cost to you, purchase and then register this book at the Manning website.

Go to https://www.manning.com/freebook and follow the instructions to complete your pBook registration.

That's it!
Thanks from Manning!

Praise for the First Edition

"A comprehensive, clear and very practical guide to making the best use of AWS throughout an application's lifecycle. Highly recommended for anyone wanting to use AWS for real-life applications!"
—Alain Couniot, Head of Enterprise Architecture, STIB-MIVB, Belgium

"Peter's tome not only dives deep on Lambda, it also covers all the AWS components your apps will need to run serverless. A soup-to-nuts tour de force. Well done!"
—Sean Hull, Founder, iHeavy, Inc.

"A great introduction for those using AWS, who want to implement a serverless architecture."
—John Huffman, Senior Technical Consultant, Summa Technologies

"This book is a fantastic introduction to serverless architectures and AWS. I wish every technical book was as well written and easy to read! The book walks you step-by-step through building a video portal, including integrating AWS Lambda, API Gateway, S3, auth0 and Firebase. By the end you feel confident not only that you understand all the pieces and how everything fits together, but also that you are ready to start building your own app."
—Kent R. Spillner, Sr. Software Engineer, DRW

Serverless Architectures on AWS

SECOND EDITION

PETER SBARSKI, YAN CUI, AJAY NAIR

MANNING

SHELTER ISLAND

For online information and ordering of this and other Manning books, please visit www.manning.com. The publisher offers discounts on this book when ordered in quantity. For more information, please contact

> Special Sales Department
> Manning Publications Co.
> 20 Baldwin Road
> PO Box 761
> Shelter Island, NY 11964
> Email: orders@manning.com

Manning Publications Co.
20 Baldwin Road
PO Box 761
Shelter Island, NY 11964

Development editor:	Toni Arritola
Technical development editor:	Brent Stains
Review editor:	Aleksandar Dragosavljević
Production editor:	Andy Marinkovich
Copy editor:	Frances Buran
Proofreader:	Jason Everett
Technical proofreader:	Niek Palm
Typesetter:	Gordan Salinovic
Cover designer:	Marija Tudor

ISBN 9781617295423

Printed and bound by CPI Group (UK) Ltd, Croydon, CR0 4YY

*To my mum and dad, who always supported and
encouraged my passion for computing.*

—Peter Sbarski

*To my wife, who always supports and encourages me, and
puts up with all my late-night coding sessions.*

—Yan Cui

*To my wife, my kids, my brother, and my parents, thank you
for giving me the purpose and time to do this.*

—Ajay Nair

contents

preface

Serverless technologies occupy an exciting space at the moment. Products like AWS Lambda and DynamoDB have been around for a few years, yet they still feel new and thrilling, sometimes mysterious or puzzling. Many folks worldwide discuss, learn, and implement systems with serverless architectures, yet we haven't yet seen a mass level of adoption like that of containers. Cloud providers such as AWS continue to grow. However, individuals and organizations still ask questions such as, is serverless right for me, and how do I architect a system correctly from the myriad of available components and options?

We've written this book to address some of the more interesting questions we've seen across the industry and our technical community. We decided to look at use cases for serverless and explore problems that usually wouldn't seem like a good fit. More importantly, we've tried to convey what it is to have a serverless-first mindset. Our recipe is simple: When you have a problem, offload as much of the undifferentiated heavy lifting onto AWS or another provider and apply the principles of serverless architectures. And, if that doesn't produce a satisfactory answer, only then go and look at other technologies that may help. It's important to reiterate that you should always use the right tool for the right job. However, having a set of principles and practices, like viewing a potential solution through a serverless prism first, gives you a map and helps make better, more robust decisions.

This book shows a few examples of us doing it in practice. We discuss how to approach several problems using serverless architectures, what criteria to consider, and how to deal with architectural trade-offs. We also present three real-world companies that have built interesting systems using serverless architectures. These companies dealt with the same kinds of problems you might be solving right now, so it's worth checking out those chapters to see what potential solutions or ideas exist.

If you are entirely new to serverless architectures, do not worry! The first three chapters introduce you to serverless and even get you building a small application. If you are an expert already, you will enjoy the last two chapters that go deeper into AWS Lambda and discuss emerging practices. And, before we let you go, one other thing: the vast majority of this second edition is new. If you read our first edition, we think that you will find this a very different book. We hope you find something interesting and helpful in this book and come with us on this exciting serverless journey.

acknowledgments

The second edition of *Serverless Architectures on AWS* couldn't have been written without the encouragement and support from my peers, colleagues, family, and friends. I am lucky to be surrounded by passionate technologists who continuously encourage, give feedback, and provide invaluable advice.

First and foremost, I want to say thank you to my two co-authors: Yan Cui and Ajay Nair. I am fortunate to know these two fantastic world-class experts to whom education and community is always foremost. I cannot describe how thankful I am to Yan and Ajay for helping to write this book and making it uniquely special among the technical literature available today. I am forever grateful to both of you for being there through this journey, teaching me, and sharing the benefit of your experience.

Second, I would like to thank our editor, Toni Arritola, who once again made the writing of this book a great experience. Toni did a lot of work on the first edition of this book, and she worked just as hard on the second edition. It bears repeating again that Toni's thoughtful feedback on the book's structure, language, and narrative was extraordinarily helpful. And, after all these years of dealing with my slipping deadlines, her attention to detail and enthusiasm kept the book and its authors going.

It goes without saying that I want to thank Sam Kroonenburg too. Sam originally introduced me to AWS Lambda and the serverless mindset. He co-founded A Cloud Guru, the first truly serverless startup, and gave me the opportunity to hone my skills. If it wasn't for Sam and my experience at A Cloud Guru, this book wouldn't exist. I would be amiss if I also didn't thank Ryan Kroonenburg, the other co-founder of A Cloud Guru and Sam's brother. Both Sam and Ryan played a big part in the popularization of serverless technologies with A Cloud Guru, and also the founding of the first technology conference focused entirely on serverless called Serverlessconf (ask me for stories over a drink!). Thank you, Sam and Ryan!

I'd also like to thank a few others who for years have given me great feedback and encouragement. A big thank you to Tim Wagner, Drew Firment, Allan Brown, Nick Triantafillou, Tait Brown, Alicia Cheah, Forrest Brazeal, Peter Hanssens, Kim Bonilla, Ilia Mogilevsky, as well as my fellow AWS serverless heroes and all my colleagues and friends at A Cloud Guru/Pluralsight. I'd also like to thank Mike Stephens from Manning for helping to bring this book to fruition.

To all the reviewers: Aliaksandra Sankova, Bonnie Malec, Borko Djurkovic, Camal Çakar, Carl Nygard, Chris Kottmyer, Christopher Fry, Daniel Vásquez, Eugene Serdiouk, Giampiero Granatella, Gregory Reshetniak, Javier Collado Cabeza, Jose San Leandro, Julien Pohie, Kelly E. Hair, Kirstie G. McKenzie, Lucian-Paul Torje, Matteo Gildone, Michael Kumm, Michal Rutka, Miguel Montalvo, Mikołaj Wawrzyniak, Patrick Steger, Paul Mcilwaine, Robert Kulagowski, Sal DiStefano, Sau Fai Fong, Shaun Hickson, Steve Hansen, Valeriy Arsentyev, Vignesh Muthuthurai, and William Dixon, your suggestions and feedback made this a better book.

Finally, I'd like to thank my family, including my dad, my brothers Igor and Dimitri, and their spouses Rita and Alexandra. They've had to find more strength to listen to me go on about the book for yet another year. And thank you to Durdana Masud, who helped me greatly throughout my writing, with both the first edition and the second edition.

—Peter Sbarski

I would like to thank Peter Sbarski for the opportunity to contribute to this book, and Toni Arritola for her help and guidance every step of the way. It has truly been a pleasure and honor to work with them over the past 12 months.

I would also like to thank Anahit Pogosova for sharing details of the amazing work that she and her team at Yle have done. The knowledge she shared with me was very valuable and contained so many useful and actional tips for anyone building data pipelines using serverless technologies. I hope I have done her work justice in chapter 6, even though I had to leave out so much. We can easily fill a whole book with the information she shared with me.

I would also like to thank a few friends and colleagues who have given me opportunities and guidance along the way. I wouldn't be the man I am today without you, and your friendship means everything to me; I can't wait to catch up with you all in person soon. Big thanks to Darryl Jennings, Tom Newton, Brett Johansen, Domas Lasauskas, Scott Smethurst, Diana Ionita, Simon Coutts, Bruno Tavares, Heitor Lessa, Erez Berkner, Aviad Mor, John Earner, Simone Basso, and Alessandro Simi.

Last, but not least, I would like to thank my wonderful wife, Yinan Xue, for all the support and encouragement she has given me and continues to give me over the years. You are my best friend and the love of my life, and I look forward to growing old and wrinkly with you!

Oh, I almost forgot, I would like to thank my cat, Ada, for bringing so much joy into our lives and all the love she has given us. That scar you left on my thigh five years ago is still visible to this day, I really . . . wait a minute. . . .

    —Yan Cui

I always hoped to create a lasting contribution to the developer community and am so excited to see that finally happen with the second edition of *Serverless Architectures on AWS*. My biggest thanks to Peter Sbarski for making this happen and for the opportunity to create this work with Yan Cui and him. It has been an honor and a pleasure to be a part of the team with these serverless luminaries. Thank you to the crew at Manning, and our editor Toni Arritola, for their everlasting patience, thoroughness, and guidance.

This book is dedicated to the serverless community. We at AWS and other providers may build the technology, but it is you, the community and the customers, that put it to work to the benefit of the world. I hope this book captures the passion, depth, and breadth that you deserve. Keep raising the bar and changing the world, one event at a time.

Finally, a special shout out to Tim Wagner for getting the whole serverless universe started.

    —Ajay Nair

about this book

Serverless technologies and architectures are fascinating and unique. They present a different way of building software in a cloud environment. This is because serverless is about offloading the undifferentiated heavy lifting to others, reducing certain operational concerns, moving toward event-driven computing, and giving yourself space to focus on what's important—the core goals of your business or project. This book teaches about the serverless approach to the design of systems. You will read how other companies have solved problems using a serverless approach on AWS and dive into numerous discussions about architecture.

Along the way, you will learn more about event-driven computing, useful design patterns, organizing and deploying your code, and security. This book isn't a collection of tutorials you can find online. Instead, it is an attempt to share our thinking and understanding of the future of cloud computing, which we think is serverless.

This book is in four parts. The first part takes you through basic serverless principles as well as crucial architectures and patterns. You will also build a small serverless application in AWS to get your hands dirty. It'll be a fun one; your application will convert video files from one format to another without running a server.

The second part focuses on three case studies from Yubl, A Cloud Guru, and Yle. You will read how other companies have solved business and technical challenges with a serverless approach. The third part is about architecture. Here you will learn how to adopt the serverless-first mindset, think about the pros and cons of different architectural implementations, and tackle unexpected challenges. The three examples we present are all different, showing that a serverless approach to the design of systems is versatile and flexible.

The fourth and final part of the book looks at the internals of AWS Lambda and emerging AWS practices. If you are already an expert on AWS and serverless, you may find this section to be particularly fascinating.

The second edition of *Serverless Architectures on AWS* is for serverless veterans and beginners alike. No matter your experience, we think you will find something valuable in these pages. We hope that this book will inspire you to think serverless first. Now, let's read and build!

About the code

This book provides many examples of code. These appear throughout the text and as separate code listings. To accommodate long lines of code, listings include line-continuation markers (➥). Code appears in a `fixed-width font just like this`, so you'll know when you see it.

This book is about architecture and, as such, it is not heavy on source code. Chapter 2 is the only practical chapter. The source for chapter is available on GitHub at http://github.com/sbarski/serverless-architectures-aws-2. If you'd like to contribute, open a pull request and we'd be happy to consider your changes. If you see a problem, please file an issue.

liveBook discussion forum

Purchase of *Serverless Architectures on AWS, Second Edition* includes free access to liveBook, Manning's online reading platform. Using liveBook's exclusive discussion features, you can attach comments to the book globally or to specific sections or paragraphs. It's a snap to make notes for yourself, ask and answer technical questions, and receive help from the authors and other users. To access the forum, go to https://livebook .manning.com/#!/book/serverless-architectures-on-aws-second-edition/discussion. You can also learn more about Manning's forums and the rules of conduct at https://livebook .manning.com/#!/discussion.

Manning's commitment to our readers is to provide a venue where a meaningful dialogue between individual readers and between readers and the authors can take place. It is not a commitment to any specific amount of participation on the part of the authors, whose contribution to the forum remains voluntary (and unpaid). We suggest you try asking the authors some challenging questions lest their interest stray! The forum and the archives of previous discussions will be accessible from the publisher's website as long as the book is in print.

about the authors

PETER SBARSKI is VP of Education & Research at A Cloud Guru, AWS Serverless Hero, and the organizer of Serverlessconf, the world's first conference dedicated entirely to serverless architectures and technologies. His work at A Cloud Guru allows him to research and write about serverless architectures, cloud computing and AWS. Peter is always happy to talk about serverless technologies at conferences and meetups year round. His other passions include technical education, and innovation in technology and cloud computing. Peter holds a Ph.D. in Computer Science from Monash University, Australia. He can be found on Twitter (@sbarski) and LinkedIn (linkedin.com/in/petersbarski).

YAN CUI is a developer advocate at Lumigo and an independent consultant who helps clients around the world go faster for less by successfully adopting serverless technologies. He has over a decade of experience running production workloads at scale on AWS and has worked as architect and principal engineer within a variety of industries including banking, e-commerce, sports streaming, and mobile gaming. Yan is an AWS Serverless Hero and a regular speaker at conferences internationally. He is the author of *Production-Ready Serverless* (Manning, 2018) and co-author of *F# Deep Dives* (Manning, 2014), and he has also self-published several popular courses such as the AppSync Masterclass. He can be found on Twitter (@theburningmonk) and LinkedIn (linkedin.com/in/theburningmonk) and writes regularly on his blog (theburningmonk.com).

AJAY NAIR is a Director of Product and Engineering with Amazon Web Services. He is the founding product leader for AWS Lambda and helped build the AWS serverless portfolio over the last several years. Ajay has spent his career focusing on cloud native platforms, developer productivity, and big data systems. He loves spending his days helping developers do more with less and delighting customers with the power of technology. Ajay holds a Masters in Information Systems Management from Carnegie Mellon, USA, with a Bachelors in Electrical and Electronics Engineering from Kerala University, India. You can find Ajay sharing thoughts on everything from serverless to product management on Twitter (@ajaynairthinks) or on LinkedIn (linkedin.com/in/ajnair).

about the cover illustration

The figure on the cover of *Serverless Architectures on AWS, Second Edition* is "Man from Stupno/Sisak, Croatia," from a book by Nikola Arsenović, published in 2003. The book includes finely colored illustrations of figures from different regions of Croatia, accompanied by descriptions of the costumes and of everyday life.

In those days, it was easy to identify where people lived and what their trade or station in life was just by their dress. Manning celebrates the inventiveness and initiative of today's computer business with book covers based on the rich diversity of regional culture centuries ago, brought back to life by pictures from collections such as this one.

Part 1

First steps

If you are new to serverless architectures, you've come to the right place. The first three chapters of this book will give you an introduction to this exciting technology and even get you to build a small serverless application of your own. The first chapter provides an overview of serverless technologies and a discussion about where we are today. The second chapter is more practical; it focuses on giving you a hands-on experience with AWS and services such as AWS Lambda. The third chapter describes popular and useful serverless patterns. Let's get started!

Going serverless

This chapter covers

- Traditional system and application architectures
- Key characteristics and benefits of serverless architectures
- How serverless architectures and microservices fit into the picture
- Considerations when transitioning from server to serverless
- What's new in this second edition?

If you ask software developers what software architecture is you might get answers ranging from "it's a blueprint or a plan" to "a conceptual model" to "the big picture." This book is about an emerging architectural approach that has been adopted by developers and companies around the world to build their modern applications—*serverless architectures*.

Serverless architectures have been described as somewhat of a "nirvana" for an application architectural approach. It promises developers the ability to iterate as fast as possible while maintaining business critical latency, availability, security, and performance guarantees, with minimal effort on the developers' part.

This book teaches you how to think about serverless systems that can scale and handle demanding computational requirements without having to provision or manage a single server. Importantly, this book describes techniques that can help developers quickly deliver products to market while maintaining a high level of quality and performance by using services and architectures offered by today's cloud platforms.

1.1   What's in a name?

Before going in any further, we think it's important to come to terms with the word *serverless*. There are various attempts at this already, including an official one from AWS (https://aws.amazon.com/serverless/) and a community favorite from Martin Fowler (https://martinfowler.com/articles/serverless.html). Here's how we define it:

> **DEFINITION**   Serverless is a qualifier that can be applied to any software or service offering, which requires that it is consumed as a utility service and incurs cost only when used.

Simple enough, right? But there's a lot to unpack in that simple definition. Let's dive into each of the following two required criteria to call something serverless:

- *Consumed as a utility service*—The "software as a service" consumption model is well understood. It means that anyone using the software uses a prescribed application programming interface (API) or web interface to use the software and customize it, while staying within any published constraints for the software and usage policies for the API. Salesforce, Office365, and Google Maps are well-known software packages delivered as a service. What's key here is that the actual infrastructure (servers, networking, storage, etc.) hosting the software and powering the API is completely abstracted from you as the consumer; all that is visible (and all that matter) is what the API permits.

  A service also typically comes with accompanying availability, reliability, and performance guarantees from the service provider. A utility service, further, has the billing characteristics that we'd expect from any utility computing offering; that is, you pay for usage not for reservation, subscriptions, or provisioning. All existing public cloud offerings have some form of utility billing associated with them. For example, Amazon Elastic Compute Cloud (EC2) allows you to pay by the second for the rent of virtual machines.

- *Incurs cost only when used*—This means there's zero cost for having the software deployed and ready to use. Think of this as the same cost model we expect from our public utilities like electricity and water. You, as the consumer, pay a per granular usage unit cost if you use any, but you pay zero if you use nothing. This aspect of pure usage-based pricing is a distinguishing criterion of serverless offerings from the other utility services that came before it.

In the rest of the book, we will use the "serverless" qualifier only for software that fits these criteria. For example, software that requires you to provide a server to host a website (like the Apache web server) would not qualify because it does not meet the first criterion. Software that is available as a service but requires you to pay by subscription (like Salesforce) would not qualify as well because it does not meet the second

> ### Just to clear up any misperceptions . . .
>
> One of the common misunderstandings is that the "-less" in "serverless" implies "absence of or without" (think "sugarless," "boneless," and so on), which leads to some colorful debates on social media on how any application architecture can claim to run without servers. We think "-less" here means "invisible in context of usage" (think "wireless," "tasteless"). There obviously are servers somewhere! The difference is that these servers are hidden from you. There's no infrastructure for you to think about and no way to tweak the underlying operating system or virtual hardware configuration. Someone else takes care of the nitty-gritty details of infrastructure management, freeing you from that operational overhead and giving back to you the most expensive commodity there is—time.

criterion. A *serverless architecture*, by extension, is one composed entirely of serverless components. But which components of an architecture need to be serverless for it to be called as such? Let's look at this next with an example.

1.2 Understanding serverless architectures

Let's take the example of a typical data-driven web application, not unlike the systems powering most of today's web-enabled software. These typically consist of a backend (server) that accepts requests from a client and then processes the requests.

The backend server performs various forms of computation, and the frontend client provides an interface for users to operate via their browser, mobile, or desktop device. Data might travel through numerous application layers before being saved to a database. The backend then generates a response that could be in the form of JSON or in fully rendered markup, which is sent back to the client (figure 1.1). These kinds of applications are conventionally architected as *tiers* (a presentation tier that controls how the information is captured and provided to the user, an application tier that controls the business logic of the application, and a data tier with the database and corresponding access controls).

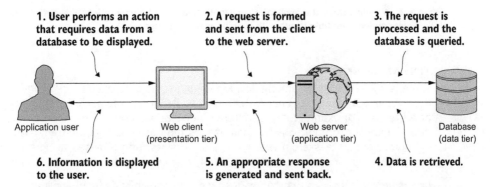

1. User performs an action that requires data from a database to be displayed.

2. A request is formed and sent from the client to the web server.

3. The request is processed and the database is queried.

Application user

Web client
(presentation tier)

Web server
(application tier)

Database
(data tier)

6. Information is displayed to the user.

5. An appropriate response is generated and sent back.

4. Data is retrieved.

Figure 1.1   A basic request-response (client-server) message-exchange pattern that most developers are familiar with. There's only one web server and one database in this figure. Most systems are much more complex.

Software architectures have evolved from the days of code running on a mainframe to a multitier architecture where the presentation, data, and application/logic tiers are traditionally separated. Within each tier, there may be multiple logical layers that deal with the particular aspects of functionality or domain. There are also cross-cutting components such as logging or exception handling systems that can span numerous layers. The preference for layering is understandable. Layering allows developers to decouple concerns and have more maintainable applications. Figure 1.2 shows an example of a tiered architecture with multiple layers including the API, the business logic, the user authentication component, and the database.

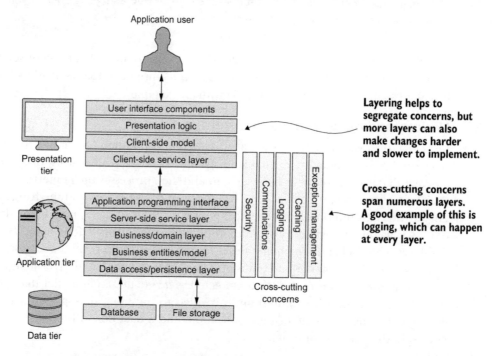

Figure 1.2 A typical three-tier application is usually made up of presentation, application, and data tiers. A tier can have multiple layers with specific responsibilities.

Tiers vs. layers

There is some confusion among developers about the difference between layers and tiers. A *tier* is a module boundary that provides isolation between major components of a system. For example, a presentation tier that's visible to the user is separate from the application tier, which encompasses the business logic. In turn, a data tier is another separate system that manages, persists, and provides access to data. Components grouped in a tier can physically reside on different infrastructures.

Layers are logical slices that carry out specific responsibilities in an application. Each tier can have multiple layers that are responsible for different elements of functionality, such as domain services.

1.2.1 Service-oriented architecture and microservices

One blunt approach would be to combine all the layers (the API, the business logic, the user authentication) into one single, monolithic code base. This may sound like an antipattern today, but that was indeed the approach we adopted in the early days of cloud-based development. Most modern approaches, however, dictate that you architect with reusability, autonomy, composability, and discoverability in mind.

Among the veterans of our industry, service-oriented architecture (SOA) is a well-known buzzword. SOA encourages an architectural approach in which developers create autonomous services that communicate via message passing and often have a schema or a contract that defines how messages are created or exchanged.

The modern incarnation of the service-oriented approach is often referred to as microservices architecture. Modern application architectures are composed of services communicating through events and APIs with business logic inserted as appropriate. We define microservices as small, standalone, fully independent services built around a particular business purpose or capability. Ideally, microservices should be easy to replace, with each service written in an appropriate framework and language.

The mere fact that microservices can be written in a different general-purpose language or a domain-specific language (DSL) is a drawing card for many developers. Benefits can be gained from using the right language or a specialized set of libraries for the job. Each microservice can maintain state and store data. And if microservices are correctly decoupled, development teams can work and deploy microservices independently from one another. This approach of building and deploying applications as a collection of loosely coupled services is considered the default approach to development in the cloud today (the "cloud native" approach, if you will).

> **Microservices all the time?**
>
> Microservice approaches aren't all a bed of roses. Having a mix of languages and frameworks can be hard to support and, without strict discipline, can lead to confusion down the road. Eventual consistency, coordination, discovery, and complex error recovery can make things difficult in a microservices universe.
>
> Software engineering is always a game of tradeoffs. Because something is in fashion (like microservices) doesn't make it universally right for all problems and use cases. What matters is knowing about the different architectural options, understanding their pros and cons, and, importantly, understanding the requirements and needs of your own problem. (And, yes, in some cases and situations, having a monolith is OK.)

1.2.2 Implementing architecture the conventional way

Once you have decided how your application is going to be architected, and all the software required for each of the layers is ready to go, you would think the hardest part is done. The truth is, that's when some of the more complex tasks begin. Developing your desired services traditionally requires servers running in data centers or in the cloud that need to be managed, maintained, patched, and backed up. Today, you would pick from a few options:

- *Directly build on VMs*—The physical deployment of each service requires you to have a set of instances with additional tasks to address required activities such as load balancing, transactions, clustering, caching, messaging, and data redundancy. Provisioning, managing, and patching of these servers is a time-consuming task that often requires dedicated operations people.

  A non-trivial environment is hard to set up and operate effectively. Infrastructure and hardware are necessary components of any IT system, but they're often also a distraction from what should be the core focus—solving the business problem. In our simple web application example, you would have to become an expert in building distributed systems and cloud infrastructure management. In a cloud environment, this form of computing is often referred to as infrastructure as a service (IaaS).

- *Use a PaaS*—Over the past few years, technologies such as platform as a service (PaaS) and containers have appeared as potential solutions to the headache of inconsistent infrastructure environments, conflicts, and server management overhead. PaaS is a form of cloud computing that provides a platform for users to run their software while hiding some of the underlying infrastructure.

  To make effective use of PaaS, developers need to write software that targets the features and capabilities of the platform. Moving a legacy application designed to run on a standalone server to a PaaS service often leads to additional development effort because of the ephemeral nature of most PaaS implementations. Still, given a choice, many developers would understandably choose to use PaaS rather than more traditional, manual solutions thanks to reduced maintenance and platform support requirements.

- *Use containers*—Containerization is considered ideal for microservices architectures because it is a way of isolating an application with its own environment. It's a lightweight alternative to full-blown virtualization that traditional cloud servers use.

  Containers are an excellent deployment and packaging solution especially when dependencies are in play (although they can come with their own housekeeping challenges and complexities). Containers are isolated and lightweight, but they need to be deployed to a server, whether in a public or private cloud or on site.

While each of these models are perfectly valid and offer varying degrees of simplicity and speed of development for your service, your costs are still driven by the lifecycle of the infrastructure or servers you own, not to your application usage. If you purchase a rack at the data center, you pay for it 24/7. If you purchase a cloud instance (wrapped in a PaaS or running containers or otherwise), you pay for it when it runs, independent of whether it is serving traffic for your web app or not.

This leads to an entire discipline of engineers investing in improving server efficiency or trying to match infrastructure lifecycle to application usage and server sizes to traffic patterns. This also means that all the effort spent on these tasks is time taken away from improving the functionality and differentiating aspects of your application. This is equivalent to asking for a place to plug in your appliance and having to pay for a share of the power generators at your utility company, as well as configuring the generator to deliver the power in the phase, frequency, and wattage you desire no matter how much you use. The actual outcome (plug in your appliance) is dwarfed by the effort and cost for the infrastructure required (the generators). This is where the serverless approach comes in. It aims for the moral equivalent of the utility approach we know and love today—there when you need it, complexity abstracted away, and you only pay for when you use it.

1.2.3 *Implementing architecture the serverless way*

A serverless architecture for our sample application could be composed of different layers. For example, to build the API, we would use a service that does not cost us anything if there are no API calls. To build the authentication service, we would use a service that does not cost us anything if there are no authentication calls. To build the storage service, we would use . . . you get the picture.

Much like the public cloud approach that offered virtual infrastructure Lego to assemble our cloud stack in the early days, a serverless architecture uses existing services from cloud providers like AWS to implement its architectural components. As an example, AWS offers services to build our application primitives like APIs (Amazon API Gateway), workflows (AWS Step Functions), queues (Amazon Simple Queue Service), databases (Amazon DynamoDB and Amazon Aurora), and more.

The idea of using off-the-shelf services to implement parts of our architecture is not new; indeed, it's been a best practice since the days of SOA. What's changed in the last few years is the capability to also implement the *custom* aspects of our applications (like the business logic) in a serverless manner. This ability to run arbitrary code without having to provision infrastructure to run it as a service or to pay for the infrastructure is referred to as functions as a service (FaaS).

FaaS allows you to provide custom code, associated dependencies, and some configuration to dictate your desired performance and access control characteristics. FaaS then executes this unit (referred to as a *function*) on an invisible compute fleet with each execution of your code receiving an isolated environment with its own disk, memory, and CPU allocation. You pay only for the time your code runs. A function is not a lightweight instance; instead, think of it as akin to processes in an OS, where you can spawn as many as needed by your application and then spin them down when your application isn't running.

Serverless architectures are really the culmination of shifts that have been going on for a long time: from monoliths to services and from managing infrastructure to increasingly delegating the undifferentiating responsibilities. Serverless architectures can help with the problem of layering and having to update too many things. There's room for developers to remove or minimize layering by breaking the system into functions and allowing the frontend to securely communicate with services and even the database directly. A well-planned serverless architecture can make future changes easier, which is an important factor for any long-term application.

To recap, a serverless architecture leverages a serverless implementation for each of its components, using FaaS (like AWS Lambda) for custom logic. This means each component is built as a service, with utility pricing that incurs cost only when used. Each component is a service and exposes no configuration or cost related to the infrastructure it is running on, which means these architectures don't rely on direct access to a server to work. By making use of various powerful single-purpose APIs and web services, developers can build loosely coupled, scalable, and efficient architectures quickly. Moving away from servers and infrastructure concerns, as well as allowing the developer to primarily focus on code, is the ultimate goal behind serverless.

More on FaaS

AWS's FaaS offering is called AWS Lambda and is one of the first from the major cloud providers. Note that Lambda isn't the only game in town. Microsoft Azure Functions (http://bit.ly/2DWx5Gn), IBM Cloud Functions (http://bit.ly/2l1PWbd), and Google Cloud Functions (http://bit.ly/2CbzOem) are other FaaS services you might want to look at.

Many developers conflate serverless with FaaS offerings like AWS Lambda, which often leads to confusing arguments around the adoption of containers or serverless when they really mean containers or functions. We like how TJ Hallowaychuk, the creator of the Apex framework, defines what serverless is about. He once tweeted, "serverless != functions, FaaS == functions, serverless == on-demand scaling and pricing characteristics (not limited to functions)." We couldn't agree more.

An emerging trend is that of *serverless containers*; that is, leveraging containers instead of functions to implement the custom logic and using the container as a utility service and incurring costs only when the container runs. Services like AWS Fargate or Google Cloud Run offer this capability. The difference between the two (functions vs. containers) is just the degree to which developers want to shift the boundaries of shared responsibilities. Containers give you a bit more control over user space libraries and network capabilities. Containers are an evolution of the existing server-based/VM model, offering an easy packaging and deployment model for your application stack. You are still required to define your operating system's requirements, your desired language stack, and dependencies to deploy code, which means you continue to carry some of the infrastructure complexity. For the purpose of this book, we are going to focus on using FaaS for our custom logic, though you can explore the usage of serverless containers for the same as well.

1.3 Making the call to go serverless

The web application example we went through is one of the simplest demonstrations of what can be achieved with serverless architectures. A serverless approach can also work exceptionally well for organizations that want to innovate and move quickly.

Functions and serverless architectures, in general, are versatile. You can use them to build backends for CRUD applications, e-commerce, back-office systems, complex web apps, and all kinds of mobile and desktop software. Tasks that used to take weeks can be done in days or hours as long as we chose the right combination of technologies. Lambda functions are stateless and scalable, which makes them perfect for implementing any logic that benefits from parallel processing.

The most flexible and powerful serverless designs are event-driven, which means each component in the architecture reacts to a state change or notification of some kind rather than responding to a request or polling for information. In chapter 2, for example, you'll build an event-driven, push-based pipeline to see how quickly you can put together a system to encode video to different bit rates and formats.

> **NOTE** You will find the use of events as a communication mechanism between components to be a recurring theme in serverless architectures; indeed, AWS Lambda's initial launch was as an event-driven computing service. Building event-driven, push-based systems will often reduce cost and complexity (you won't need to run extra code to poll for changes) and, potentially, make the overall user experience smoother. It goes without saying that although event-driven, push-based models are a good goal, they might not be appropriate or achievable in all circumstances.

Serverless architecture allows developers to focus on software design and code rather than infrastructure. Scalability and high availability are easier to achieve, and the pricing is often more fair because you pay only for what you use. More importantly, you have the potential to reduce some of the complexity of the system by minimizing the number of layers and amount of code needed.

Adopting a serverless approach to application development comes with significant agility, elasticity, and cost efficiency gains. However, it is easy to fall into the trap of trying to adopt a serverless approach for *all* applications. We recommend keeping a few principles in mind as you start your serverless journey:

- *Avoid lift-and-shift*—In practice, serverless architectures are more suited for new applications rather than porting existing applications over. This is because existing application code bases have a lot of code that is made redundant by the serverless services. For example, porting a Java Spring app into Lambda brings a heavy framework into a function, most of which exists to interact with a web server (which doesn't exist inside Lambda).
- *Adopt a serverless first approach, not a serverless only approach*—While there are companies like A Cloud Guru that have adopted a serverless only approach, where 100% of their application runs as a serverless implementation, the more

widespread approach that companies like Expedia and T-Mobile have adopted is to go serverless first. What this means is that their developers attempt to first build any new application in the following priority order: build as much as possible using third-party services, fall back to custom services built using AWS serverless primitives like AWS Lambda, and finally, fall back to custom services built using custom software running on infrastructure like EC2. We talk about the reasons why you may have to fall back beyond custom serverless services in the next section.

- *It doesn't have to be all or nothing*—One advantage of the serverless approach is that existing applications can be gradually converted to serverless architecture. If a developer is faced with a monolithic code base, they can gradually tease it apart and convert individual components into a serverless implementation (the strangler pattern).

The best approach is to initially create a prototype to test developer assumptions about how the system would function if it is going to be partly or fully serverless. Legacy systems tend to have interesting constraints that require creative solutions, and as with any architectural refactors at a large scale, compromises are inevitably going to be made. The system may end up being a hybrid (as in figure 1.3), but it may be better to have some of its components use Lambda and third-party services rather than remain with an unchanged legacy architecture that no longer scales or that requires expensive infrastructure to run.

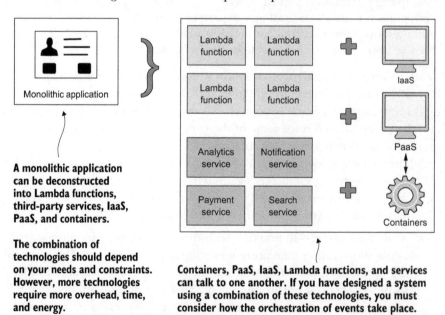

A monolithic application can be deconstructed into Lambda functions, third-party services, IaaS, PaaS, and containers.

The combination of technologies should depend on your needs and constraints. However, more technologies require more overhead, time, and energy.

Containers, PaaS, IaaS, Lambda functions, and services can talk to one another. If you have designed a system using a combination of these technologies, you must consider how the orchestration of events take place.

Figure 1.3 Serverless architecture is not an all-or-nothing proposition. If you currently have a monolithic application, you can begin to gradually extract components and run them in isolated services or compute functions. You can decouple a monolithic application into an assortment of IaaS, PaaS, containers, functions, and third-party services if it helps.

The transition from a legacy, server-based application to a scalable serverless architecture may take time to get right. It needs to be approached carefully and slowly, and developers need to have a good test plan and a great DevOps strategy in place before they begin.

What about NoOps?

Early on, around the time of the first conference on serverless technologies and architectures (https://serverlessconf.io) in 2016, there was talk that serverless technologies foreshadowed the era of *NoOps*. Some people believed that thanks to serverless, companies would no longer need to think about infrastructure operations. The cloud vendor will take care of everything was the thought. That assumption, that NoOps was a real thing, proved not to be the case.

When it comes to building and running serverless applications, DevOps engineers are essential, except now they have a different focus. Their attention is on deployment automation, testing, and working with the operations/support teams of their preferred cloud provider (rather than tweaking servers and patching operating systems).

Companies can get away with smaller, more specialized DevOps teams; however, ignoring operations entirely is a recipe for disaster (and don't let anyone else tell you otherwise). Remember, when your application fails, customers hold you accountable, not your cloud provider, so be ready and have the right people and processes in place.

- *Pick applications suited for a service-oriented architecture*—Serverless architectures are a natural extension of ideas raised in SOAs. In a serverless architecture, all custom code is written and executed as isolated, independent, and often granular functions that are run in a compute service such as AWS Lambda. Because every component is a service, serverless architectures share a lot of advantages and complexities with event-driven microservices architectures. This also means applications likely need to be architected to meet the requirements of these approaches (like making the individual services stateless, for example).

  Keep in mind that the serverless approach is all about reducing the amount of code you have to own and maintain, so you can iterate and innovate faster. This means you should strive to minimize the number of components that are required to build your application. For example, you may architect your web application with a rich front end (in lieu of a complex backend) that can talk to third-party services directly. That kind of architecture can be conducive to a better user experience. Fewer hops between online resources and reduced latency will result in a better perception of performance and usability of the application. In other words, you don't have to route everything through a FaaS; your frontend may be able to communicate directly with a search provider, a database, or another useful API.

  Also keep in mind that moving from a monolithic approach to a more decentralized serverless approach doesn't automatically reduce the complexity of the underlying system. The distributed nature of the solution can introduce its own challenges because of the need to make remote rather than in-process calls and the need to handle failures and latency across a network, which your application will need to be resilient to.

- *Minimize custom code*—The rise of serverless means many standard application components like APIs, workflows, queues, and databases are available as serverless offerings from cloud providers and third parties. It's far more useful for developers to spend time solving a problem unique to their domain rather than recreating functionality already implemented by someone else. Don't build for the sake of building if viable third-party services and APIs are available. Stand on the shoulders of giants to reach new heights.

  Appendix A has a short list of Amazon Web Services and non-Amazon Web Services that we've found useful. We'll look at most of those services in more detail as we move through the book. However, it goes without saying that when a third-party service is considered, factors such as price, capability, availability, documentation, and support must be carefully assessed.

  If you have to build a piece of custom functionality, our advice is simple: try to solve your problem using functions first, and if that doesn't work explore containers and more traditional server-based architectures second. Developers can write functions to carry out almost any common task, such as reading and writing to a data source, calling out to other functions, and performing calculations. In more complex cases, developers can set up more elaborate pipelines and orchestrate invocations of multiple functions.

1.4 Serverless pros and cons

The serverless approach of building applications by quickly assembling services provides two significant advantages: less code to write and maintain per application and per activity pricing for our applications. This translates into a disruptive gain in agility and developer productivity, and a much more streamlined alignment between development and finance (because any application inefficiencies or optimizations show a direct, tangible financial impact). Here are a few of the specific benefits you will realize by adopting serverless architecture:

- *High scale and reliability without server management*—Building large scale, distributed systems is hard. Tasks such as server configuration and management, patching, and maintenance are taken care of by the vendor, as is managing the infrastructure architecture for high scale and reliability, which saves time and money. For example, Amazon looks after the health of its fleet of servers that power AWS Lambda.

  If you don't have specific requirements to manage or modify server resources, then having Amazon or another vendor look after them is a great solution. You're responsible only for your own code, leaving operational and administrative tasks to a different set of capable hands.

- *Competitive pricing*—Traditional server-based architecture requires servers that don't necessarily run at full capacity all of the time. Scaling, even with automated systems, involves a new server, which is often wasted until there's a temporary upsurge in traffic or new data.

  Serverless systems are much more granular with regard to scaling and are cost-effective, especially when peak loads are uneven or unexpected. Because of their utility pay-per-use billing, serverless services can be extremely cost-effective; however, they're not cheaper than traditional (server and container) technologies in all circumstances. The best thing is to do some modeling before embarking on a big project.

- *Less code*—We mentioned at the start of the chapter that serverless architecture provides an opportunity to reduce some of the complexity and code, in comparison to more traditional systems. Adopting a serverless approach eliminates undifferentiated code such as that required for orchestrating server fleets or routing requests and events between components, which forms a surprisingly large part of modern code bases.

Serverless is not a silver bullet in all circumstances, however. Here are some reasons where you would want to avoid serverless architectures:

- *You are not comfortable with public cloud-based architectures.* Serverless development is a natural extension of the move to cloud-based development, where more and more of the undifferentiated heavy lifting is moved to the providers. There are applications and business scenarios where you need to maintain your own data center; in such cases, you cannot build a serverless architecture (though you are welcome to host your own primitives on your infrastructure and use those to build applications).

- *The services don't meet the availability, performance, compliance, or scale needs of your customers.* AWS serverless services offer an availability SLA, but their threshold may be below what you need for your business. They also have a variety of compliance certifications, but you must validate if they need what your business needs. Services like AWS Lambda also do not offer a performance SLA, which means you may need to evaluate their performance against your desired levels. Non-AWS, third-party services are in the same boat. Some may have strong SLAs, whereas others may not have one at all.

- *Your application and business needs more control or you need to customize the infrastructure.* When it comes to Lambda, the efficiencies gained from having Amazon look after the platform and scale functions come at the expense of being able to customize the operating system or tweak the underlying instance. You can modify the amount of RAM allocated to a function and change timeouts, but that's about it. Similarly, different third-party services will have varying levels of customization and flexibility.

- *Your application and business needs require you to stay vendor agnostic.* If a developer decides to use third-party APIs and services, including AWS, there's a chance that architecture could become strongly coupled to the platform being used. The implications of vendor lock-in and the risk of using third-party services—including company viability, data sovereignty and privacy, cost, support, documentation, and available feature set—need to be thoroughly considered.

In this chapter, you learned what serverless architecture is, looked at its principles, and how it compares to traditional architectures. In the next chapter, we'll get our hands dirty by creating a small serverless, event-driven application. This will help you get a good taste for serverless if this is your first time trying this approach. From there, we'll explore important architectures and patterns and discuss use cases where serverless architectures are used to solve a problem.

1.5   What's new in this second edition?

For all intent and purposes, this is a completely different book from the first edition of *Serverless Architectures on AWS*. Most of the chapters have been written from the ground up to provide a completely different experience from the first edition.

When the first edition of this book came out in 2017, serverless was still new and many of us were learning about serverless for the first time. As such, the first edition gave a gentle introduction to serverless and walked the reader through a build of a serverless application. Since then a lot of new educational content has crossed our desks, including numerous books and video courses to help us get started with serverless technologies on AWS.

If you're looking for an introduction to serverless architectures on AWS, we have included some introductory content in chapter 2 and in appendices A and B. You can also find the first edition of this book on the Manning website (https://www.manning.com/books/serverless-architectures-on-aws). Most of the content from the first edition is still relevant today, and with that book, you will learn to build a serverless application from scratch.

But, just as serverless technologies allow us to focus on the things that differentiate our business, we want to focus on things that can differentiate this book with this second edition. Instead of yet another getting started guide to serverless, this book focuses on serverless use cases and interesting architectures. It is aimed at developers with some experience of serverless technologies already and answers the questions that many of you have been asking us. Given the switch in focus, this book does not have many actual code samples. Instead, we hope to challenge the way you think about serverless architecture and help you get the most out of serverless technologies on AWS.

Summary

- The cloud has been and continues to be a game changer for IT infrastructure and software development.
- Software developers need to think about the ways they can maximize the use of cloud platforms to gain a competitive advantage.
- Serverless architectures are the latest step forward for developers and organizations to think about, study, and adopt. This exciting shift in implementing application architectures will grow quickly as software developers embrace compute services such as AWS Lambda.
- In many cases, serverless applications will be cheaper to run and faster to implement. There's also a need to reduce complexity and costs associated with running infrastructure and carrying out development of traditional software systems.
- The reduction in cost and time spent on infrastructure maintenance and the benefits of scalability are good reasons for organizations and developers to consider serverless architectures.

First steps to serverless

This chapter covers

- Writing and deploying AWS Lambda functions
- AWS services such as Simple Storage Service (S3) and Elemental MediaConvert
- Using the Serverless Framework to organize and deploy services

To give you an understanding of serverless architectures, you're going to build a small, event-driven serverless application: specifically, a video-encoding pipeline. Your service will transcode videos, uploaded to an S3 bucket, from their existing format, resolution or bit rate to a different format or bit rate (kind of like YouTube only without the frontend website).

To build this video-encoding pipeline, you will use AWS Lambda, S3, and Elemental MediaConvert. Later, if you so desire, you can build a frontend around it, but we'll leave that for you as an exercise. If you want to see how we've done it ourselves, you can refer to our first edition that covers the frontend in some detail.

2.1 Building a video-encoding pipeline

In this section, you'll begin to build a small, event-driven serverless application. At a high level, you'll learn the following in this chapter:

- How to construct a rudimentary serverless architecture using three AWS services including Lambda
- How to use the Serverless Framework to organize and deploy a serverless application
- How to run, debug, and test the serverless pipeline that you built

Frameworks for serverless

You might have heard that there are several frameworks that you can use to organize and deploy serverless applications. These include the AWS Serverless Application Model (https:// github.com/awslabs/serverless-application-model), the Serverless Framework (https://serverless.com), Chalice (https://github.com/aws/chalice), and a few others. In this chapter, you'll use Serverless Framework to organize and automate the deployment of your serverless application.

Our advice is to always use a framework like the Serverless Framework or Serverless Application Model (SAM). Once you understand the principles of serverless architectures, a framework accelerates everything you do by leaps and bounds. Appendix C contains more information on the different frameworks we have found useful. There's even an introduction and a bit of a primer on the Serverless Framework that you'll use in this chapter. Have a look at appendix C when you get a chance.

Let's talk about the event-driven pipeline you are going to build (we'll call it *The 24-Hour Video*). Your pipeline will encode videos that were uploaded to a designated S3 bucket into different formats, resolutions, and bit rates. Because the entire process is event-driven, once a file is uploaded to S3, the system triggers automatically to process the file and create a new version with a different encoding in a separate bucket. And because everything is done automatically, there's no need for any intervention on your behalf.

2.1.1 A quick note on AWS costs

Most AWS services have a free tier. Following this example, you should stay within the free tier of most AWS services. AWS Elemental MediaConvert, however, is one service that may end up costing you a little bit of money. You'll use MediaConvert to transcode video files. This service is pay-as-you-go without any upfront cost. Pricing is based solely on the duration of the new videos MediaConvert creates, and you are charged in 10-second increments.

MediaConvert offers two pricing tiers for on-demand services: Basic and Professional. You will use the Basic tier in this book, although we invite you to investigate the Professional tier if you are going to take your application to the next level (remember us if you end up building the next YouTube!). The Basic tier supports features such as single-pass encoding, clipping, stitching, and overlays. The Professional tier supports quite a few more features.

The per-minute rate in the Basic tier depends on the resolution and the frame rate of the desired output. It ranges from $0.0075 per minute for basic SD quality output to $0.0450 per minute for UHD output. This rate also differs based on the region you are in. US East 1 (North Virginia), for example, is cheaper than US West 1 (Northern California), but US East 1 is the region you'll use throughout this book. You can see the tiers and the pricing information at https://aws.amazon.com/mediaconvert/pricing/. Just remember that there's no free tier for MediaConvert, so you'll start paying something almost immediately.

The S3 free tier allows users to store 5 GB of data with standard storage, issue 20,000 GET requests and 2,000 PUT requests, and transfer 15 GB of data each month. Lambda provides a free tier with 1 M free requests and 400,000 GB seconds of compute time. You should be well within the free tier limitations of those services. The following lists the high-level requirements for *The 24-Hour Video*:

- The transcoding process converts uploaded source videos to three different resolutions and bit rates:
  - 6 Mbps with a 16 × 9 aspect ratio and a resolution of 1920 × 1080
  - 4.5 Mbps with a 16 × 9 aspect ratio and a resolution of 1280 × 720
  - 1.5 Mbps with a 4 × 3 aspect ratio and a resolution of 640 × 480
- There will be two S3 buckets:
  - Original files will go into the upload bucket.
  - Files created by AWS MediaConvert will be saved to the transcoded video bucket.

To make things simpler to manage, you'll set up a build and deployment system using the Node Package Manager (npm) and the Serverless Framework. First, here's an overview on the AWS services we'll use in this example.

2.1.2   *Using Amazon Web Services (AWS)*

To create your serverless backend, you'll use several services provided by AWS. These include Simple Storage Service (S3) for file storage, MediaConvert for video conversion, and Lambda for running custom code and orchestrating key parts of the system. In this chapter, you'll create your first Lambda function to kick off MediaConvert jobs. Here's a brief description for each of the AWS services that we'll use:

- *S3 provides the storage service.* Amazon S3 stores the uploaded and newly transcoded videos.
- *Lambda handles parts of the system that require coordination or that can't be done directly by other services.* This function automatically runs when a file is uploaded to an S3 bucket.
- *MediaConvert encodes your videos to different resolutions and bit rates.* Default presets remove the need to create custom encoding profiles.

Figure 2.1 shows a detailed flow of the proposed approach. Note that the only point where a user needs to interact with the system is at the initial upload stage. This figure and the architecture may look complex, but we'll break the system into manageable chunks and tackle them one by one over the course of this chapter.

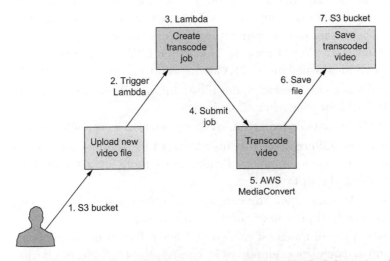

Figure 2.1 *The 24-Hour Video* **backend is built with AWS S3, MediaConvert, and Lambda. This pipeline may seem to have a lot of steps initially, but in this chapter, we'll break this down, and you'll build a scalable serverless system in no time at all.**

2.2 Preparing your system

It's time to set up AWS services and install the software on your computer. Here's what you'll install on your machine:

- Node.js and its package manager (npm) to help manage Lambda functions and keep track of dependencies
- The AWS command-line interface (CLI) to help with deployments and future use cases and examples
- The Serverless Framework (npm package) to help you organize and deploy your application to AWS

In AWS, you'll create

- An Identity and Access Management (IAM) user and roles
- S3 buckets to store video files
- The first Lambda function

This section may seem lengthy, but it explains a number of things that will help you throughout the book. If you've already used AWS, you'll be able to move through this section quickly.

2.2.1 Setting up your system

To begin, you need to create an AWS account and install a number of software packages and tools on your computer. Let's take these in order:

1. Create an AWS account. It's free but you will need to provide your credit card details in case there are any charges if you go over the free tier allotment.

    You can create your account at https://aws.amazon.com. We highly recommend that you set up 2 Factor Authentication (2FA) on your account as soon as possible. The instructions for 2FA are here: https://amzn.to/2ZASm33.

2. After your account is created, download and install the appropriate version of the AWS CLI for your system from here:

    http://docs.aws.amazon.com/cli/latest/userguide/installing.html

    There are different ways to install the CLI, including an MSI installer if you're using Windows, pip (a Python-based tool), or a bundled installer if you're using Mac or Linux.

3. Install Node.js and npm. You can download Node.js from https://nodejs.org/en/download/ (npm comes bundled with Node.js).

    You can install the latest version of Node.js but, at the time of writing, the most up-to-date version supported by Lambda was 14. Node 14.*x* is what you will target when you deploy code.

Just a heads up: in a short while you'll need to install Serverless Framework. However, you don't need to do it now. We'll cover that when it is time.

2.2.2 Working with Identity and Access Management (IAM)

Having an AWS account is good, but you cannot do too much with it just yet. For example, the AWS CLI you have just installed isn't going to function. You will not be able to create resources, deploy, or do anything, really. To make AWS work, you'll need to create an IAM user, assign permissions to the user, and then configure the CLI to use the IAM user's credentials. Let's do that now:

1. In the AWS console, click IAM (Identity and Access Management), click Users, and then click Add User.

2. Give your IAM user a name (in figure 2.2, we used lambda-upload for the name) and select the Programmatic Access check box. Selecting this check box allows you to generate an access key ID and a secret access key. (You'll need these keys to run `aws configure` in a few steps.)

3. Click Next: Permissions to proceed.

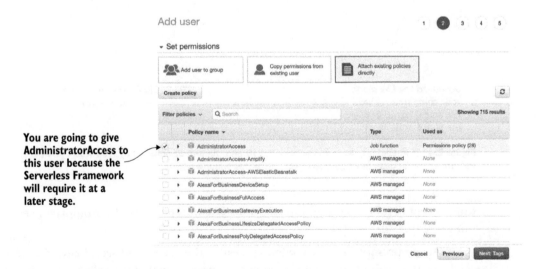

Add user

1 2 3 4 5

Set user details

You can add multiple users at once with the same access type and permissions. Learn more

User name* lambda-upload

➕ Add another user

Select AWS access type

Select how these users will access AWS. Access keys and autogenerated passwords are provided in the last step. Learn more

Access type* ✓ **Programmatic access**
Enables an **access key ID** and **secret access key** for the AWS API, CLI, SDK, and other development tools.

☐ **AWS Management Console access**
Enables a **password** that allows users to sign-in to the AWS Management Console.

Enable Programmatic Access to generate the access key ID and the secret access key.

* Required   Cancel   Next: Permissions

Figure 2.2 **Creating a new IAM user is straightforward when using the IAM console.**

4. Select Attach Existing Policies Directly and then click the checkbox next to AdministratorAccess (figure 2.3). Choose Next: Tags to proceed.

Add user

1 2 3 4 5

▾ Set permissions

Add user to group | Copy permissions from existing user | Attach existing policies directly

Create policy

Filter policies ⌄   🔍 Search   Showing 715 results

	Policy name ▾	Type	Used as
✓ ▸	🗐 AdministratorAccess	Job function	Permissions policy (28)
☐ ▸	🗐 AdministratorAccess-Amplify	AWS managed	None
☐ ▸	🗐 AdministratorAccess-AWSElasticBeanstalk	AWS managed	None
☐ ▸	🗐 AlexaForBusinessDeviceSetup	AWS managed	None
☐ ▸	🗐 AlexaForBusinessFullAccess	AWS managed	None
☐ ▸	🗐 AlexaForBusinessGatewayExecution	AWS managed	None
☐ ▸	🗐 AlexaForBusinessLifesizeDelegatedAccessPolicy	AWS managed	None
☐ ▸	🗐 AlexaForBusinessPolyDelegatedAccessPolicy	AWS managed	None

You are going to give AdministratorAccess to this user because the Serverless Framework will require it at a later stage.

Cancel   Previous   Next: Tags

Figure 2.3 **Make sure to select the AdministratorAccess policy. You will need it to upload functions and deploy other services.**

5. Tags are useful for keeping an inventory and metadata, but for this example, you don't need to do anything. Click Next: Review to go forward.

6. On the final page, you can review your user details and the permissions summary. Choose Create User to proceed.

You should now see a table with the username, the access key ID, and the secret access key. You can also download a CSV file with this information. Go ahead and download it now to retain a copy of the keys on your computer and click Close to exit (figure 2.4).

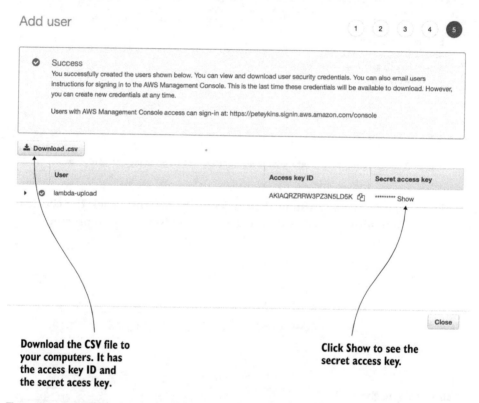

Download the CSV file to
your computers. It has
the access key ID and
the secret acess key.

Click Show to see the
secret access key.

Figure 2.4   Remember to save the access key ID and the secret access key. You won't be able to get the secret access key again once you close this window.

Run `aws configure` from a terminal on your system. The AWS CLI prompts for several things:

1. At the prompt for user credentials, enter the access and secret keys generated for the lambda-upload username or the username that you selected previously.

2. You'll also be prompted to enter a region. Type `us-east-1` and press Enter. We recommend that you use the same region for all services (you'll find that it's cheaper and makes things easier to configure). The N. Virginia (us-east-1)

region supports everything we'll use for the duration of this book so make sure to use us-east-1 at all times.

3. There will be one more prompt asking you to select the default output format. Set it as json.

You are now done with the AWS CLI configuration. You created an IAM user and used that user's credentials to configure the CLI on your system. Good job!

Granular permissions

The best practice when it comes to permissions in AWS is to make them *granular*. This means that your IAM users and roles should have only the specific permissions needed to carry out their purpose. They shouldn't have all administrator-level permissions, for example, unless there is a good reason for it.

You just created an IAM user that has administrator-level permissions. This flies in the face of the advice we've just given. The reason for this is that the Serverless Framework, which you will use shortly, is going to need administrator-level access. The Framework calls to a lot of APIs, and it's difficult to configure an IAM user with just the right permissions. If you aren't going to use the Serverless Framework and want to deploy functions using the AWS CLI instead, then we'd recommend creating an IAM user and assigning a few specific permissions needed to upload your functions.

2.2.3 Let's make a bucket

The next step is to create a bucket in S3. This bucket will contain transcoded video put there by Elemental MediaConvert. All users of S3 share the same bucket name-space, which means that you have to come up with bucket names that are not in use. In this book, we'll assume that this bucket is named something like serverless-video-transcoded.

Bucket names

Bucket names must be unique throughout the S3 global resource space. We've already taken serverless-video-transcoded, so you'll need to come up with a different name. We suggest adding your initials (or a random string of characters) to these bucket names to help identify them throughout the book (for example, serverless-video-upload-ps and serverless-video-transcoded-ps).

To create a bucket

1. In the AWS console, choose S3 and then click Create Bucket (figure 2.5).
2. Type in a name for the bucket and choose US East (N. Virginia) as the region.
3. Scroll to the bottom of the page and click Create Bucket to confirm. Your bucket should immediately appear in the console.

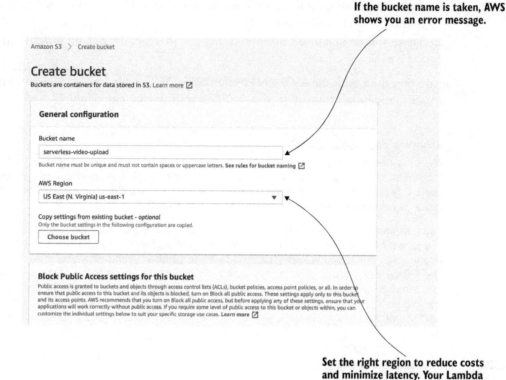

If the bucket name is taken, AWS shows you an error message.

Set the right region to reduce costs and minimize latency. Your Lambda functions should be in the same region.

Figure 2.5   Creating a bucket from the AWS S3 console. Remember that bucket names are globally unique, so you'll have to come up with your own new name.

NOTE   You are going to end up needing another S3 bucket to which you will upload videos in the first place. The Serverless Framework creates this bucket for you automatically in the next section, so you don't need to do anything yet. You can create the transcoded video bucket using CloudFormation inside the Serverless Framework's serverless.yml file too, but explaining that is outside the scope of this chapter (good exercise, though).

2.2.4   *Creating an IAM role*

Now you need to create an IAM role for your first Lambda function (you will create this function in a little while). The role allows your function to interact with S3 and Elemental MediaConvert. You'll add two policies to this role:

- `AWSLambdaExecute`
- `AWSElementalMediaConvertFullAccess`

The `AWSLambdaExecute` policy allows Lambda to interact with S3 and CloudWatch. CloudWatch is an AWS service for collecting log files, tracking metrics, and setting alarms. The `AWSElementalMediaConvertFullAccess` policy allows Lambda to submit new transcoding jobs to Elemental MediaConvert.

1. In the AWS console, find and click IAM.
2. Choose Roles.
3. Click the Create Role button to begin. You will see a list of different AWS technologies under AWS Service. Select Lambda and the Next: Permissions button.
4. In this view, you can search for and attach premade policies. Find and attach (by clicking the checkbox on the left) the following two policies:
   - `AWSLambdaExecute`
   - `AWSElementalMediaConvertFullAccess`
5. Click Next: Tags to advance.
6. Click Next: Review to proceed to the Review page.
7. Name your role transcode-video and click Create Role.

After the role is created, you'll see the list of your existing roles again. Choose transcode-video to see what's inside. It should look like figure 2.6.

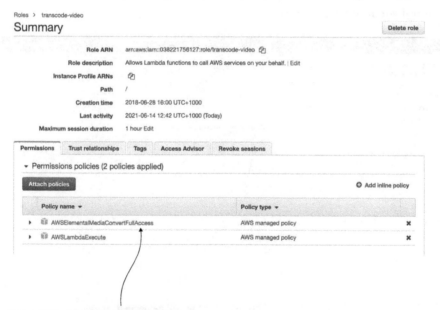

Two policies have been added to the role.
Permissions are embedded within policies.

Figure 2.6   Two managed policies are needed for the transcode-video role to access S3 and create Elemental MediaConvert jobs.

2.2.5   *Using AWS Elemental MediaConvert*

You are going to use Elemental MediaConvert to convert uploaded video files from one format to another. At a high level, MediaConvert works by taking a file uploaded to an S3 bucket, transcoding the file to one or more different versions, and then placing these versions in to another S3 bucket.

When you create a MediaConvert job, you'll have to specify this information, including input and output buckets, and what conversion you'd like to carry out. You will also have to specify a MediaConvert endpoint. Each user has a custom endpoint, and you need to know where it is. Let's find it now so that you'll know where to look.

1. In the AWS console, select MediaConvert (it will be under the Media Services category).
2. Click the hamburger icon in the top left corner (it looks like three parallel lines).
3. Choose Account from the menu.

You should see the API endpoint that you will need to use in this chapter (figure 2.7). Note that you can always refer to these instructions to find the MediaConvert API endpoint if you forget where it is.

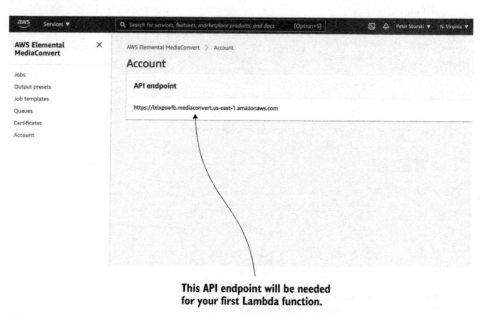

**This API endpoint will be needed
for your first Lambda function.**

Figure 2.7   Viewing the API endpoint that you will use in this chapter

You are nearly there! There's one more IAM role you need to create now to make things easier later.

2.2.6 Using MediaConvert Role

You need to create a role for the MediaConvert service. MediaConvert needs to have access to S3 as well as the API Gateway. Without this role, MediaConvert simply will not run when you try to invoke it from Lambda. To create the role, follow these steps (or try it on your own!):

1. In the AWS console, click IAM and then click Roles.
2. Click the Create Role button. You will see a list of different AWS technologies under AWS Service. Select MediaConvert and the Next: Permissions button. AWS has already predefined what policies you need for this role. These are S3 Full Access and API Gateway Full Invoke.
3. Choose Next: Tags, then click Next: Review to proceed to the next page.
4. Name your role media-convert-role and click Create Role.
5. Copy the ARN of the role to a notepad or someplace where it can be easily retrieved. You'll need the role ARN as well as the API endpoint later (in listing 2.3).

2.3 Starting with the Serverless Framework

The Serverless Framework is going to help you organize your functions and deploy them to AWS. This framework is powerful, so you will get a lot of flexibility in terms of how to package code, what variables to use, and environments to deploy to.

   If you get stuck with the Serverless Framework, have a look at appendix C or check out https://serverless.com/framework/docs. Appendix C features a thorough walk-through of the Serverless Framework as well as useful hints and tips. However, if you don't find your answer there, then the online documentation is the way to go.

> ### Source code on GitHub
> The source code for this chapter can be found at https://github.com/sbarski/serverless -architectures-aws-2.

2.3.1 Setting up the Serverless Framework

Install the Serverless Framework by running `npm install -g serverless` from the terminal. At the time of writing, we used Serverless Framework 2.63. If you are using a later version of the framework and something doesn't work, you may have to apply your best detective skills to figure out what's wrong and fix it (or downgrade to 2.63).

CREDENTIALS

The Serverless Framework needs access to your AWS account so that it can create and manage resources on your behalf. By default, Serverless Framework uses the AWS profile you have already configured on your machine using the AWS CLI.

HELLO WORLD!

Having installed the Serverless Framework and configured credentials, let's test that it works. In your terminal, run the following command:

```
serverless create --template aws-nodejs --path hello-world
```

Change to the newly created directory by typing cd hello-world. You should see two files in this directory: serverless.yml and handler.js. The first file, serverless.yml, is a project file (a service) that describes functions, events, and resources that the function can use. The second file, handler.js, is an example Lambda function that you can change! Open handler.js and modify the implementation of the function as the following listing shows.

Listing 2.1   A new hello-world Lambda function

```
'use strict';                                  Because this is a basic function, you
                                               can run it in AWS Lambda and see a
module.exports.hello = async (event) => {  ◁─┘ message.
  return {
    statusCode: 200,
    body: JSON.stringify(
      {                                        The only line of code that you need to
        message: 'Hello Serverless World!', ◁─┘ modify before running this example
        input: event,
      },
      null,
      2
    ),
  };
};
```

Once you have finished modifying the function, remember to save the file. You are now ready to deploy. Run serverless deploy from the terminal and press Enter (make sure you are in the same directory as the serverless.yml file before you deploy; otherwise, you'll get an error message).

You'll see the Serverless Framework package up files, prepare a CloudFormation stack, and deploy your function to AWS. As soon as the deployment finishes, you'll see a bit of useful information such as the stage used for the function (dev), the region (us-east-1), and the name of the service (hello-world). Your function will be called hello-world-dev-hello a combination of the service name, stage, and the function export.

You can finally check that the function was successfully deployed by opening the Lambda console in AWS and running the function from there. Another option is to invoke the deployed function from the terminal.

To run the function in AWS and return a response, execute the following command in the terminal: serverless invoke --function hello. The Serverless Framework will know to invoke this function from the cloud environment.

Serverless deploy

You don't need to type `serverless` (as in `serverless deploy`) each time you want
to deploy or do an operation. You can use the `sls` abbreviation. The following commands are entirely valid: `sls deploy` or `sls invoke --function hello`.

2.3.2 Bringing Serverless Framework to The 24-Hour Video

Now that you have gotten the Serverless Framework to work, let's get busy with *The 24-
Hour Video*. You are going to create a new function and reference it in serverless.yml.
You will be able to deploy the function (and then add additional functions) with a single
command and, later, sustainably grow and organize your entire serverless application.

1. In a terminal window, run the following command:

   ```
   sls create --template aws-nodejs --path twentyfour-hour-video
   ```

   The reason we used `twentyfour` instead of 24 is because a service name must
   begin with an alphabetic character.

2. Change to the new twentyfour-hour-video directory that was just created.
3. Delete handler.js but leave serverless.yml intact.
4. Create a new subfolder called transcode-video.

In a moment, you'll begin changing serverless.yml. You can stick to our implementation (listing 2.2), however, there are five parameters that you must change to correctly
reflect your environment. These parameters are bolded in listing 2.2:

- The name of the upload bucket
- The name of the transcoded video bucket
- The video role ARN for your function
- The MediaConvert endpoint
- The MediaConvert role

Listing 2.2 Changing serverless.yml for your function

The provider is AWS, but Serverless Framework supports
other Cloud providers like Azure and Google Cloud too.

```
service: twentyfour-hour-video          Set this to nodejsl4.x if it's not already set.

provider:                               Defines the region to deploy to. You can override
  name: aws                             this setting and deploy to other regions.
  runtime: nodejs14.x
  region: us-east-1                     Set this custom variable to the
                                        name of your upload bucket.
custom:
  upload-bucket: upload-video-bucket        Set the transcode-bucket to the name
  transcode-bucket: transcoded-video-bucket of your transcoded video bucket. You
  transcode-video-role:                     created this bucket in section 2.2.3.
    arn:aws:iam::038221756127:role/transcode-video    Set the transcode-video role
                                                       ARN you created in section 2.2.4.
                                                       Update the ARN to your value.
```

```
media-endpoint:
  ➥ https://u4ac0ytu.mediaconvert.us-east-1.amazonaws.com  ◄┐
media-role:
  ➥ arn:aws:iam::038221756127:role/media-convert-role  ◄──
```

> Set your personal MediaConvert endpoint for the service to work. Your URL will be different so be sure to change this.

```
functions:
  transcode-video:
    handler: transcode-video/index.handler
    role: ${self:custom.transcode-video-role}
    package:
      individually: true
    environment:
      MEDIA_ENDPOINT: ${self:custom.media-endpoint}
      MEDIA_ROLE: ${self:custom.media-role}
      TRANSCODED_VIDEO_BUCKET: ${self:custom.transcode-bucket}
    events:
      - s3: ${self:custom.upload-bucket}  ◄──
```

> Set the MediaConvert role ARN you created in section 2.2.6. If you kept the same name, change the account number (e.g., 038221751234) to your account number and everything should work.

> Specifies the event trigger for the Lambda function, which is the S3 upload bucket

Here's a brief explanation of everything you need to update in listing 2.2 to make it work for you. Let's begin with the upload bucket.

UPLOAD BUCKET

In listing 2.2, you must specify the name of the upload bucket. This is a new bucket that doesn't yet exist. Remember, you need to use a bucket name that is globally unique. One way to do this is to prefix or postfix your full name (unless you have a common name) or add a few random letters and numbers.

Serverless Framework via CloudFormation creates the bucket for you automatically. You can go for something like upload-bucket-*firstname-lastname*. If the bucket name is already taken, Serverless Framework will tell you during deployment. You'll be able to change it and try again.

TRANSCODED VIDEO BUCKET

In listing 2.2, there's a custom property called `transcode-bucket`. This property contains the name of your transcoded video bucket. Update this property to the name of the bucket you manually created in section 2.2.3.

LAMBDA ROLE ARN

You must specify an IAM role for the function. Luckily, you created a role in section 2.2.4. You need to find the ARN of that role, copy it, and then update the parameter called transcode-video-role. To get the role ARN and update serverless.yml, follow these easy steps:

1. In the IAM console, select Roles.
2. Find the transcode-video role and select it.
3. Copy the value for the role ARN.
4. Paste the value in to the serverless.yml file for the transcode-video-role.

MEDIACONVERT ENDPOINT

In listing 2.2, you'll find a line that creates a media-endpoint variable. To get this endpoint, refer to section 2.2.5 or follow these steps:

1. In the AWS console, select MediaConvert (it will be under the Media Services category).

2. Click the hamburger icon in the top left corner (it's the button that looks like three parallel lines).

3. Choose Account from the menu. You'll see the API endpoint that you should copy into listing 2.2.

MEDIACONVERT ROLE

In section 2.2.6, you created an IAM role for the Element MediaConvert service. In listing 2.2, you needed to specify the ARN for that role. Make sure to look it up and copy it over correctly. Be careful not to confuse the two IAM roles that you have. The IAM role created in section 2.2.4 is intended for the transcode-video Lambda function. The role created in 2.2.6 is intended for MediaConvert and is the one you should use.

2.3.3 Creating your first Lambda function

Now that you've created a serverless.yml file, change to the transcode-video folder, and in your terminal window, run `npm init`. Agree to all the options by pressing Enter. You can change anything you want; it will not affect your function.

You'll get a new file called package.json. This file can be used later if you want to add additional dependencies or libraries into your function. Now, let's discuss how your new function will work and what it will do:

- The function will invoke as soon as a new file is uploaded to an S3 bucket.
- Information about the uploaded video will pass to the Lambda function via the event object. It will include the bucket name and the name (key) of the file being uploaded.
- The Lambda function will prepare a transcoding job for AWS MediaConvert.
- The function will submit the job to MediaConvert and writes a message to an Amazon CloudWatch log stream.

Create a new file named index.js and open it in your favorite text editor. This file contains the first function. The important thing to note is that you must define a function handler, which will be invoked by the Lambda runtime.

Listing 2.3 shows this function's implementation. Copy this listing into index.js. Before you can deploy and run this code though, you'll need to make a few small changes as detailed in the text after the code listing.

Listing 2.3 Creating the transcode video Lambda

```
'use strict';

const AWS = require('aws-sdk');
const mediaConvert = new AWS.MediaConvert({
    endpoint: process.env.MEDIA_ENDPOINT
});
```

Gets the MediaConvert endpoint environment variable that's set in serverless.yml (listing 2.2)

```
const outputBucketName =
➦ process.env.TRANSCODED_VIDEO_BUCKET;          ◄──┐  Gets the transcoded video bucket name
                                                       that's specified in serverless.yml

exports.handler = async (event, context) => {
    const key = event.Records[0].s3.object.key;
    const sourceKey = decodeURIComponent(key.replace(/\+/g, ' '));
    const outputKey = sourceKey.split('.')[0];

    const input = 's3://' + event.Records[0].s3.bucket.name + '/' +
    ➦ event.Records[0].s3.object.key;
    const output = 's3://' + outputBucketName + '/' + outputKey + '/';

    try {
                                                           Gets the MediaConvert role ARN
        const job = {                                      that's specified in serverless.yml
            "Role": process.env.MEDIA_ROLE,     ◄──┘
            "Settings": {
                "Inputs": [{                              Specifies the Audio Selector for the
                    "FileInput": input,                   MediaConvert job definition. You'll
                    "AudioSelectors": {         ◄──       default to naming a single audio
                        "Audio Selector 1": {             track in the video.
                            "SelectorType": "TRACK",
                            "Tracks": [1]
                        }
                    }
                }],
                "OutputGroups": [{
                    "Name": "File Group",
                    "Outputs": [{
                        "Preset": "System-
                        ➥ Generic_Hd_Mp4_Avc_Aac_16x9_1920x1080p_24Hz_6Mbps",
                        "Extension": "mp4",
                        "NameModifier": "_16x9_1920x1080p_24Hz_6Mbps"
                    }, {
                        "Preset": "System-
                        ➥ Generic_Hd_Mp4_Avc_Aac_16x9_1280x720p_24Hz_4.5Mbps",
                        "Extension": "mp4",
                        "NameModifier": "_16x9_1280x720p_24Hz_4.5Mbps"
                    }, {
                        "Preset": "System-
                        ➥ Generic_Sd_Mp4_Avc_Aac_4x3_640x480p_24Hz_1.5Mbps",
                        "Extension": "mp4",
                        "NameModifier": "_4x3_640x480p_24Hz_1.5Mbps"
                    }],
                    "OutputGroupSettings": {
                        "Type": "FILE_GROUP_SETTINGS",
                        "FileGroupSettings": {
                            "Destination": output     ◄──
                        }
                    }
                }]
            }
        };

    const mediaConvertResult = await
    ➦ mediaConvert.createJob(job).promise();
```

Sets the location of the input video for the MediaConvert job definition ──► "FileInput": input,

Sets the output bucket for the new video files

```
        console.log(mediaConvertResult);

    } catch (error) {
        console.error(error);
    }
};
```

MEDIACONVERT OUTPUTS

The function in listing 2.3 declares three new outputs that define the format for your newly transcoded videos (this includes bit rate, resolution, and so forth). The templates specified in listing 2.3 are generic templates built in to MediaConvert. Luckily, you aren't forced to use the ones we've selected; you can choose from different templates or even create your own. To look at other available presets in MediaConvert do the following:

1. In the AWS console, select MediaConvert.
2. Click the hamburger icon in the top left corner.
3. Choose Output Presets.
4. From the dropdown that says Custom Presets, select System Presets.

You'll see a grid of different presets you can use (figure 2.8). Note that the grid has multiple pages and that you can choose to see different categories (MP4, HLS, Broadcast-XDCAM, and so on).

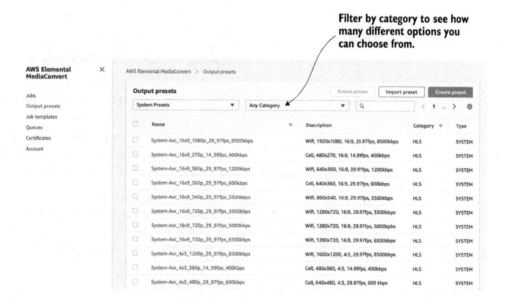

Figure 2.8 The MediaConvert Output Presets page lets you select system presets or configure your own.

If you want to create a different type of video using the code in listing 2.3, select the name of the desired preset, and copy it into the function as you did for the others (remember to specify the extension and a modified name). As an example, if you want to add HLS output, you'd need to include something like this in the `Outputs` array in the function:

```
{
    "Preset": "System-Ott_Hls_Ts_Avc_Aac_16x9_1280x720p_30Hz_3.5Mbps",
    "Extension": "hls",
    "NameModifier": "_Hls_Ts_Avc_Aac_16x9_1280x720p_30Hz_3.5Mbps "
}
```

DEPLOYMENT

Deploy your first function from the terminal by typing `sls deploy` (make sure you issue `sls deploy` from the directory where serverless.yml is located). The deployment should succeed, and you should see your functions in AWS. The first function is going to be named something like `twentyfour-hour-video-dev-transcode-video`. Later, if you want, you can remove this function from AWS by running `sls remove` from the terminal.

One other note: the deployment process may create an additional bucket named something like twentyfour-hour-video-de-serverlessdeploymentbuck-sq06y6wjku9z. This is normal. The Serverless Framework creates this bucket to upload the Cloud-Formation templates it generates. You can safely ignore this bucket, but do not manually delete! The `sls remove` command will remove it for you (along with the deployed Lambda function).

2.4   *Testing in AWS*

To test your first function, upload a video to the upload bucket. Follow these steps:

1. Go to the S3 console.
2. Click into your upload bucket and then select Upload to open the Upload page (figure 2.9).
3. Click Add Files, select a video file from your computer, and click the Upload button. All other settings can be left as is. If you don't have any video files to test, go to https://sample-videos.com and grab one of the MP4 videos.

After a time, you should see three new videos in your transcoded video bucket. These files should appear in a folder rather than in the root of the bucket (figure 2.10). The length of time to produce a new video depends on the duration of the file you've uploaded. It may take five minutes (or even longer) to produce a new file so grab a cup of tea while you wait.

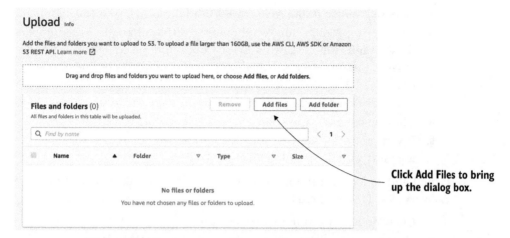

Figure 2.9 To test in ASW, it's better to upload a small file initially because it makes the upload and transcoding go a lot quicker.

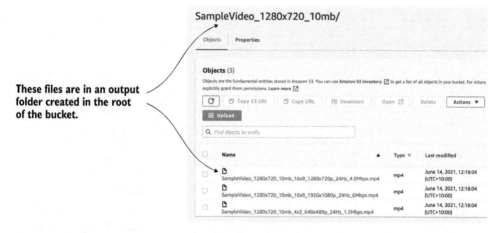

Figure 2.10 MediaConvert generates three new files and places them in a folder in the transcoded video S3 bucket.

2.5 Looking at logs

Having performed a test in the previous section, you should see three new files in your transcoded video bucket. But things may not always go as smoothly (although we hope they do)! In case of problems, such as new files not appearing, you can check two different logs for errors. The first and most important one is Lambda's log in Cloud-Watch. To view the log, perform the following steps:

1. Choose Lambda in the AWS console and then click your function name.
2. Choose the Monitor tab. You should see different graphs with numbers. One of those graphs will be labeled Error Count and Success Rate. If there is a spike (that is, the count is more than 0), it means there is a problem.
3. Click View Logs in CloudWatch to open CloudWatch. You'll see all the log entries ordered by date. On the right, you'll see which stream they belong to.
4. Click each log entry to see more details including error messages.
5. If you previously saw that your Invocation error rate was more than 0, find the log entry with the error and fix the problem.

If the Lambda logs reveal nothing out of the ordinary, take a look at the AWS Media-Convert logs. To view these logs:

1. Click MediaConvert in the AWS console.
2. Choose the hamburger icon on the left to open the sidebar.
3. Choose Jobs from the menu. On the right you should see a list of jobs.
4. Click a job (if it failed) to see more information (figure 2.11).

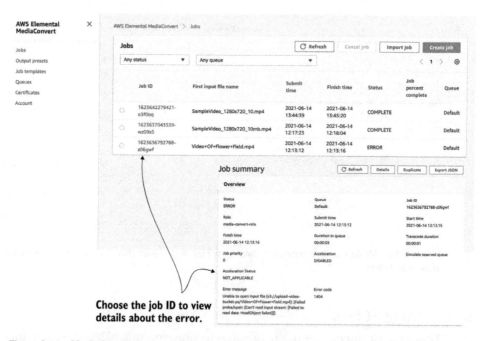

Choose the job ID to view details about the error.

Figure 2.11 MediaConvert failures can occur for a variety of reasons including the source file being deleted before the job started, an error with the code in the Lambda function, or a misconfiguration.

When problems happen

In our experience, problems often occur because IAM permissions haven't been configured correctly or there was a typo somewhere in your function code. AWS doesn't always have the most descriptive error messages so, sometimes, a bit of digging around and investigative work with CloudWatch is required.

Summary

- The best way to organize serverless applications is to use an Infrastructure as Code (IaC) framework like the Serverless Framework.
- Deploying functions and manually setting up services is great for learning, but it is not sustainable in the long term. The Serverless Framework can help to organize and deploy even the most complex serverless applications.
- Serverless applications and pipelines usually consist of different services connected together. In *The 24-Hour Video* example, we use AWS Lambda, S3, and Elemental MediaConvert. Most serverless applications use a combination of services.
- AWS CloudWatch is an important service for logging what happens within your AWS Lambda functions. It's vital that you learn how to use it as you are most definitely going to need it.
- Security in AWS is controlled primarily via Identity and Access Management (IAM), although there are some exceptions. If you want to become an expert at AWS and serverless applications, knowing how IAM works is essential.
- Estimating cost in AWS can be tricky. A lot of services have generous free tiers but can end up costing a lot if used incorrectly. Make sure you review the costs of all services you want to use and understand what the potential cost can be.

Architectures and patterns

This chapter covers

- Use cases for serverless architectures
- Examples of patterns and architectures

What are the use cases for serverless architectures and what kinds of architectures and patterns are useful? We're often asked these questions and queried about use cases as people learn about a serverless approach to designing systems. We find that it's helpful to look at how others have applied this technology and what kinds of use cases, designs, and architectures they've produced.

This chapter gives you a solid introduction to where serverless architectures are a good fit and how to think about the design of serverless systems. The rest of the book focuses on real-world use cases and goes deep into a number of serverless architectures that we've found particularly fascinating.

3.1 Use cases

Serverless technologies and architectures can be used to build entire systems, create isolated components, or implement specific granular tasks. The scope for use of serverless design is broad, and one of its advantages is that it's possible to use it for small as well as large tasks alike. We've designed serverless systems that power web and mobile applications for tens of thousands of users, and we've built simple systems to solve specific minute problems.

It's worth remembering that serverless is not just about running code in a compute service such as Lambda. It's also about using third-party services and APIs to cut down on the amount of work you must do. With this in mind, let's look at some basic use cases.

3.1.1 Backend compute

Technologies such as AWS Lambda are a few years old, but we've already seen large serverless backends that power entire businesses. A Cloud Guru (https://acloudguru .com), for example, supports many thousands of users collaborating in real time and streams hundreds of gigabytes of video. Another example is the insurance company, Branch, which from the start adopted a serverless-first approach (https://amzn.to/ 3vRumYU).

Indeed, it is possible to create and run an entire business while having a serverless-first mindset. If you articulate that kind of philosophical approach to technology yourself, it will help you answer questions such as what services to adopt or how to best solve a particular architectural problem.

Startups are not the only organizations looking for agility and efficiencies from serverless. Established companies with long histories are also using serverless technologies and architectures to deliver value to their customers. Some of these bigger companies include well-known names like Comcast, Coinbase, Fender, Nordstrom, and Netflix (https://aws.amazon.com/serverless/customers/).

3.1.2 Internet of Things (IoT)

Putting aside web and mobile applications, serverless is a great fit for the Internet of Things (IoT) applications. Amazon Web Services (AWS) has a useful IoT platform (https://aws.amazon.com/iot-platform/how-it-works/) that combines

- Authentication and authorization
- Communications gateway
- Registry (a way to assign a unique identity to each device)
- Device shadowing (to persist device state)
- Rules engine (to transform and route device messages to AWS services)

The rules engine, for example, can save files to Amazon's Simple Storage Service (S3), push data to an Amazon Simple Queue Service (SQS) queue, and invoke AWS Lambda functions. Amazon's IoT platform makes it easy to build scalable IoT backends for devices without having to run a server. A serverless application backend is appealing because it removes a lot of infrastructure management, has granular and predictable billing (especially when a serverless compute service such as Lambda is used), and can scale well to meet uneven demands.

3.1.3   *Data processing and manipulation*

A common use for serverless technologies is data processing, conversion, manipulation, and transcoding. We've seen Lambda functions built by other developers for processing CSV, JSON, and XML files; collation and aggregation of data; image resizing; and format conversion. Lambda and AWS services are well suited for building event-driven pipelines for data-processing tasks.

In chapter 2, you built a powerful pipeline for converting videos from one format to another. This pipeline runs only when a new video file is added to a designated S3 bucket, meaning that you only pay for the execution of Lambda when there's something to do and never while the system is idle. More broadly, however, we find data processing to be an excellent use case for serverless technologies, especially when we use Lambda in concert with other services.

3.1.4   *Real-time analytics*

Ingestion of data such as logs, system events, transactions, or user clicks can be accomplished using services such as Amazon Kinesis Data Streams and Amazon Kinesis Firehose. Kinesis Data Streams and Lambda functions are a good fit for applications that generate a lot of data that needs to be analyzed, aggregated, and stored. When it comes to Kinesis, the number of functions spawned to process messages from a stream is the same as the number of shards (therefore, there's one Lambda function per shard as figure 3.1 shows).

If a Lambda function fails to process a batch, it retries the operation. This can keep going for up to 24 hours (which is how long Kinesis will keep data around before it expires) each time processing fails.

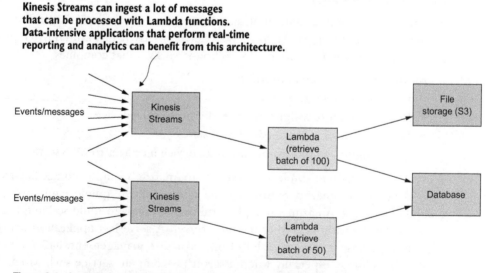

**Kinesis Streams can ingest a lot of messages
that can be processed with Lambda functions.
Data-intensive applications that perform real-time
reporting and analytics can benefit from this architecture.**

Figure 3.1   Lambda is a perfect tool to process data in near real time.

Amazon Kinesis Firehose is another Kinesis service designed to ingest gigabytes of streaming data and then push it into other services like S3, RedShift, or Elasticsearch for further analytics. Firehose is a true serverless service because it is fully managed, it scales automatically depending on the volume of data coming in, and there's no need to think about sharding as is the case with Kinesis Data Streams.

A great feature of Kinesis Firehose is that a Lambda function can be added to the stream to seamlessly process data as it is added and before it is sent to its final destination. You can use this to transform data while it's in flight without having to provision any other infrastructure. We are not going to go into much more depth right now because chapter 6 and chapter 9 discuss use cases and applications for the Kinesis products in more detail.

3.1.5 Legacy API proxy

One innovative use case of the Amazon API Gateway and Lambda that we've seen a few times is what we refer to as the legacy API proxy. Here, developers use API Gateway and Lambda to create a new API layer over legacy APIs and services, which makes them easier to use.

The API Gateway creates a RESTful interface, and Lambda functions modify request/response and marshal data to formats that legacy services understand. The API Gateway and Lambda functions can transform requests made by clients and invoke legacy services directly as figure 3.2 illustrates. This approach makes legacy services easier to consume for modern clients that may not support older protocols and data formats.

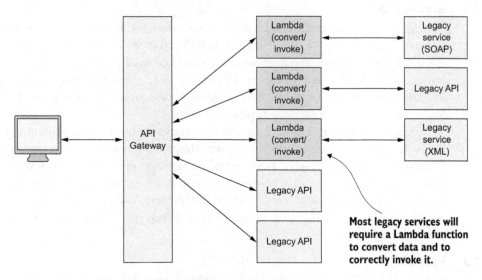

Figure 3.2 We can use the API proxy architecture to build a modern API interface over old services and APIs.

It's important to note that the API Gateway can transform (to an extent) and issue requests against other HTTP endpoints. But it works only in a number of fairly basic and limited use cases where JSON transformation is needed. In more complex scenarios, however, a Lambda function is needed to convert data, issue requests, and process responses.

Take a Simple Object Access Protocol (SOAP) service as an example. You'd need to write a Lambda function to connect to a SOAP service and then map responses to JSON. Thankfully, there are libraries that can take care of much of the heavy lifting in a Lambda function; for example, there are SOAP clients that can be downloaded from the npm registry for this purpose (see https://www.npmjs.com/package/soap).

3.1.6 *Scheduled services*

Lambda functions can run on a schedule, which makes them effective for repetitive tasks like data backups, imports and exports, reminders, and alerts. We've seen developers use Lambda functions on a schedule to periodically ping their websites to see if they're online and send an email or a text message if they're not. You'll find Lambda blueprints available for this (a *blueprint* is a template with sample code that can be selected when creating a new Lambda function).

We've also seen developers write Lambda functions to perform nightly downloads of files off their servers and send daily account statements to users. Repetitive tasks such as file backup and file validation can also be done easily with Lambda thanks to the scheduling capability that you can set and forget. Check out chapter 7 for an in-depth analysis on how to go about thinking and building a scheduling service.

3.1.7 *Bots and skills*

Another popular use of Lambda functions and serverless technologies is to build bots (a *bot* is an app or a script that runs automated tasks) for services such as Slack. A bot made for Slack can respond to commands, carry out small tasks, and send reports and notifications. We, for example, built a Slack bot in Lambda to report on the number of online sales made each day. And we've seen developers build bots for Telegram, Skype, and Facebook's messenger platform.

Similarly, developers write Lambda functions to power Alexa skills for Amazon Echo. Amazon Echo is a hands-free speaker that responds to voice commands. It runs a virtual assistant called Alexa. Developers can implement *skills* to extend Alexa's capabilities even further (a *skill* is essentially an app that can respond to a person's voice; for more information, see http://amzn.to/2b5NMFj). You can write a skill to order a pizza or quiz yourself on geography. Alexa is driven entirely by voice, and *skills* are powered by Lambda.

3.1.8 *Hybrids*

As we mentioned in chapter 1, serverless technologies and architectures are not an all-or-nothing proposition. They can be adopted and used alongside traditional systems. This hybrid approach may work especially well if a part of the existing infrastructure is already in AWS. We've also seen adoption of serverless technologies and architectures in organizations with developers initially creating standalone components (often to do additional data processing, database backups, and basic alerting) and, over time, integrating these components into their main systems (figure 3.3).

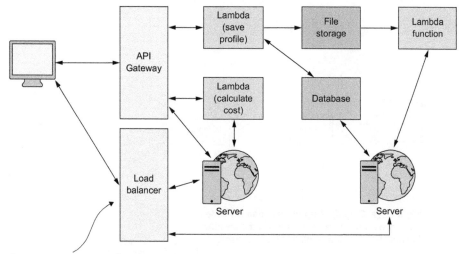

Any legacy system can use functions and services. This can allow you to slowly introduce serverless technologies without disturbing too much of the world order.

Figure 3.3 The hybrid approach is useful if you have a legacy system that uses servers.

3.2 *Patterns*

Patterns are architectural solutions to problems in software design. They're designed to address common problems found in software development. They're also an excellent communications tool for developers working together on a solution. It's far easier to find an answer to a problem if everyone in the room understands which patterns are applicable, how they work, their advantages, and their disadvantages.

The patterns presented in this section are useful for solving design problems in serverless architectures. But these patterns aren't exclusive to serverless. They were used in distributed systems long before serverless technologies became viable.

Apart from the patterns presented in this chapter, we recommend that you become familiar with patterns relating to authentication, data management (e.g., CQRS, event sourcing, materialized views), and error handling (e.g., Retry Pattern). Learning and applying these patterns will make you a better software engineer, regardless of the platform you choose to use. Let's look at a few of these patterns.

3.2.1 *GraphQL*

GraphQL (http://graphql.org) is a popular data query language developed by Facebook in 2012 and released publicly in 2015. It was designed as an alternative to REST (Representational State Transfer) because of its perceived weaknesses (multiple round-trips, over-fetching, and problems with versioning). GraphQL attempts to solve these problems by providing a hierarchical, declarative way of performing queries from a single endpoint (e.g., api/graphql). Figure 3.4 shows an example of a GraphQL and AWS Lambda implementation.

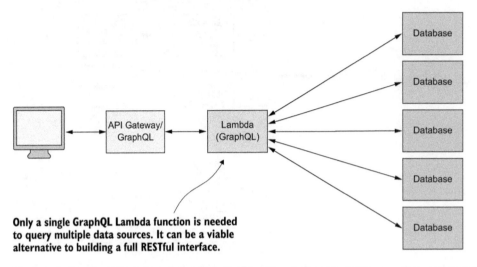

Only a single GraphQL Lambda function is needed to query multiple data sources. It can be a viable alternative to building a full RESTful interface.

Figure 3.4   The GraphQL and Lambda architecture has become popular in the serverless community.

GraphQL gives power to the client. Instead of specifying the structure of the response on the server, it's defined on the client (http://bit.ly/2aTjlh5). The client can specify what properties and relationships to return. GraphQL aggregates data from multiple sources and returns it to the client in a single round trip, which makes it an efficient system for retrieving data. According to Facebook, GraphQL serves millions of requests per second from nearly 1,000 different versions of its application.

A GraphQL library (server) can be hosted and run from a Lambda function. You'll also find managed solutions of GraphQL such as the ever-popular AWS AppSync at https://aws.amazon.com/appsync/.

WHEN TO USE THIS

GraphQL is a type of composite pattern that lets you aggregate data from multiple places. Reading and hydrating data from multiple data sources is common in web applications and especially so in those that adopt the microservices approach. There are other benefits too, including smaller payloads, avoiding the need to rebuild the data model, and no more versioned APIs (as compared to REST). These are just some of the reasons why GraphQL has become so popular in the past few years.

3.2.2   *Command pattern*

In the previous section, we mentioned the fact that a single endpoint can be used to cater to different requests with different data (a single GraphQL endpoint, for example, can accept any combination of fields from a client and create a response that matches the request). The same idea can be applied more generally. You can design a system in which a specific Lambda function controls and invokes other functions. You can connect it to an API Gateway or invoke it manually and pass messages to it to invoke other Lambda functions.

In software engineering, the *command pattern* (figure 3.5) is used to "encapsulate a request as an object, thereby letting you parameterize clients with different requests, queue or log requests, and support undoable operations" because of the "need to issue requests to objects without knowing anything about the operation being requested or the receiver of the request" (http://bit.ly/29ZaoWt). The command pattern lets you decouple the caller of the operation from the entity that carries out the required processing.

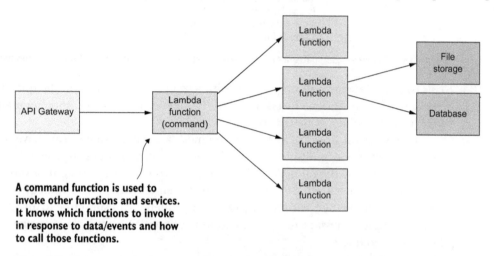

A command function is used to invoke other functions and services. It knows which functions to invoke in response to data/events and how to call those functions.

Figure 3.5   The command pattern invokes and controls functions and services from a single function.

In practice, this pattern can simplify an API Gateway implementation because you may not want or need to create a RESTful URI for every request. It can also make versioning simpler. The command Lambda function could work with different versions of your clients and invoke the right Lambda function that's needed by the client.

WHEN TO USE THIS

This pattern is useful if you want to decouple the caller and the receiver. Having a way to pass arguments as an object and allowing clients to be parametrized with different requests can reduce coupling between components and help make the system more extensible.

3.2.3   *Messaging pattern*

Messaging patterns (figure 3.6) are popular in distributed systems because they allow developers to build scalable and robust systems by decoupling functions and services from direct dependence on one another and allowing storage of events/records/requests in a queue. The reliability comes from the fact that if the consuming service goes offline, the queue retains messages (for some period), which can still be processed at a later time.

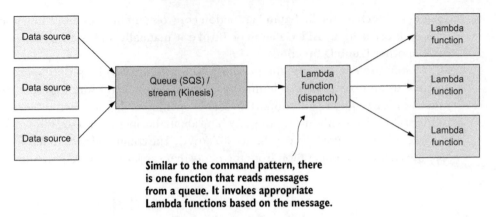

Similar to the command pattern, there is one function that reads messages from a queue. It invokes appropriate Lambda functions based on the message.

Figure 3.6   The messaging pattern and its many variations are popular in distributed environments.

This pattern features a message queue with a sender that can post to the queue and a receiver that can retrieve messages from the queue. In terms of implementation in AWS, you can build this pattern on top of the SQS.

Depending on how the system is designed, a message queue can have a single sender/receiver or multiple senders/receivers. SQS queues typically have one receiver per queue. If you need to have multiple consumers, a straightforward way to do it is to introduce multiple queues into the system (figure 3.7). A strategy you could apply is to combine SQS with Amazon SNS. SQS queues can subscribe to an SNS topic so that pushing a message to the topic would automatically push the message to all of the subscribed queues.

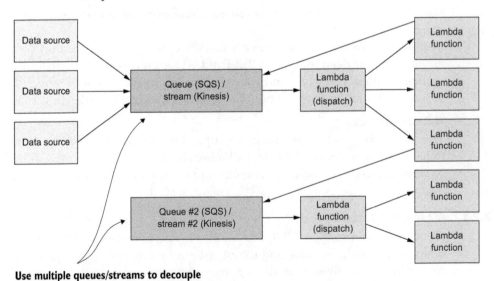

Use multiple queues/streams to decouple multiple components in your system.

Figure 3.7   Your system may have multiple queues or streams and Lambda functions to process all incoming data.

The messaging pattern handles workloads and data processing. The queue serves as a buffer, so if the consuming service crashes, data isn't lost. It remains in the queue until the service can restart and begin processing it again.

A message queue can make future changes easier, too, because there's less coupling between functions. In an environment that has a lot of data processing, messages, and requests, try to minimize the number of functions that are directly dependent on other functions and use the messaging pattern instead.

3.2.4 Priority queue pattern

A great benefit of using a platform such as AWS and serverless architectures is that capacity planning and scalability are more of a concern for Amazon's engineers than for you. But, in some cases, you may want to control how and when messages get dealt with by your system. This is where you might need to have different queues, topics, or streams to feed messages to your functions.

Your system might go one step further, having entirely different workflows for messages of different priority (the priority queue pattern). Messages that need immediate attention might go through a flow that expedites the process by using more expensive services and APIs with more capacity. Messages that don't need to be processed quickly can go through a different workflow as figure 3.8 shows.

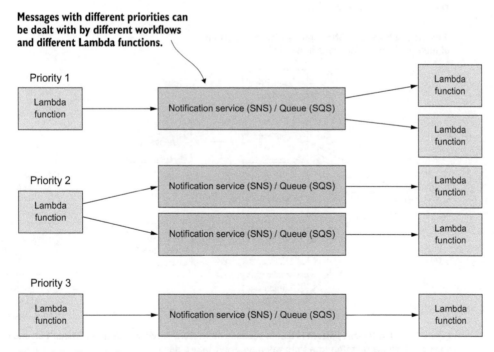

Figure 3.8 The priority queue pattern is an evolution of the messaging pattern.

The priority queue pattern might involve the creation and use of entirely different SNS topics, SQS queues, Lambda functions, and even third-party services. Use this pattern sparingly, however, because additional components, dependencies, and workflows result in more complexity.

WHEN TO USE THIS

This pattern works when you need to have a different priority for processing messages. Your system can implement workflows and use different services and APIs to cater to many types of needs and users (for example, paying versus nonpaying users).

3.2.5 *Fan-out pattern*

Fan-out is a type of messaging pattern that's familiar to many AWS users. Generally, the fan-out pattern pushes a message to all listening/subscribed clients of a particular queue or a message pipeline. In AWS, this pattern is usually implemented using SNS topics that allow multiple subscribers to be invoked when a new message is added to a topic.

Take S3 as an example. When a new file is added to a bucket, S3 can invoke a single Lambda function with information about the file. But what if you need to invoke two, three, or more Lambda functions at the same time? The original function could be modified to invoke other functions (like the command pattern), but that's a lot of work if all you need is to run functions in parallel. The solution is to use the fan-out pattern with SNS (see figure 3.9).

A message added to an SNS topic can force invocation of multiple Lambda functions in parallel.

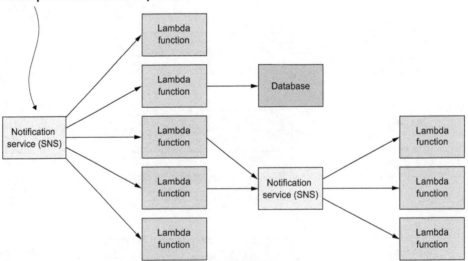

Figure 3.9   The fan-out pattern is useful because many AWS services (such as S3) can't invoke more than one Lambda function at a time when an event takes place.

SNS topics are communications or messaging channels that can have multiple publishers and subscribers (including Lambda functions). When a new message is added to a topic, it forces invocation of all the subscribers in parallel, thus causing the event to *fan out*.

Going back to the S3 example discussed earlier, instead of invoking a single Lambda function, you can configure S3 to push a message to an SNS topic, which invokes all subscribed functions simultaneously. It's an effective way to create event-driven architectures and perform operations in parallel. Chapter 8 shows how to use this pattern to perform video encoding at scale.

WHEN TO USE THIS

This pattern is useful if you need to invoke multiple Lambda functions at the same time. An SNS topic will retry, invoking your Lambda functions, if it fails to deliver the message or if the function fails to execute (see https://go.aws/3DTdCEK).

Furthermore, the fan-out pattern can be used for more than just invocation of multiple Lambda functions. SNS topics support other subscribers such as email and SQS queues. Adding a new message to a topic can invoke Lambda functions, send an email, or push a message on to an SQS queue, all at the same time.

> ### SQS vs. SNS vs. EventBridge
> Sometimes it's hard to know which AWS service to use in which situation. When it comes to event messaging, we've discussed SQS and SNS already, but there's also Amazon EventBridge to round out the family. The following Lumigo blog post features an excellent summary and comparison of these services: https://bit.ly/3AYdJga. We highly recommend that you take a look at it if you are trying to understand their differences and use cases. Another good explanation comes from AWS themselves: https://go.aws/3phPOWW.

3.2.6 Compute as glue

The compute-as-glue architecture (figure 3.10) describes the idea that we can use Lambda functions to create powerful execution pipelines and workflows. This often involves using Lambda as *glue* between different services, coordinating and invoking them. With this style of architecture, the focus of the developer is on the design of their pipeline, coordination, and data flow. The parallelism of serverless compute services like Lambda helps to make these architectures appealing.

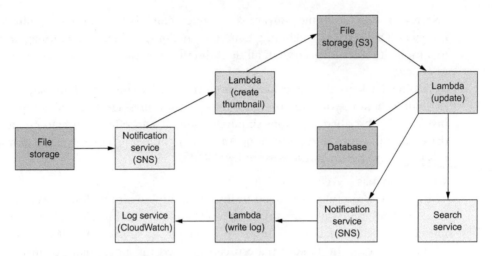

Figure 3.10   The compute-as-glue architecture uses Lambda functions to connect different services and APIs to achieve a task. In this pipeline, a simple image transformation results in a new file, an update to a database, an update to a search service, and a new entry to a log service.

3.2.7   *Pipes and filters pattern*

The purpose of the pipes and filters pattern is to decompose a complex processing task into a series of manageable, discrete services organized in a pipeline (figure 3.11). Components designed to transform data are traditionally referred to as *filters*, whereas connectors that pass data from one component to the next component are referred to as *pipes*. Serverless architecture lends itself well to this kind of pattern. This is useful for all kinds of tasks where multiple steps are required to achieve a result.

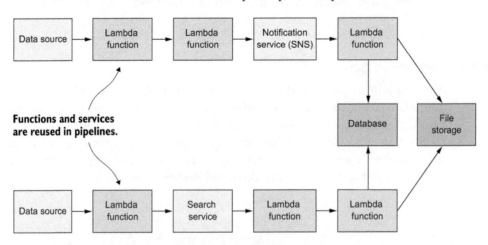

Figure 3.11   The pipes and filters pattern encourages the construction of pipelines to pass and transform data from its origin (pump) to its destination (sink).

With this pattern, we recommend that every Lambda function be written as a granular service or a task with the single-responsibility principle in mind. Inputs and outputs should be clearly defined (there should be a clear interface) and any side effects minimized. Following this advice will allow you to create functions that can be reused in pipelines and, more broadly, within your serverless system.

You might notice that this pattern is similar to the compute-as-glue architecture we described previously. You are right, compute as glue and this pattern are closely related and are simply a variation of the same concept.

WHEN TO USE THIS

When you have a complex task, try to break it down into a series of functions (a pipeline) and apply the following rules:

- Make sure your function follows the single-responsibility principle.
- Clearly define an interface for the function. Make sure inputs and outputs are clearly stated.
- Create a black box. Consumers of the function shouldn't have to know how it works, but they must know to use it and what kind of output to expect.

Throughout the rest of this book, we'll discuss and give more context to the patterns and architecture we explored here. With that in mind, let's jump into the next chapter and read a story about a social network called Yubl.

Summary

- Serverless architecture can support different use cases including building backends for web, mobile, and IoT applications, as well as data processing and analytics.
- Serverless technologies like AWS Lambda are flexible. They can be combined with containers or virtual machines into hybrid architectures. You don't need to be a serverless purist to achieve great outcomes.
- Certain patterns and approaches like GraphQL are well suited to serverless architectures because AWS services such as AppSync are on hand and can integrate nicely with the rest of your architecture.
- Classic software engineering patterns like messaging patterns work exceptionally well with serverless architectures and AWS products such as SQS.
- The fan-out pattern is one of the more common patterns. Knowing how to set it up using Amazon SNS is important to be effective with AWS.
- AWS has a lot of different services and products that overlap. Having a thorough understanding of when to use each service will help you make better decisions.

Part 2

Use cases

You've read through part 1 and now, we hope, you have a good understanding of what serverless is all about. It's time to take a look at how three companies use serverless architectures to solve problems and delight their customers. In part 2, we present three use-case studies from Yubl, A Cloud Guru, and Yle.

Yubl: Architecture
highlights, lessons learned

This chapter covers

- The original Yubl architecture and its problems
- The new serverless architecture and the decisions behind it
- Strategies and patterns for moving monolith applications to serverless
- Lessons learned from this migration

In April 2016, I joined a social network based in London called Yubl. There I inherited a monolithic backend system written in Node.js and running on a handful of Elastic Compute Cloud (EC2) instances. The original system took 2.5 years to implement and had a long list of performance and scalability issues once it went live. With a small team of six engineers, we managed to move the platform to serverless over the course of six months. Along the way, we added many new features and addressed the existing performance and scalability issues. We reduced feature delivery time from months to days, and in some cases, hours. Although cost was not the main motivation for undertaking this transformation, we made a 95% savings on our AWS bill in the process. Let's take a peek at the original Yubl architecture.

4.1   *The original Yubl architecture*

Yubl (short for "your social bubble") was a mobile-first, social network designed for the 17 to 25-year-old demographic. The user-generated posts (called *yubls*) contained videos as well as animated and interactive elements. The app had all the social features you'd find in other social networks: follow users, private and group chat, liking and resharing content, and others.

The original architecture (figure 4.1) consisted of the following:

- A monolithic REST API written in Node.js and running on EC2
- A WebSockets API written in Node.js and running on EC2
- A monolithic MongoDB database hosted in MongoLab
- A CloudAMQP message queue
- A cluster of background workers written in Node.js and running on EC2

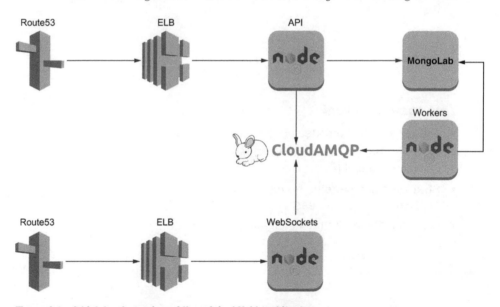

Figure 4.1   A high-level overview of the original Yubl architecture

> ### What is MongoDB and MongoLab?
>
> MongoDB is a popular document-oriented NoSQL database that allows you to store JSON documents. You can learn more about it at https://www.mongodb.com.
>
> MongoLab is an online service that provides MongoDB hosting as a service. You can create a MongoDB cluster with a few clicks, and MongoLab takes care of the underlying infrastructure for you. You can learn more about it at https://mlab.com. Back in 2016, MongoLab was a viable service for running MongoDB without having to manage the underlying infrastructure yourself.

> ## What is RabbitMQ and CloudAMQP?
>
> Advanced Message Queueing Protocol (AMQP) is an application protocol for message-oriented middlewares. It supports message queueing and routing and is often used in publish-and-subscribe systems.
>
> - RabbitMQ is an open-source message broker that implements the AMQP protocol. You can learn more abo9ut RabbitMQ at https://www.rabbitmq.com/.
> - CloudAMQP is an online service that provides RabbitMQ hosting. You can learn more about it at https://cloudamqp.com.

4.1.1 Scalability problems

Being an early stage social network, the baseline traffic at Yubl was low, but they managed to attract several high-profile Instagram influencers to the platform. These influencers brought many of their Instagram followers along, and with tens of thousands of followers, these influencers drove unpredictable and spiky traffic through the system whenever they posted new content.

We often saw 100x spikes in traffic as thousands of users flooded in all at once to see their favorite influencer's new content. These traffic spikes were usually short-lived, which was problematic for the EC2-based system because EC2 autoscaling couldn't react fast enough. It typically takes EC2 instances a few minutes to spin up. By the time they are ready to serve user requests, it's too late. The traffic spikes have come and gone, and many users would have left after having experienced a laggy response time.

As a workaround, we ran a much larger EC2 cluster, scaling up much earlier than we wanted. This resulted in a lot of wasted cost because we had to pay for lots of EC2 resources that we were not using. Our cluster of API web servers had an average utilization of from 2% to 5%.

4.1.2 Performance problems

The monolithic MongoDB database was also a constant source of performance and scalability problems. Every read and write operation hit the database directly; some API operations can take a heavy toll on a MongoDB server. One example of this is a user search, which is a frequently used API call and executes a complex regex query against MongoDB. Another example included user recommendations, which executed a complex query to find second- and third-degree connections to the current user (those who follow your followers or those followed by users you follow).

4.1.3 Long feature delivery cycles

The codebase was complex, and many features were intertwined through shared MongoDB collections and implicit coupling through shared libraries. Although there were plenty of unit tests with a reasonable code coverage, these did not prove useful because code changes often passed all the tests, only to fail when deployed to the AWS environment. The interaction with external services was mocked thoroughly and, therefore, not covered by the tests. In many cases, the tests simply confirmed the mocks were working and returned what was requested even if the MongoDB query contained syntax errors. We had little faith in the tests because they gave us too many false-positives.

To make matters worse, every deployment required taking the whole system down for 30 minutes or more, during which time users received no feedback and the app just appeared broken. Features used to take months to go to production. Even simple changes often took weeks to complete, which was frustrating to everyone involved.

4.1.4   *Why serverless?*

Based on the requirements for our system and the problems the current implementation experienced, serverless was a great fit for the following reasons:

- *AWS Lambda autoscales the number of concurrent executions based on load.* This happens instantly and handles those unpredictable spikes we experience effortlessly.
- *AWS Lambda deploys functions to three availability zones by default, which provides significant redundancy without incurring extra costs.* We pay only when a function runs, whereas with EC2, we paid for the redundancy in a multi-AZ setup, which also dilutes the traffic and reduces the resource utilization even further.
- *AWS manages the underlying physical infrastructure as well as the operating system that our code runs on.* AWS applies patches and security updates regularly and does a much better job of keeping the operating system secure than we could. This removes a whole class of vulnerabilities that plague so many software systems around the world.
- *With tools such as the Serverless framework, the deployment pipeline for our application is drastically simplified.* A typical deployment takes less than a minute and has no downtime because AWS Lambda automatically routes requests to the new code.
- *When using serverless technologies such as API Gateway, Lambda, and DynamoDB, we don't have to worry about the underlying infrastructure.* This lets us focus on addressing core business needs. Almost every line of our code is business logic! And it allows the development team to move quickly, knowing that what we build is scalable and resilient by default.
- *The number of production deployments went from four to six per month to averaging more than 80 per month with the same sized team.* We didn't have to hire more people to go faster, we allowed each developer to be more productive instead.
- *As we migrated more and more of the system to serverless, scalability, cost and reliability all improved.* There were far fewer production issues, and we were spending a fraction of what we spent on EC2 previously.

4.2 *The new serverless Yubl architecture*

By November 2016, less than 8 months after I joined the company and started us on the journey to serverless, almost the entire backend system was migrated to serverless; this using a combination of services such as API Gateway, Lambda, DynamoDB, Kinesis, and so much more. Along the way, we enhanced existing features and implemented countless new features. We also addressed many security issues with the previous system.

Overall, the system's reliability increased drastically. We experienced only one minor outage to our production environment because of a brief Simple Storage Service (S3) outage. The following points are some key highlights of the new serverless architecture on AWS:

- The monolith was broken up into many microservices.
- Every microservice has its own GitHub repository and one Continuous Integration/Continuous Delivery (CI/CD) pipeline. All the components that make up this microservice (API Gateway, Lambda functions, DynamoDB tables, etc.) are deployed together as one CloudFormation stack using the Serverless Framework.
- Most microservices have an API Gateway REST API running under its own subdomain, such as search.yubl.com.
- Every microservice has its own database for the data it needs. Most use DynamoDB, but it's not universal because different microservices have different data needs.
- Every state change in the system is captured as an event and published to a Kinesis Data Stream (for example, a user created new content, a user posted new content, and so on).
- Most of the time, we prefer to synchronize data between microservices through events rather than synchronous API calls at run time. This helps prevent cascade failures when one microservice experiences an outage in production. Instead, microservices subscribe to the relevant Kinesis Data Stream and copy needed data from the appropriate events.

This diagram (https://d2qt42rcwzspd6.cloudfront.net/overall.png) shows a birds-eye view of this new architecture. Don't worry about making sense of everything in the figure. It merely demonstrates the fact that you can build even complex systems using serverless components.

It's worth mentioning that the move to serverless was not one of our goals. The goal was to deliver a better user experience with less downtime, more responsiveness, and more scalability. Serverless technologies like Lambda, API Gateway, and DynamoDB happen to be a great way to achieve our goals while also making our lives a lot easier and allowing us to ship features faster.

4.2.1   *Rearchitecting and rewriting*

To fully realize our goals, we had to rearchitect and rewrite large parts of the system. But we didn't want to migrate everything to serverless for the sake of migrating them. We wanted to accelerate feature development and deliver value to our users faster than before. For this, we took a pragmatic approach, whereby we made a case-by-case decision on whether to rearchitect a feature when we needed to work on it.

To mitigate our risks, we rearchitected and migrated features that had the least business impact first. Business critical features such as timelines (which is the first thing you see in the app) were tackled only when we had gained sufficient confidence and know-how. This approach of migrating a large system piece-by-piece is commonly referred to as the *strangler pattern.*

In the Yubl app, you could search other users by first name, last name, and username. This was a simple feature, but it caused crippling performance issues with the monolith as the number of users grew. This was because a search was implemented with regex queries against MongoDB. The old implementation also didn't allow for more sophisticated ranking, so users often couldn't find who they were looking for. There was a push from the marketing team to surface influencers further up the search results as many users had followed these influencers onto the platform.

This was the first feature that we rearchitected and migrated to serverless because it was both low-risk and could have a high impact. Let's dive into how we extracted the search feature out of the monolith and built a microservice around it with its own REST API.

4.2.2   *The new search API*

One of the first and most important steps was to ensure that our legacy monolith would publish its state changes to Kinesis Data Streams. This gave us a foundation to build the new microservices by building on top of these events. To extract the search capability out of the monolith, we created a new search microservice. Figure 4.2 shows the high-level architecture of this search microservice.

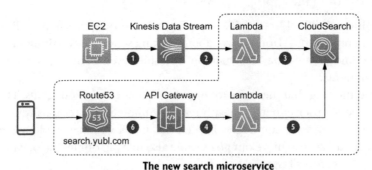

The new search microservice

Figure 4.2   A high-level overview of the new architecture running on serverless components

If you follow the numbered arrows in figure 4.2, this is how all the pieces fit together:

1. The legacy monolith publishes all user-related events to a Kinesis Data Stream called users. These include the user-created and user-profile-updated events that tell us when a new user joins or a user has updated their profile.
2. A Lambda function subscribes to the users stream.
3. The Lambda function uses these events to insert, update, or delete user documents in the users index in Amazon CloudSearch.
4. A new API in API Gateway with a POST /?query={string} endpoint proxies to another Lambda function to handle the HTTP request.
5. The Lambda function translates a user's query string into a search request against the users index in Amazon CloudSearch.
6. To create a user-friendly subdomain for the new REST API, a custom domain name in API Gateway for search.yubl.com is registered in Route53.

For this microservice, we chose Amazon CloudSearch instead of Amazon Elastic-Search because, at the time, Amazon ElasticSearch didn't allow you to change the number of write nodes in an ElasticSearch cluster, which is a scalability concern for the write throughput. But Amazon CloudSearch was not without its problems.

Although you can autoscale the read and write nodes independently, scaling up a CloudSearch cluster takes as long as 30 minutes. This did not match well with our spiky workload, and we had to overprovision the read cluster as a result. If I implemented this service again today, I would definitely use Amazon ElasticSearch or a third-party service such as Algolia (https://algolia.com) instead.

Before we launched the new service, we also needed to ensure all existing user data was available in the CloudSearch index. To do this, we ran a one-off task to copy all existing user data (~800,000 users) from MongoDB to CloudSearch, while tracking the most recent user profile update. Only after this was complete, did we enable the function at step 2 (figure 4.2) to start processing user updates.

Another important detail to note here is that when we enabled the function's Kinesis subscription, we processed events from when the one-off task started. With Kinesis, you are able to specify the StartingPosition of the subscription. You can configure this to AT_TIMESTAMP to start processing events from a specific timestamp. Processing events from when a one-off task started ensured that we didn't miss any updates that happened while Yubl was running.

Once live, performance of the new search service was significantly improved over the old search. It also removed a lot of the load on the monolith MongoDB database in the process, which had a positive impact on the general responsiveness of the app. It also gave us a template on how to build other microservices using serverless technologies such as API Gateway and Lambda.

4.3   *Migrating to new microservices gracefully*

Building the new microservices was the easy part. The difficult part was how to migrate them safely and be able to roll back quickly if there were any unforeseen issues. Another concern was how to do it gracefully without downtime and impact on our users. Suppose your starting position is a monolith where all the features are accessing directly a shared database (figure 4.3). Where will you begin?

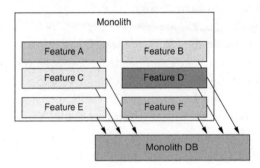

Figure 4.3   A monolithic system where everything has direct access to a shared database

We started to break apart this monolith into microservices built with serverless components such as API Gateway, Lambda, and DynamoDB. As we moved a feature out of the monolith into its own microservice, we wanted the microservice to be the authority over some part of the system, be it user profiles or product catalogue or customer orders. The microservice has its own database, and other microservices (or the monolith) should not be able to reach into its database and access or manipulate data directly.

Instead, to instigate some change in state, other microservices need to communicate with this microservice through its API. This can be HTTP-based in the form of a REST API call or message-based in the form of publishing an event/message to a queue. The important thing is to cut off direct access to and manipulation of data that the microservice is supposed to be the authority of (figure 4.4). How do you do this gracefully without causing significant disruption to your users?

The challenge here is that it's risky to do a big-bang migration because it usually requires downtime. That is not to say that you should never entertain the idea of a big-bang migration. If you're a small startup and have few users on your current platform, then a big-bang migration with downtime is quite possibly the fastest and most efficient approach for you. But for many organizations that are undergoing such migration, it's important to minimize the risk and disruption caused by moving to a new microservice.

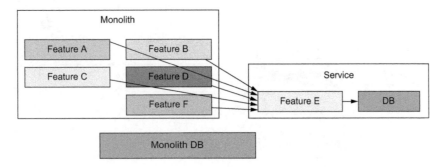

Figure 4.4 A monolithic system where everything has direct access to a shared database

A common strategy is to perform the migration in multiple steps to maximize safety. For example, the following process describes some likely steps as figure 4.5 illustrates:

1. Move the business logic for a particular feature into a separate service and create its own API. The new service will still use the monolith database until it has authority over the data.

2. Find the places where the monolith accesses this feature's data directly and redirect those access points to go through the new service's API instead. Start with the least critical component first to minimize the blast radius of any unforeseen problems or impacts.

3. Move all other direct access points to the new service's data to go through its API (probably, one at a time).

4. Now that the new service is the authority over its data, you can plan a course to migrate the data out of the monolith database into its own database. You might use a different database, based on your requirements for this new service. If your access pattern is simple and mostly key lookups, then DynamoDB is probably a good choice.

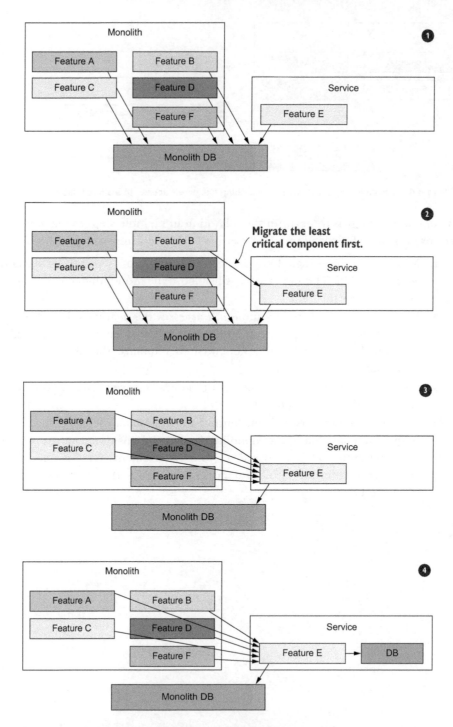

Figure 4.5   **Gradually cut off the direct access to the shared monolith database by moving access to go through the new microservice's API instead.**

5. Once you have created the new database, you need to migrate data from the monolith database. To do so without downtime, you can treat the new database as a read-through and write-through cache: any updates and inserts are written to the monolith database and then copied to the new database (figure 4.6).

   When attempting to read, you will read from the new database first. If the data is not found, then read from the monolith database and save the data in the new database.

6. Run a one-off task in the background to copy over all existing data (figure 4.6). Take care to ensure that you don't overwrite newer updates. (With DynamoDB, https://amzn.to/2IbE818, this can be done using conditional writes.)

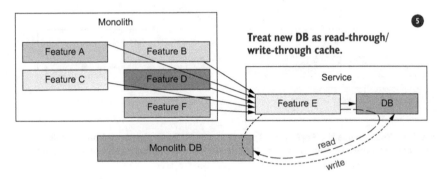

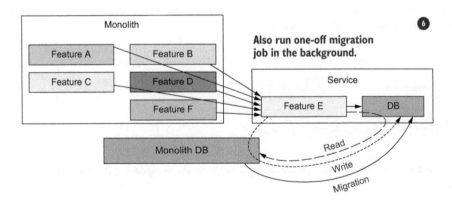

Figure 4.6   Migrate data to the new database gradually, without downtime.

This is a useful pattern for extracting features from a monolith and moving them into microservices that can scale and fail independently. There is more you can do to ensure that you do so safely and gracefully to minimize the potential impact on your users. For example, you can route only a small percentage of traffic to the new microservice when it first goes live. This limits the blast radius of any unforeseen problems with the new microservice. It is especially important for microservices that are user-facing and that handle requests from the mobile/web client directly because they can have a big impact on user experience.

This approach is commonly known as the *canary pattern* and is not limited to system migrations. The term *canary deployment* refers to a deployment strategy where the pattern is used for every deployment when a small percentage of traffic is directed at the new version of the application, which limits the blast radius of any unforeseen problems. If you're using the Application Load Balancer (ALB) in front of your application, then you can configure this routing behavior there (figure 4.7).

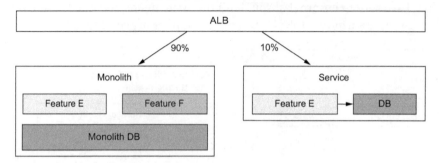

Figure 4.7   You can use the Application Load Balancer (ALB) to distribute traffic between the monolith and the new microservices. This allows you to minimize impact of unforeseen problems to a subset of users.

Where this approach is not possible (or in the case of Yubl where ALB didn't exist at the time), you can also proxy requests from the monolith for a configurable percentage of requests. Figure 4.8 shows this approach.

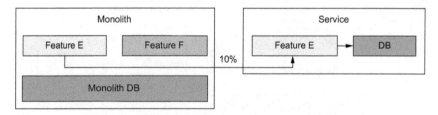

Figure 4.8   Even without ALBs, you can still proxy requests by modifying the monolith.

Summary

- You need to re-architect most applications to reap the full benefit of a serverless architecture. Although there are solutions to lift and shift existing applications into serverless, these don't deliver optimal performance and scalability.
- To get the full benefit of a serverless architecture, you need small, autonomous teams who are capable of making their own architectural decisions. Developers should be responsible for more than just the code and empowered to own their system. As Amazon's motto goes, "You build it, you run it."

- DevOps is simpler with serverless. You get a lot of automation out of the box, and tools such as Serverless Framework takes care of the rest. You still need to know what metrics to pay attention to and what alerts to add, however, as operational experience of running a production system is still valuable.

- Unit tests have a low return on investment when it comes to serverless architectures. Most functions are simple and often integrate with other services such as Amazon's DynamoDB and Simple Queuing Service (SQS). Unit tests that mock these integration points do not test those service interactions and give you a false sense of security.

- Prefer integration tests that exercise the real AWS services for the happy paths and use mocks only for failure cases that are difficult to simulate otherwise. For example, execute the function code locally but have it talk to the real DynamoDB tables. Then use mocks when you need to test your error handling for DynamoDB's throughput exceeded errors.

- Services often have to call each other in a microservices architecture. For internal APIs that are more prone to breaking in the development environments (compared to AWS services), use mocks to isolate the failures. The last thing you want is for an error in one service to fail the tests for all other services that depend on it.

- Simulating AWS services (for example, DynamoDB, SNS, SQS) locally is not worth the effort. It's easier and quicker to deploy a temporary stack, than using local simulation tools.

- When dealing with batched event sources like Kinesis and SQS, you need to think about how to handle partial failures. You either have to make sure that the operations are idempotent and can be retried without problem, or you need to ensure that successfully processed items in a failed batch are not processed again when the batch is retried.

A Cloud Guru:
Architecture highlights,
lessons learned

This chapter covers

- A Cloud Guru's original REST architecture
- The reasons the team decided to migrate from REST to microservices and GraphQL
- Lessons learned through the migration

In the first edition of this book, we described a serverless LMS (Learning Management System) built by A Cloud Guru (https://acloudguru.com). At that time, A Cloud Guru built a RESTful API backend using Amazon API Gateway, AWS Lambda, and Google's Firebase as its primary database. Since we published our first edition, A Cloud Guru has gone through a major transformation. The company moved from a RESTful monolithic design to a GraphQL-driven microservices architecture. This chapter describes this journey. We'll look at the original RESTful design, the transition to microservices, how GraphQL plays a major part, and the lessons learned along the way.

One thing is clear though, serverless technologies allowed A Cloud Guru to re-architect their platform rapidly and with minimal fuss. As a developer, you can be more agile with a serverless application than with a traditional three-tier behemoth. This is because, in a serverless approach, your primary focus is on the architecture of the system, your data, and the code. A Cloud Guru developers didn't need to spend time and energy worrying about provisioning servers, updating server software, or managing Kubernetes clusters. That alone saved them time and gave them the opportunity to focus on the platform elements that were critical to the business.

5.1 The original architecture

A Cloud Guru is an online educational platform for anyone wanting to learn Amazon Web Services (AWS), Microsoft Azure, and Google Cloud Platform, as well as Cloud-related technologies. The core features of the platform include the following:

- On-demand video courses
- Practice exams and quizzes
- A real-time discussion forum
- Dashboards and reporting
- User profiles and gamification
- Educational features like learning paths
- Interactive sandbox environments for students wanting to test their skills

A Cloud Guru is also an ecommerce platform that allows students to pay for a monthly or yearly subscription and have access to content and features. The training architects who create courses for A Cloud Guru can upload videos directly to S3. These videos are immediately transcoded to a variety of formats and resolutions (1080p, 720p, HLS, and so on).

In 2017–2018, the A Cloud Guru platform used Firebase as its primary database. A nice feature of this database is that it allows client devices (the browser on your computer or phone) to receive updates in near real time without refreshing or polling. (Firebase uses web sockets to push updates to all connected devices at the same time.) The other main components were API Gateway and AWS Lambda. Figure 5.1 shows a basic high-level view of how that initial REST architecture looked.

In the first edition of this book, we described how to build a serverless system with a RESTful interface. We wanted to illustrate the fact that you can create sophisticated, scalable, and highly available platforms using functions and services provided by AWS and Google Cloud Platform. The A Cloud Guru team was able to do that and go far beyond. They built a system that would go on to serve tens of thousands of concurrent users. Figure 5.2 shows a slightly more advanced version of the same architecture as was presented in the first edition of this book.

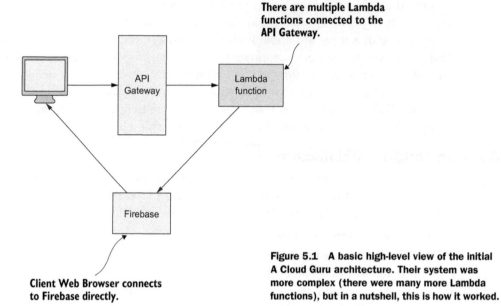

There are multiple Lambda functions connected to the API Gateway.

Client Web Browser connects to Firebase directly.

Figure 5.1   A basic high-level view of the initial A Cloud Guru architecture. Their system was more complex (there were many more Lambda functions), but in a nutshell, this is how it worked.

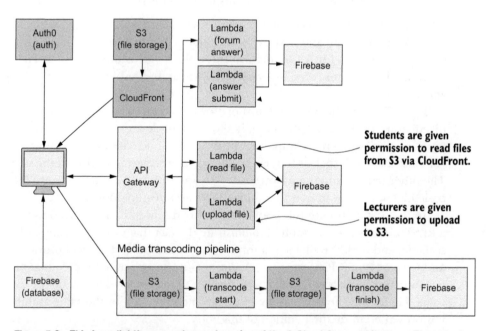

Students are given permission to read files from S3 via CloudFront.

Lecturers are given permission to upload to S3.

Figure 5.2   This is a slightly more advanced version of the A Cloud Guru architecture. The actual production architecture had Lambda functions and services for performing payments, managing administration, gaming, reporting, and analytics.

The original system worked well and scaled as the development team expected. It was also inexpensive to run with the AWS bill being just a few thousand dollars (the Lambda and the API Gateway bill was under $1,000). Note the following about the original A Cloud Guru architecture (figure 5.2):

- The frontend was built using AngularJS and was hosted by Netlify (https://netlify.com).
- Auth0 was used to provide registration and authentication. It creates delegation tokens that allow an AngularJS website to directly and securely communicate with other services such as Firebase.
- Every client created a connection to Firebase using web sockets and received updates from it in near real time. This meant that clients received updates as they happened without having to poll (which led to a nicer user experience).
- The training architects who created content for the platform uploaded files (usually videos) straight to an S3 bucket via their browser.

  For this to work, the web application invoked a Lambda function to first request the necessary upload credentials. As soon as the credentials were retrieved, the client web application uploaded the file to S3 via HTTP. All of this happened behind the scenes and was invisible to the training architects.
- Once a file was uploaded to S3, the system automatically kicked off a chain of events that transcoded the videos, saved the new files in another bucket, updated the database, and immediately made the transcoded videos available to other users.
- To view the videos, students were given permission by another Lambda function. Permissions were valid for 24 hours, after which they were to be renewed.
- Files were accessed via CloudFront. CloudFront ensures that users have low-latency access to videos wherever they may be.

Over time, the A Cloud Guru development team began considering the future of their serverless REST architecture. The company wanted to further accelerate the development of the platform, reduce blockers, and allow independent teams to focus on different high-value features. The following were some of the considerations that drove the decision to change the architecture:

- The existing architecture that was created was, in a sense, a serverless monolith. There were a large number of Lambda functions, but they connected to the same Firebase database. Making a change to the database would affect nearly every Lambda function and the developers working on them. This made it easy in the existing system for developers to step on each other's toes.
- The business wanted to have separate development teams owning different parts of the product. For example, the student-experience team would need to be able to update a database and deploy a Lambda function without affecting the team responsible for billing and reporting.

- Transitioning to a true microservices approach (where each microservice owns its data and its own view of the world) would allow teams to develop the platform in parallel. Each development team would look after a number of microservices and iterate on them as needed. This would mean moving away from a single Firebase database to multiple databases and yet still provide a way to read and hydrate data as needed.
- Moving to a microservices approach would give the teams a greater level of isolation. This would mean that different subsystems and components within the code base would have clearer boundaries in terms of ownership and a looser coupling.
- The team wanted to find a way to minimize round trips to the backend and fetch only the data that was needed. Devs also wanted to be able to serve multiple clients like mobile and web. While this can be accomplished with REST, the team determined that GraphQL was a better fit.
- Finally, the company felt that Firebase was getting a little bit too expensive.

Given the platform's access usage patterns, Amazon's DynamoDB looked like the right database to move to. Migrating to DynamoDB would allow teams to better manage infrastructure using CloudFormation and use built-in DynamoDB features like event triggers. And it would allow teams to stay entirely within the AWS environment.

Refactoring to a proper microservices approach and moving to DynamoDB as the primary database necessitated a rethink of the entire architecture. One of the main questions to consider was how to get data from disparate microservices and do it as effectively as possible (without multiple round trips or data hydration on the client) when a user made a request. This is where GraphQL entered the picture and became the focus of the new architecture. But before we get to GraphQL, let's see how the A Cloud Guru team split up their monolith and created their microservices first.

A serverless monolith

The RESTful API design that A Cloud Guru originally created was a serverless monolith. There was a single database and functions that needed to save or load data connected to it. There is nothing wrong with building a serverless monolith. For A Cloud Guru, it scaled well for a long time and helped build the company. The core reason for the move to a microservices design was the need for multiple teams to work in parallel.

If you are starting out today, know that it is OK to go with a monolithic approach. When you need to, you can migrate to microservices. Remember, you don't have to follow the trend and do the microservices road if it isn't right for you.

5.1.1   The journey to 43 microservices

Let's take a look at the serverless microservices approach the company came up with. First, here are some stats of the new GraphQL re-architected A Cloud Guru platform at the start of 2020:

- 240 million Lambda invocations per month (100 per second)
- 180 million API Gateway calls per month (70 per second)
- 90 TB of data transferred from CloudFront per month (274 MB per second)

The team began to break apart the monolith and move to a microservices architecture during 2018. API Gateway and Lambdas were separated into discrete microservices, each with their own responsibilities and view of the world. In the new world of microservices, each service could be as simple as a single DynamoDB table, a couple of Lambda functions, and an API Gateway. Figure 5.3 shows an example of how a couple of basic microservices could look.

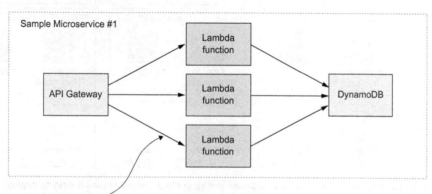

Two basic examples of how simple microservices could be structured with Lambda, API Gateway, DynamoDB, and S3.

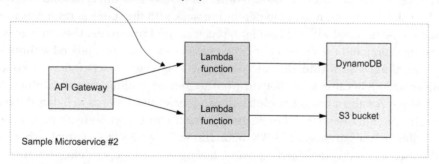

Figure 5.3   The two microservices here are akin to the simplified RESTful architecture we discussed before.

The packaging of the microservices is also interesting to note. A Cloud Guru uses Serverless Framework and CloudFormation to organize and deploy microservices. Some services in a microservice are *stateful*, whereas others are *stateless*. A Lambda function is stateless, meaning that it can be overwritten on each deployment. It's always ephemeral. A DynamoDB table or an S3 bucket is stateful; you must be careful to preserve the data that is already there. Your deployment process cannot overwrite it. Also, there can be global services and resources that don't belong to any specific microservice. How do you think they should be deployed and managed?

The A Cloud Guru team designed their microservice so they would have different CloudFormation stacks for stateless and stateful resources, as well as a stack for configuration and core dependencies. Figure 5.4 shows what that looks like.

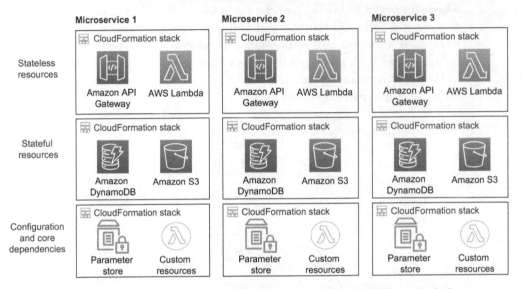

Figure 5.4   Each microservice is in its own CloudFormation stack, which makes it easy to deploy.

This approach to different CloudFormation stacks for different kinds of resources allows the development team to deploy the stack with the stateless resources when they need to be updated without having to touch stateful resources. The same goes for the configuration and the core-dependencies stack. They can be updated without modifying anything else within the microservices. This kind of separation of concerns is advantageous because it can help to avoid accidental modification of stateful resources.

There are also a few other global dependencies that exist as well, but these are not within any microservice. They include infrastructure components such as Amazon RedShift (data warehouse), AWS WAF (firewall), and VPCs (virtual private cloud). Microservices were designed to avoid having a hard dependency on these global resources. In fact, there is quite a loose coupling between them.

For example, if a microservice needs to push data into RedShift, it doesn't do it directly. Instead, a regular ETL job pulls data out of microservices and writes it to Red-Shift. That means microservices don't have to know about RedShift. A microservice can live and breathe on its own while a separate ETL task does its own job. Figure 5.5 shows that it's necessary for some resources to live outside specific microservices.

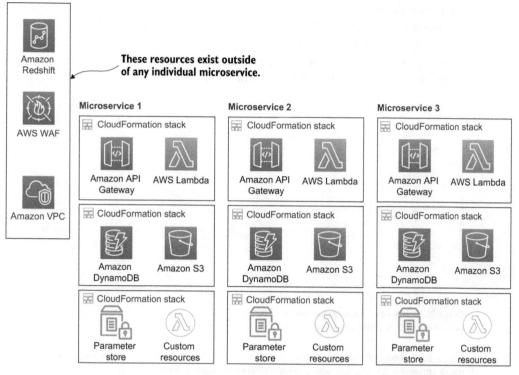

Figure 5.5 Global dependencies reside outside of each individual microservice. Not everything has to exist within a microservice.

The A Cloud Guru team gradually teased apart the serverless monolith that was created in the first place and re-implemented it with microservices. Moving from one architecture to a another always takes time but a nice advantage here was that the team could primarily focus on code. There was no hardware, servers, or a container orchestration engine (like Kubernetes) to worry about. The team carefully and gradually reimplemented various components making sure that no users were affected during the change.

As part of the move to microservices, GraphQL became the solution to the question of how to pull the right data from different microservices when a client makes a request. After all, each microservice may have its own database and its own view of the world. When a user needs to get data, how does it all happen? Which microservice has asked for it? And, what if multiple microservices have the required information, and the client needs an aggregate response? GraphQL became the tool to query microservices and, with schema-stitching, create responses needed for the clients.

5.1.2   What is GraphQL

We already mentioned GraphQL in chapter 3, but let's do a quick recap about what it is. GraphQL is a popular data query language developed by Facebook in 2012 and released publicly in 2015. It was designed as an alternative to REST because of REST's perceived weaknesses (multiple round-trips, over-fetching, and problems with versioning). GraphQL attempted to solve these problems by providing a hierarchical, declarative way of performing queries from a single endpoint (for example, api/graphql). Figure 5.6 provides an illustration of how this looks.

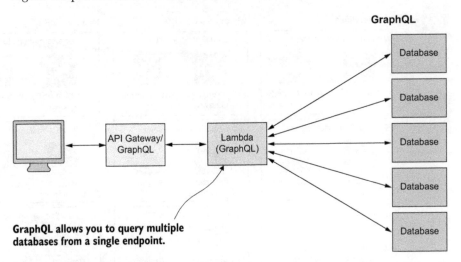

Figure 5.6   A GraphQL library running in a Lambda function can query multiple databases and, using schema stitching, produce a result relevant for each individual client.

GraphQL gives power to the client. Instead of specifying the structure of the response on the server, it's defined on the client. The client can specify which properties and relationships to return. GraphQL aggregates data from multiple sources and returns it to the client in a single round trip, which makes it an efficient system for retrieving data.

According to Facebook, GraphQL serves millions of requests per second from nearly 1,000 different versions of its application. To further illustrate what GraphQL looks like, here's a simple query taken from https://graphql.org/learn/queries/:

```
{
  hero {
    name
  }
}
```

And one possible response to that query:

```
{
  "data": {
    "hero": {
      "name": "R2-D2"
    }
  }
}
```

In a serverless architecture, GraphQL can be run from a single Lambda function connected to the API Gateway (this is what A Cloud Guru did) or used through a service like AWS AppSync. GraphQL can query and write to multiple data sources such as DynamoDB tables and, using schema-stitching, assemble a response that matches the request.

5.1.3 Moving to GraphQL

When A Cloud Guru began moving to GraphQL, AWS AppSync wasn't yet released or even announced for that matter. The team had one option, which was to run GraphQL from a Lambda function using the Apollo GraphQL library (https://www.apollo graphql.com).

Initially, getting the Apollo GraphQL implementation to work in a Lambda function presented a few interesting challenges. Apollo was originally designed for long-running processes on servers and containers. The team had to make a certain number of tweaks to optimize it for Lambda.

The A Cloud Guru team began using GraphQL and a design pattern called Backends for Frontends (BFF). The idea behind BFF is that each client has its own API or endpoint that services its specific needs (for example, there's a dedicated endpoint for mobile and another for the web). Each of the endpoints can query the appropriate microservices to save or load data as needed. The client doesn't need to know about the different microservices. It only needs to know which endpoint to query. This pattern solves the decoupling issue present in many systems. Figure 5.7 shows an example of the BFF architecture and what the A Cloud Guru team is driving toward.

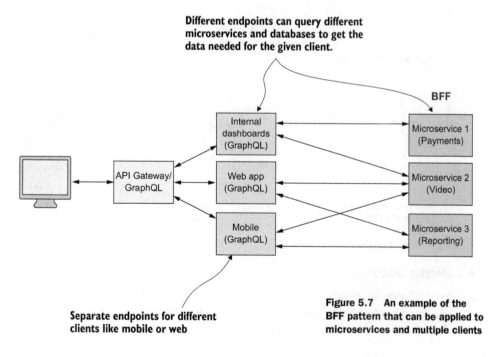

Different endpoints can query different microservices and databases to get the data needed for the given client.

BFF

Separate endpoints for different clients like mobile or web

Figure 5.7 An example of the BFF pattern that can be applied to microservices and multiple clients

Throughout the chapter, we've called the Lambda function that contains the GraphQL JavaScript library a GraphQL endpoint. But it's probably better to call it a *BFF endpoint* as we now understand this pattern. Here's how the A Cloud Guru's implementation works at a high level (excluding a few details like service discovery):

- A request from the user reaches the API Gateway.
- The API Gateway invokes a Lambda function with the Apollo GraphQL library. This is the BFF endpoint we've discussed.
- The Apollo GraphQL library queries the microservices it knows about (more on how it knows about which microservices to target in the service discovery section).
- Each microservice has an endpoint that is an API Gateway with a Lambda function (there is a /graphql endpoint in each microservice).
- The Lambda function runs the GraphQL library with a number of thin schema resolvers. It queries the databases contained within the microservice and produces a result, which is sent back to the BFF endpoint.
- The BFF endpoint receives responses from the different microservices it queried. Using schema stitching, it assembles the final response.
- This final response is sent back to the client via the API Gateway.

The GraphQL Lambda function is aware of the multitude of microservices (more on this in a moment) and is able to query those when it receives a client request. Figure 5.8 shows a high-level overview of this architecture.

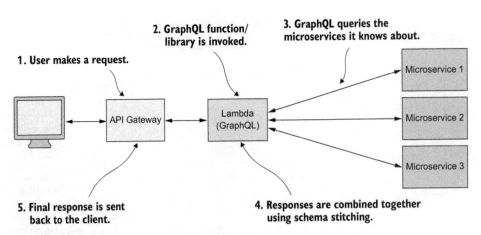

Figure 5.8   The GraphQL endpoint serves as the central point for clients that need data.

5.1.4 Service discovery

With 43 microservices in the system, how does GraphQL know which services to query when a client request comes in? The A Cloud Guru team built an internal service-discovery service called Sputnik (note, this is an in-house, proprietary service that's not available publicly). Sputnik consists of a database with API/URI definitions and database schemas. The microservices know when to update Sputnik. Additionally, the GraphQL Lambda function knows when to query Sputnik to get schemas for each microservice and figure out where to route requests.

> **DEFINITION** Service discovery is a standard technique in microservices architecture, which solves the problem of knowing what services are available, how to access them, and what their interface looks like.

Sputnik is made up of Lambda functions and DynamoDB tables that contain schemas and URIs of different microservices. It is really a microservice that facilitates the communication of BFF with other microservices in the system. Figure 5.9 shows how Sputnik helps the BFF endpoint know where to make a query.

> **TIP** AWS has a service called Cloud Map, which is AWS' own service discovery product. It even has a tagline that simply says, "Service discovery for cloud resources." If you are looking for something like Sputnik, check out Cloud Map. It may work for you. You can find Cloud Map at https://aws.amazon .com/cloud-map/.

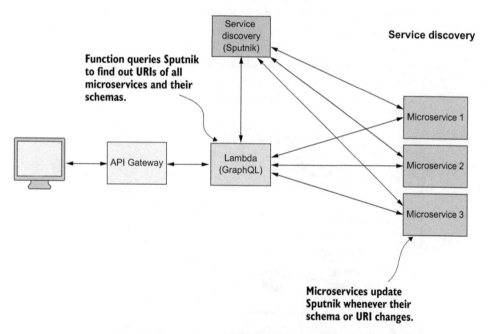

Figure 5.9   The service discovery (Sputnik) mechanism for A Cloud Guru. There's an AWS service called Cloud Map that you may want to check out if you are looking for something similar.

The metadata about each microservice (URI and schema) is cached at the BFF endpoint too, negating the need for the function to query Sputnik on every request. However, Sputnik can invalidate the cache and force the Lambda function to requery it again.

5.1.5   *Security in the BFF world*

A Cloud Guru practices security in depth with multiple layers of security built into the system. Let's talk about the two main components: user authentication/authorization and BFF to microservice security.

In the A Cloud Guru platform, students are authenticated using the Auth0 service that generates a unique JWT token for each user. All requests to AWS are made with that JWT token, which is validated using a custom authorizer at the API Gateway. If the JWT token is valid, the request is allowed to continue to the BFF endpoint. If it's not, then a response is generated and sent back to the client telling it that it is unauthorized. This is a simple mechanism, which was also used in the original REST design of the platform.

The second interesting element is how to authenticate a request made by the BFF to the microservice. In this scenario, A Cloud Guru uses API keys to authenticate requests. Each microservice has a unique API key that the BFF includes in its request in the header (using the X-API-Key parameter). Microservices check the included key and authorize requests if everything is OK.

5.2   *Remnants of the legacy*

The migration from REST to GraphQL took some time because the teams were careful not to cause issues for users. An interesting side effect of this was the way the system looked midway through the re-architecture. The team implemented new microservices and a BFF, but the old Firebase database was still in use because it was powering some of the elements of the user interface on the A Cloud Guru website. Figure 5.10 shows how that mid-way architecture looked.

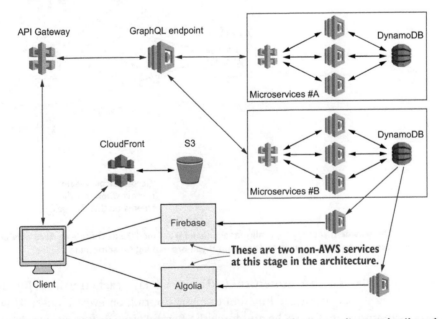

Figure 5.10   A high-level overview of the A Cloud Guru architecture as it was going through a transition

An interesting note about figure 5.10: you can see that Firebase is still used to drive some of the client-facing user interface elements. To keep the data in Firebase up to date, the team used DynamoDB event streams and Lambdas to ensure that happened. When a table is updated in any microservice, that change is pushed by DynamoDB to the DynamoDB event stream, which in turn invokes a Lambda function. That Lambda function analyses the change and then updates Firebase (and any other services like Algolia as needed).

Now, Firebase becomes basically a materialized view that is used to drive some parts of the interface. It is never directly queried, but it is there for older components that depend on it. This is one of the creative decisions made by the team as they transitioned from the old serverless architecture to the new one. They were able to use Firebase while they introduced DynamoDB and microservices and move everything across.

There's also an important lesson here in migration. You can gradually implement a new architecture while keeping the old one going by splitting things into smaller pieces and moving them one by one.

Summary

- Teams can work on a platform without affecting each other. Different teams are responsible for different microservices, and they can work on those without affecting anyone else.
- There has been a substantial improvement in performance for A Cloud Guru. For example, a BFF pattern fetches only the data that's needed (great for mobile) and needs only one roundtrip to make that happen. This is an optimization on what was there previously.
- The BFF pattern helps to support multiple client types and devices. These can be different depending on the requirements of the client.
- The team also had to do additional re-engineering to make Apollo work well with Lambda. These days, it shouldn't be much of a problem, but that's the pain when you are an early adopter.
- As always, security is a number one concern. More microservices create a larger surface area for attacks. It's therefore critical that microservices and endpoints are secured. The use of machine keys to secure communications between back-end components is an example of one good practice you should know about.

Yle: Architecture
highlights, lessons learned

6

This chapter covers
- Yle's big data architecture
- Scalability and resilience, lessons learned

Yle is the national broadcaster for Finland and operates their own popular streaming service called Yle Areena, which is used by millions of households. For a number of years now, Yle has used serverless technologies at scale in their architecture. They use a combination of AWS Fargate (https://aws.amazon.com/fargate), Lambda, and Kinesis to process more than 500 million user-interaction events per day. These events feed Yle's machine learning (ML) algorithm and help them provide better content recommendations, image personalization, smart notifications, and more.[1]

---

[1] I want to take this opportunity to thank Anahit Pogosova for sharing details of this architecture and the lessons she and her team learned along the way.

6.1   *Ingesting events at scale with Fargate*

To provide better content recommendations, Yle needs to know which content the visitors interact with the most. Yle ingests user-interaction data from streaming services as well as mobile and TV apps via an HTTP API. The challenge with this API is that the traffic can be spiky, such as during live sporting events. And sometimes events overlap (for example, when the election results coverage was on at the same time as a hockey game, which is the most popular sport in Finland)!

As mentioned, Yle's API ingests more than 500 million user-interaction events per day with more than 600,000 requests per minute during peak time. Live sporting events or special events (such as the election results) can cause peak traffic to go even higher. The maximum traffic throughput they have observed is 2,500,000 requests per minute.

Because the traffic is so spiky, the Yle team decided to use Fargate instead of AWS's API Gateway and Lambda. Fargate, also an AWS service, lets you run containers without having to worry about underlying virtual machines. It's part of an emerging trend for serverless containers, where you use containers as a utility service.

6.1.1   *Cost considerations*

In general, AWS services that charge you based on up time tend to be orders of magnitude cheaper when running at scale, compared with those that charge based on request count. With API Gateway and Lambda, you pay for individual API requests. Fargate, on the other hand, charges a per-hour amount based on the vCPU, memory, and storage resources that your containers use. You incur costs for as long as the containers run, even if they don't serve any user traffic.

Paying for up time can be inefficient for APIs that don't receive a lot of requests. For example, an API that receives a few thousand requests a day would cost significantly less using API Gateway and Lambda. This is especially true when you consider that you need some redundancy to ensure that your API stays up and running even if a container fails or if one of the AWS availability zones (AZs) hosting your containers experiences an outage. However, for high throughput APIs like the Yle API, which handles hundreds of millions of requests per day, running the API in Fargate can be more economical than using API Gateway and Lambda.

6.1.2   *Performance considerations*

A more important consideration for the Yle team was that, given how spikey their traffic can be, they would likely run into throttling limits with API Gateway and Lambda. A Lambda function's concurrency is the number of instances of that function that serve requests at a given time. This is known as the number of *concurrent executions*.

Most AWS regions have a default limit of 1,000 concurrent executions across all your Lambda functions in that region. This is a soft limit, however, and can be raised by a support request. Even though Lambda does not impose a hard limit on the maximum number of concurrent executions, how quickly you reach the required number of concurrent executions is limited by two factors:

- The initial burst limit, which ranges from 500 to 3,000 depending on the region.
- After the initial burst limit, your functions' concurrencies can increase by 500 instances per minute. This continues until there are enough instances to serve all requests or until a concurrency limit is reached.

API traffic is often measured in requests per second (or RPS). It's worth noting that RPS is not equivalent to Lambda's concurrent executions. For example, if an API request takes an average of 100 ms to process, then a single instance of a Lambda function can process up to 10 requests per second. If this API needs to handle 100 RPS at peak, then you will likely need around 10 Lambda concurrent executions at peak to handle this throughput.

If, however, an API's throughput jumps from 100 RPS to 20,000 RPS in the span of 30 seconds, then you will likely exhaust the initial burst limit and the subsequent scaling limit of 500 instances per minute. Eventually Lambda would be able to scale enough instances of your API functions to handle this peak load, but in the meantime, many API requests would have been throttled.

Another caveat to consider is that because live events are scheduled ahead of time, the Yle team can use a broadcast schedule to prescale their infrastructure in advance. There is no easy way to do this with Lambda except for using provisioned concurrency (https://amzn.to/3faBkCU). But you'd need to allocate provisioned concurrency to every Lambda function that needs to be prescaled; that would consume the available concurrencies in the region.

When used broadly like this, it can significantly impact your ability to absorb further spikes in traffic because there might not be enough concurrency left in the region if most of it is taken up by provision concurrency. Because of these scaling limits, AWS API Gateway and Lambda are not a good fit for APIs with extremely spiky traffic. It's the main reason why the Yle team opted to build their API with Fargate, and that was a sensible decision.

6.2   *Processing events in real-time*

Once Yle's API ingested the user-interaction events, it published them to Amazon Kinesis Data Stream in batches of 500 records at a time with an Amazon Simple Queue Service (SQS) queue as the dead-letter queue (DLQ). Figure 6.1 illustrates this process.

6.2.1   *Kinesis Data Streams*

Amazon's Kinesis Data Streams is a fully managed and massively scalable service that lets you

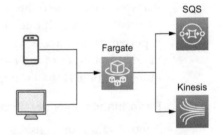

Figure 6.1 High-level architecture of Yle's ingestion API, which assimilates more than 500 million events per day at a peak throughput of more than 600,000 events per minute. The events are forwarded to Kinesis Data Stream in batches of 500 records. If the Kinesis data stream is unavailable, the events are sent to an SQS dead-letter queue (DLQ) to be reprocessed later.

stream data and process it in real time. Data is available to the consumers of the stream in milliseconds and is stored in the stream for 24 hours, by default, but that can be extended to a whole year, based on your configuration. (Keep in mind that extra charges apply when you extend the retention period for your stream.)

Within a Kinesis stream, the basic unit of parallelism is a shard. When you send data to a Kinesis stream, the data is sent to one of its shards based on the partition key you send in the request. Each shard can ingest 1 MB of data per second or up to 1,000 records per second and supports an egress throughput of up to 2 MB per second. The more shards a stream has, the more throughput it can handle.

There is no upper limit to the number of shards you can have in a stream so, theoretically, you can scale a Kinesis stream indefinitely by adding more shards to it. But there are cost implications that you have to consider when deciding how many shards you will need for your workload.

Kinesis charges based on two core dimensions: shard hours and PUT payload units. One PUT payload unit equates one request to send a record with up to 25 KB to a Kinesis stream. If you send a piece of data that is 45 KB in size, for example, then that counts as two PUT payload units. It works the same way as Amazon's DynamoDB's read and write request units.

A Kinesis shard costs $0.015 per hour and $0.014 per million PUT payload units. There are also additional charges if you enable optional features such as extending the data retention period. Some of these additional costs are also charged at a per hour rate, such as the cost for extended data retention and enhanced fan-out.

Because of the hourly cost, it's not economically efficient to over-provision the number of shards you'll need. Given the amount of throughput each shard supports, you don't need many shards to support even a high throughput system like Yle's data ingestion pipeline.

Based on Yle's prime-time traffic of 600,000 requests per minute, if we assume the traffic is uniformly distributed across 1 minute, then we arrive at 10,000 requests per second. And assuming that each event is less than 25 KB in size, then Yle needs about 10 shards to accommodate this traffic pattern. However, as we discussed, their traffic is spiky and, because Kinesis doesn't support autoscaling, the Yle team over-provisions their stream, running 40 shards all the time. This gives the team plenty of headroom to handle unexpected spikes and to minimize the risk of data loss.

6.2.2 *SQS dead-letter queue (DLQ)*

Because data is the blood supply for Yle's ML algorithms, the team wants to ensure that it's not lost when the Kinesis service experiences an outage in Yle's region. In the event the Kinesis service is out of commission, the API sends the events to the SQS DLQ so they can be captured and reprocessed later.

6.2.3   *The Router Lambda function*

To process the constant stream of events, a Lambda function called *Router* subscribes to the Kinesis data stream. This function routes events to different Kinesis Firehose streams that the other microservices use.

To make storing and querying the data more efficient, the Yle team stores the events in Apache Parquet format. To do this, they use Amazon Kinesis Data Firehose (to batch data into large files and deliver them to S3) with AWS Glue Data Catalog (to provide the schema). Figure 6.2 shows this arrangement.

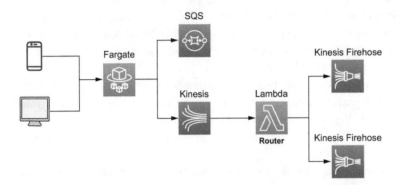

Figure 6.2   The Lambda Router function routes events to different Kinesis Firehose streams so they can be aggregated and converted to Apache Parquet files.

6.2.4   *Kinesis Data Firehose*

Kinesis Data Firehose is another member of the Amazon Kinesis family of services. It is a fully managed service to load streaming data to a destination. Kinesis Firehose can send data to Amazon S3, Amazon Redshift, Amazon Elasticsearch Service (Amazon ES), and any HTTP endpoint owned by you or by external service providers such as Datadog, New Relic, and Splunk.

A Firehose stream allows you to load streaming data with zero lines of code. Unlike Kinesis Data Streams, a Kinesis Firehose stream scales automatically, and you pay for only the volume of data you ingest into the stream. The cost for ingesting data into Kinesis Data Firehose starts at $0.029 per GB for the first 500 TB of data per month. It gets cheaper the more data you ingest.

In addition to the automated scaling, a Firehose stream can batch the incoming data, compress it and, optionally, transform it using Lambda functions. It can also convert the input data from JSON to Apache Parquet or to Apache ORC formats before loading it into the destination.

Like Kinesis Data Streams, it stores data in the stream for only up to 24 hours. You can configure the batch size by the maximum number of records or for a certain period of time. For example, you can ask the Firehose stream to batch the data into 128 MB files or 5 minutes' worth of data, whichever limit is reached first. It's a convenient service with no management overhead for scaling, and you don't have to write any custom code to transport data to the intended target.

To convert the data from JSON format to Apache Parquet or Apache ORC, you need to use the AWS Glue Data Catalog service. A Kinesis Firehose stream uses the schema captured in the Glue Data Catalog before sending it to a destination.

The Yle team uses S3 as the data lake and the destination for the Kinesis Firehose streams (figure 6.3). Once the data is delivered to S3, it is further processed and consumed by a number of microservices to perform several ML tasks such as demographic predictions.

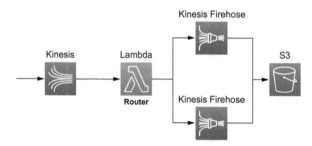

Figure 6.3   The Router function routes incoming events to a number of Kinesis Firehose streams, one for each type of event. The streams then batch, transform, and convert the data into Apache Parque format and write it to S3.

6.2.5   *Kinesis Data Analytics*

To personalize the icon image for videos, the Yle team uses the *contextual bandits model*, which is a form of an unsupervised ML model. They use the user-interaction events to reward the model so it can learn what the user likes. To do that, the team uses Kinesis Data Analytics to filter and aggregate the data from the Firehose stream and deliver it to a Lambda function called Reward Router. This function then calls several Reward APIs to reward the personalization models the Yle team maintains (figure 6.4).

Kinesis Data Analytics lets you run queries against streaming data using SQL or Java and the Apache Flink framework. Using an SQL approach, you can join, filter, and aggregate data across several streams without writing any custom code or running

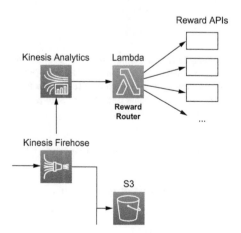

Figure 6.4   The Yle team uses Kinesis Data Analytics and Lambda to reward different personalization models in real time.

any infrastructure. The Java approach, however, gives you the most control over how your application runs and how it processes the data.

You can output the result of your queries to Kinesis Data Stream, Kinesis Firehose, or a Lambda function. Having a Lambda function as a destination gives you a lot of flexibility, however. You can process the results further, forward the results to anywhere you want, or both. In Yle's case, they use the Reward Router function as the destination for the Kinesis Data Analytics application and reward the relevant personalization models.

6.2.6   *Putting it altogether*

Taking a step back, you can see in figure 6.5 what Yle's data pipeline looks like from a high level. We have omitted some minor details, such as the fact that the Kinesis Firehose streams also use Lambda functions to transform and format the data and the fact that this is just the start of the journey for many of these user events. Once the data is saved into S3 in Apache Parquet format, many microservices ingest the data, process it, and use it to enrich their ML models.

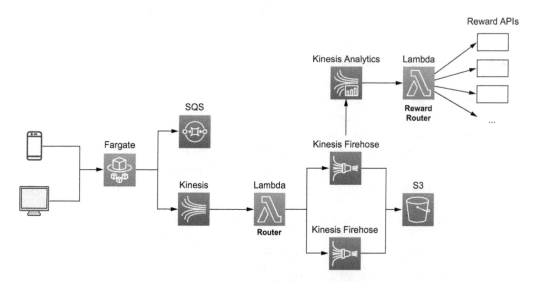

Figure 6.5   Yle's data pipeline architecture. They use Fargate to run the ingestion API because of cost and performance considerations and then process the ingested events in real time using Kinesis Data Streams, Kinesis Firehose, and Lambda. The data is transformed, compressed, and converted to Apache Parquet format and stored in S3 as the data lake. At the same time, they also use Kinesis Data Analytics to perform real-time aggregations and use Lambda to reward the relevant personalization ML models.

What I would like to highlight in this architecture is the prevalent use of Kinesis and its data analytics capabilities. This includes

- Kinesis Data Streams for ingesting large amounts of user events.

- Kinesis Firehose Streams for batching, formatting, and outputting data into large compressed files that are more easily consumable by the downstream ML models.
- Kinesis Data Analytics for running aggregations over live streams of data in real time and using a Lambda function as a destination to reward personalization models.

6.3 Lessons learned

The use of these Kinesis capabilities and how they are combined is a common sight in data analytics applications. However, Yle is processing events at a much higher scale than most! Operating at such high scale comes with unique challenges, and the Yle team has learned some valuable lessons along the way, including those that follow.

6.3.1 Know your service limits

Every service in AWS comes with service limits. These generally fall into three categories:

- *Resource limits*—How many of X can you have in a region. For example, Kinesis Data Streams has a default quota of 500 shards per region in us-east-1, us-west-1, and eu-west-1, and 200 shards per region in all other regions. Similarly, AWS Identity and Access Management (IAM) has a default quota of 1,000 roles per region.
- *Control-plane API limits*—How many requests per second you can send to a control plane API to manage your resources. For example, Kinesis Data Streams limits you to five requests per second to the CreateStream API.
- *Data-plane API limits*—How many requests per second you can send to a data plane API to act on your data. For example, Kinesis Data Streams limits you to five `GetRecords` requests per second per shard.

These limits are published in the AWS Service Quotas console. In the console, you can view your current limits and whether you can raise the limit.

SOFT VS. HARD LIMITS

Limits that can be raised are considered *soft limits*, and those that can't be raised are considered *hard limits*. You can ask for a soft limits raise via a support ticket, or you can do it in the AWS Service Quotas console. But it's worth keeping in mind that sometimes there is a limit to how far you can raise those soft limits. For example, the number of IAM roles in a region is a soft limit, but you can raise that limit to only 5,000 roles per region. If your approach relies on raising these soft limits indefinitely, then there's a good chance that you're using the service in a way that it's not designed for, and you might have to reconsider your approach.

Keeping an eye on your usage levels and your current limits is something that every AWS user should do but is especially important when you need to operate at scale and you run the risk of running into those limits. For the Yle team, one of the important lessons they learned is that you need to raise the limit on the number of

Fargate tasks you can run and give yourself plenty of headroom because it can take a few days for AWS to raise the limit in your account.

At present, the default limit is 1,000 concurrent Fargate tasks per region. When the Yle team started out, however, the default limit was only 100, and it took the team three days to raise that limit to 200.

PROJECT THROUGHPUT AT EVERY POINT ALONG THE PIPELINE

To understand which service limits affect your application, look at every service along the way and build a projection of how throughput changes with user traffic. Take Yle's case: as the number of concurrent users goes up, there's more traffic going through the ingestion API running in Fargate.

- How does this increase affect the throughput that needs to be processed by Kinesis and, therefore, the number of shards that need to be provisioned?
- Based on the current `BatchSize` and `ParallelizationFactor` configurations, how many concurrent Lambda executions would be required to process the events at peak load?
- Given that many concurrent Lambda executions, how many events would be sent to each Kinesis Firehose stream?
- Does your current throughput limit for Kinesis Data Firehose support that many events per second?

ALWAYS LOAD TEST, DON'T ASSUME

Every service in the pipeline can become a bottleneck, and the best way to know that your application can handle the desired throughput is to load test it. The services you build your application on might be scalable, but it doesn't mean that your application is, not without the proper adjustment to its service limits.

If your target is to handle 100,000 concurrent users, then load test it to at least 200,000 concurrent users. Who knows, maybe your application will be successful! That's what you're hoping for, right? Even if your application already comfortably handles 50,000 concurrent users, load test it to 200,000 concurrent users anyway. You can't assume the system is infinitely scalable and that its performance characteristics are perfectly consistent as throughput goes up. Don't assume anything; find out.

SOME LIMITS HAVE A BIGGER BLAST RADIUS THAN OTHERS

It's also worth mentioning that some service limits have a bigger blast radius than others. Lambda's regional concurrency limit is a great example of this.

Whereas exhausting the write throughput limit on a Kinesis shard affects only `putRecord` operations against that shard, the impact is localized to a single shard in a single Kinesis stream and will not affect your application in a big way. On the other hand, exhausting the Lambda concurrent executions limit can have a wide-reaching impact on your application because you're likely using Lambda functions to handle a variety of different workloads: APIs, real-time event processing, transforming data for Kinesis Firehose, and so on.

This is why you need to pay even more attention to those service limits that have a big blast radius. In the case of Lambda, you can also use the `ReservedConcurrency` configuration to restrain the maximum number of concurrent executions a function can have in cases where it's appropriate and necessary.

MIND CLOUDWATCH'S METRIC GRANULARITY

You should monitor your usage level and be proactive about raising service limits. One way to do that is by setting up CloudWatch alarms against the relevant metrics. One caveat to keep in mind here is that CloudWatch often reports usage metrics at a per-minute granularity but the limits are per second, which applies to both Kinesis Data Streams and DynamoDB's throughput metrics. In these cases, when you set up those CloudWatch alarms, make sure that you set up the thresholds correctly. For example, if the per-second throughput limit is 1, then the corresponding per-minute threshold should be 60.

6.3.2 Build with failure in mind

Notice that in figure 6.1, there is a SQS DLQ? It's there as a backup for when there is a problem with the Kinesis Data Streams service. Kinesis Data Streams is a robust and highly scalable service, but it's not infallible.

EVERYTHING FAILS, ALL THE TIME

AWS CTO, Werner Vogel, famously said, "Everything fails, all the time." It's a fact of life that even the most reliable and robust service can have a hiccup from time to time. Remember when S3 was down (https://aws.amazon.com/message/41926) for a few hours in 2017? Or that time when Kinesis Data Streams had an outage and affected CloudWatch and EventBridge as well (https://aws.amazon.com/message/11201)? Or when Gmail, Google Drive, and YouTube went down (http://mng.bz/ExlO)?

At the machine level, individual disk drives or CPU cores or memory chips constantly fail and are replaced. Cloud providers such as AWS and Google have invested heavily into their physical infrastructure as well as their software infrastructure to ensure that such failures do not affect their customers. In fact, by using serverless technologies such as API Gateway, Lambda, and DynamoDB, your application is already protected from data center-wide failures because your code and data are stored in multiple availability zones (data centers) within a given AWS region. However, there are occasional region-wide disruptions that affect one or more services in an entire AWS region, such as the S3 and Kinesis outages mentioned previously.

What this means is that you need to build your application with failure in mind and have a plan B (and maybe even a plan C, D, and E) in case your primary service has a bad day at the office. DLQs are a good way to capture traffic that can't be delivered to the primary target when first asked. Many AWS services now offer DLQ support out of the box. For example, SNS, EventBridge, and SQS all support DLQs natively in case the events they capture cannot be delivered to the intended target after retries. If you process events from a Kinesis Data Stream with a Lambda function, then you can also use the `OnFailure` configuration to specify a DQL.

The more throughput your system has to process, the more failures you will encounter, and the more important these DLQs become. Remember, even a one-in-a-million event would occur five times a minute if you have to process 5,000,000 requests a minute!

PAY ATTENTION TO RETRY CONFIGURATIONS

As you introduce more moving parts into your architecture and process more throughput, you should also pay more attention to your timeout and retry configurations. There are two problems that often plague applications that operate at scale:

- *Thundering herd*—A large number of processes waiting for an event are awaken at the same time, but there aren't enough resources to handle the requests from all these newly awaken processes. This creates a lot of resource contention, potentially causing the system to grind to a halt or fail over.
- *Retry storm*—An anti-pattern in client-server communications. When a server becomes unhealthy, the client retries aggressively, which multiplies the volume of requests to the remaining healthy servers and, in turn, causes them to time-out or fail. This triggers even more retries and exacerbates the problem even further.

Retries are a simple and effective way to handle most intermittent problems, but setting these needs to be done with care. A good practice is to use exponential backoff between retry attempts and the circuit breaker pattern to mitigate the risk of retry storms (https://martinfowler.com/bliki/CircuitBreaker.html).

6.3.3   *Batching is good for cost and efficiency*

Cost is one of those things that developers often don't think about when they're making architectural decisions, but this can come back and bite them in a big way later. This is especially true when you need to operate at scale and process large volumes of events. As we discussed in section 6.1.1, one of the reasons why the Yle team decided to use Fargate for ingesting user-interactions events instead of API Gateway and Lambda was cost and efficiency.

In general, AWS services that charge you based on up time tend to be orders of magnitude cheaper when running at scale, compared with those that charge based on request count. And the bigger the scale, the more you need to batch events for cost and efficiency. After all, processing 1,000 events with a single Lambda invocation is far cheaper and more efficient than processing those with 1,000 Lambda invocations.

Processing events in a batch also reduces the number of concurrent Lambda executions you need to run and minimizes the risk of exhausting the regional concurrent executions limit. However, with batch processing comes the potential for partial failures.

If you process one event at a time and that event fails enough times, then you put it into the DLQ and move on to the next event. But when you process 1,000 events in a single invocation and one event fails, what do you do about the other 999 events? Do you throw an error and let the invocation be retried, potentially reprocessing the 999 successful events? Do you put the failed event into a DLQ and process it later? These are the sort of questions that you have to answer.

6.3.4 *Cost estimation is tricky*

If you don't pay attention to cost, then it can pile up quickly and catch you by surprise. But trying to accurately predict your cost ahead of time is also difficult; there are a lot of factors that can affect your cost in production. For example, looking at the architecture diagram in figure 6.5, you might be focusing on the cost of Fargate, Lambda, and the Kinesis family of services. There are also other peripheral services to consider, such as the cost for CloudWatch, X-Ray, and data transfer costs.

The cost of Lambda is usually a small part of the overall cost of a serverless application. In fact, in most production systems, the cost of Lambda often pales in comparison with the cost of CloudWatch metrics, logs, and alarms.

Summary

- Yle's ingestion API processes more than 500 million events per day and more than 600,000 events per minute at peak times. The traffic is spiky and heavily influenced by real-world events such as a live hockey match or the election results.
- The Yle team uses Fargate for the ingestion API because of cost and performance considerations.
- In general, AWS services that charge you based on up time are significantly cheaper to use at scale compared to those services that charge you based on usage (number of requests, volume of data processed, etc.).
- The Yle team uses Kinesis Data Stream, Kinesis Data Firehose, and Lambda to process, transform, and convert the ingested events to Apache Parquet format.
- The ingested data is stored in S3 as the data lake.
- The Yle team uses Kinesis Data Analytics to perform real-time aggregation on the ingested events.
- The aggregated events reward the relevant personalization ML models.

Part 3

Practicum

It's time to take a look at three interesting problems and discuss how we would tackle them using serverless architectures. We will not be providing source code, but we will show sample architectures and discuss how to go about designing three different and unique systems. Let's sink our teeth into these delicious serverless architectures.

Building a scheduling
service for ad hoc tasks

7

This chapter covers

- Approaching architectural decisions when faced with a novel problem
- Defining nonfunctional requirements
- Choosing the right AWS service to satisfy nonfunctional requirements
- Combining different AWS services

With serverless technologies, you can build scalable and resilient applications quickly by offloading infrastructure responsibilities to AWS. Doing so allows you to focus on the needs of your customers and your business. Ideally, all the code you write is directly attributed to features that differentiate your business and add value for your customers.

What this means in practice is that you use many managed services instead of building and running your own. For example, instead of running a cluster of RabbitMQ servers on EC2, you use Amazon Simple Queue Service (SQS). Throughout the course of this book, you have also read about other AWS services such as DynamoDB and Step Functions.

Therefore, an important skill is to be able to analyze the nonfunctional requirements of a system and choose the correct AWS service to work with. But the AWS ecosystem is enormous and consists of a huge number of different services. Many of these services overlap in their use cases but have different operational constraints and scaling characteristics. For example, to add a queue between two Lambda functions to decouple them, you can use any of the following services:

- Amazon SQS
- Amazon Simple Notification Service (SNS)
- Amazon Kinesis Data Streams
- Amazon DynamoDB Streams
- Amazon EventBridge
- AWS IOT Core

These services have different characteristics when it comes to their scaling behavior, cost, service limits, and how they integrate with Lambda. Depending on your requirements, some might be a better fit for you than others.

Although AWS gives you a lot of different services to architect your system, it doesn't offer any guidance or opinion on when to use which. As a developer or architect working with AWS, one of the most challenging tasks is figuring this out for yourself.

This chapter shines a light on the problem by taking you through the design process for a scheduling service for ad hoc tasks. It's a common need for applications, and AWS does not yet offer a managed service to solve this problem. The closest thing in AWS is the scheduled events in EventBridge, but scheduling repeated tasks (e.g., do X every Y seconds) is different than scheduling ad hoc tasks (e.g., do X at 2021-08-30T23:59:59Z, do Y at 2021-08-20T08:05:00Z).

The functional requirement for such a scheduling service is simple: you schedule an ad hoc task to be run at a specified date and time (for example, "Remind me to call mum on Monday, at 9:00"). What's interesting about this is that it has to deal with different nonfunctional requirements depending on the application (for example, "It needs to handle a million open tasks that are scheduled but not yet run").

For the rest of this chapter, you will see five different solutions for this scheduling service using different AWS services and learn how to evaluate them. But first, let's define the nonfunctional requirements that we will evaluate the solutions against. Here is the plan for this chapter:

- *Define nonfunctional requirements.* The four nonfunctional requirements we will consider are precision, scalability (number of open tasks), scalability (hotspots), and cost. All the following solutions will be evaluated against these requirements:
  - *Cron with EventBridge*—A simple solution using cron jobs to find open tasks and run them.
  - *DynamoDB TTL*—A creative use of DynamoDB's time-to-live (TTL) mechanism to trigger and run the scheduled ad hoc tasks.
  - *Step Functions*—A solution that uses Step Function's `Wait` state to schedule and run tasks.

- *SQS*—A solution that uses SQS's `DelaySeconds` and `VisibilityTimeout` settings to hide tasks until their scheduled execution time.
- *Combining DynamoDB TTL and SQS*—A solution that combines DynamoDB TTL with SQS to compensate for each other's shortcomings.

- *Choose the right solution for your application.* Different applications have different needs, and some nonfunctional requirements may be more important than others. In this section, you will see three different applications, understand their needs, and pick the most appropriate solution for them.

7.1 Defining nonfunctional requirements

The ad hoc scheduling service is an interesting problem that often shows up in different contexts and has different nonfunctional requirements. For example, a dating app may require ad hoc tasks to remind users a date is coming up. A multiplayer game may need to schedule ad hoc tasks to start or stop a tournament. A news site might use ad hoc tasks to cancel expired subscriptions.

User behaviors and traffic patterns differ between these contexts, which in turn create different nonfunctional requirements the service needs to meet. It's important for you to define these requirements up front to prevent unconscious biases (such as a confirmation bias) from creeping in.

Too often, we subconsciously put more weight behind characteristics that align with our solution, even if they aren't as important to our application. Defining requirements up front helps us maintain our objectivity. For a service that allows you to schedule ad hoc tasks to run at a specific time, the following lists some nonfunctional requirements you need to consider:

- *Precision*—How close to the scheduled time is the task run?
- *Scalability (number of open tasks)*—Can the service support millions of tasks that are scheduled but not yet processed?
- *Scalability (hotspots)*—Can the service run millions of tasks at the same time?
- *Cost*

Throughout this chapter, you will evaluate five different solutions against this set of nonfunctional requirements. And remember, there are no wrong answers! The goal of this chapter is to help you hone the skill of thinking through solutions and evaluating them. We'll spend the rest of the chapter looking at these different solutions. Each provides a different approach and utilizes different AWS services. However, every solution uses only serverless components, and there is no infrastructure to manage. The five solutions include

- A cron job with EventBridge
- DynamoDB Time to Live (TTL)
- Step Functions
- SQS
- Combining DynamoDB TTL with SQS

After each solution, we'll ask you to score the solution against the aforementioned nonfunctional requirements. You can compare your scores against ours and see the rationale for our scores. Let's start with the solution for a cron job with EventBridge.

7.2   *Cron Job with EventBridge*

This solution uses a cron job in EventBridge to invoke a Lambda function every couple of minutes (figure 7.1). With this solution, you will need the following:

- A database (such as DynamoDB) to store all the scheduled tasks, including when they should run
- An EventBridge schedule that runs every X minutes
- A Lambda function that reads overdue tasks from the database and runs them

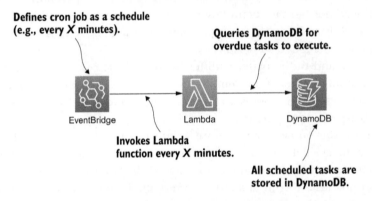

Figure 7.1   High-level architecture showing an EventBridge cron job with Lambda to run ad hoc scheduled tasks.

There are a few things to note about this solution:

- The lowest granularity for an EventBridge schedule is 1 minute. Assuming the service is able to keep up with the rate of scheduled tasks that need to run, the precision of this solution is *within 1 minute.*
- The Lambda function can run for up to 15 minutes. If the Lambda function fetches more scheduled tasks than it can process in 1 minute, then it can keep running until it completes the batch. In the meantime, the cron job can start another concurrent execution of this function. Therefore, you need to take care to avoid the same scheduled tasks being fetched and run twice.
- The precision of individual tasks within the batch can vary, depending on their relative position in the batch and when they are actually processed. In the case of a large batch that cannot be processed within 1 minute, the precision for some tasks may be longer than 1 minute (figure 7.2).
- It's possible to increase the throughput of this solution by adding a Lambda function as the target multiple times (figure 7.3).

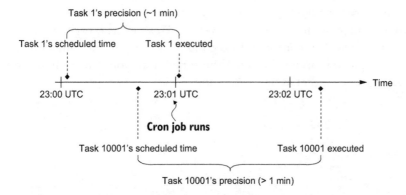

Figure 7.2   The precision of individual tasks inside a batch can vary greatly depending on their position inside the batch.

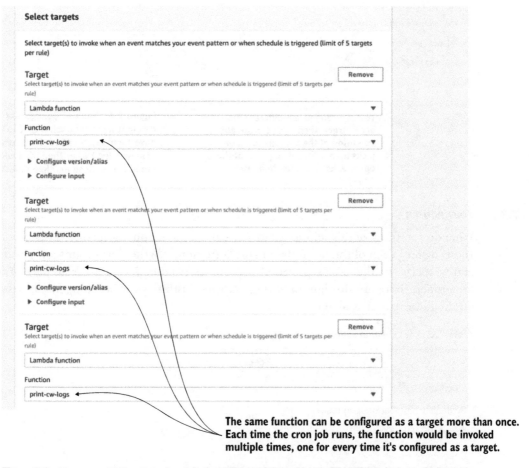

Figure 7.3   You can add the same Lambda function as a target for an EventBridge rule multiple times.

- Because EventBridge has a limit of five targets per rule, you can use this technique to increase the throughput fivefold. This means every time the cron job runs, it creates five concurrent executions of this Lambda function. To avoid them all picking up and running the same tasks, you can configure different inputs for each target as figure 7.4 shows.

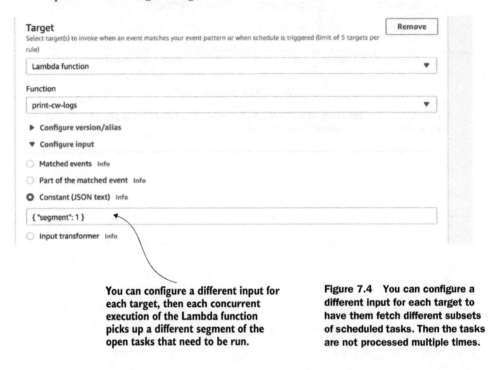

You can configure a different input for each target, then each concurrent execution of the Lambda function picks up a different segment of the open tasks that need to be run.

Figure 7.4   You can configure a different input for each target to have them fetch different subsets of scheduled tasks. Then the tasks are not processed multiple times.

7.2.1   Your scores

What do you think of this solution? How would you rate it on a scale of 1 (worst) to 10 (best) against each of the nonfunctional requirements? Write down your scores in the empty spaces in the tables provided for this (see table 7.1 as an example). And remember, there are no right or wrong answers. Just use your best judgement based on the information available.

Table 7.1   Your solution scores for a cron job

	Score
Precision	
Scalability (number of open tasks)	
Scalability (hotspots)	
Cost	

7.2.2 Our scores

The biggest advantage of this solution is that it's really simple to implement. The complexity of a solution is an important consideration in real-world projects because we're always bound by resource and time constraints. However, for the purpose of this book, we will ignore these real-world constraints and only consider the nonfunctional requirements outlined in section 7.1. With that said, here are our scores for this solution (table 7.2). We'll then explain our reasons for these scores in the following subsections.

Table 7.2 Our solution scores for a cron job with EventBridge

	Score
Precision	6
Scalability (number of open tasks)	10
Scalability (hotspots)	2
Cost	7

PRECISION

We gave this solution a 6 for precision because EventBridge cron jobs can run at most once per minute. That's the best precision we can hope for with this solution. Furthermore, this solution is also constrained by the number of tasks that can be processed in each iteration. When there are too many tasks that need to be run simultaneously, they can stack up and cause delays. These delays are a symptom of the biggest challenge with this solution—dealing with hotspots. More on that next.

SCALABILITY (NUMBER OF OPEN TASKS)

Provided that the open tasks do not cluster together (*hotspots*), this solution would have no problem scaling to millions and millions of open tasks. Each time the Lambda function runs, it only cares about the tasks that are now overdue. Because of this, we gave this solution a perfect 10 for scalability (number of open tasks).

SCALABILITY (HOTSPOTS)

We gave this solution a lowly 2 for this criteria because a cron job doesn't handle hotspots well at all. When there are more tasks than the Lambda function can handle in one invocation, this solution runs into all kinds of trouble and forces us into difficult trade-offs.

For example, do we allow the function to run for more than 1 minute? If we don't, then the function would time out, and there's a strong possibility that some tasks might be processed but not marked as so because the invocation was interrupted midway through. We need to either make sure the scheduled tasks are idempotent or we have to choose between:

- Executing some tasks twice if we mark them as processed in the database after successfully processing.
- Not executing some tasks at all if we mark them as processed in the database before we finish processing them.
- Employing a mechanism such as the Saga pattern (http://mng.bz/AOEp) for managing the transaction and reliably updating the database record after the task is successfully processed. (This can add a lot of complexity and cost to the solution.)

On the other hand, if we allow the function to run for more than 1 minute, then we are less likely to experience this problem until we see a large enough hotspot that the Lambda function can't process in 15 minutes! Also, now there can be more than one concurrent execution of this function running at the same time. To avoid the same task being run more than once, we can set the function's Reserved Concurrency setting to 1. This ensures that at any moment, only one concurrent execution of the Lambda function is running (see figure 7.5). However, this severely limits the potential throughput of the system.

Imagine 1,000,000 tasks that need to be run at 00:00 UTC, but the Lambda function can process only 10,000 tasks per minute. If we do nothing, then the function would timeout, be retried, and would take at least 100 invocations to finish all the

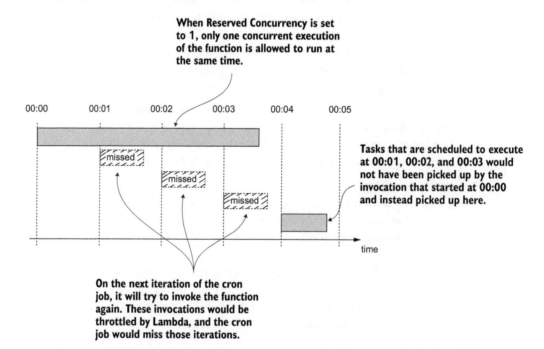

Figure 7.5 If we limit `Reserve Concurrency` to 1, then there will be only one concurrent execution of the Lambda function running at any moment. This means some cron job cycles will be skipped.

tasks. In the meantime, other tasks are also delayed, further exasperating the impact on user experience. This is the Achille's heel of this solution. But we can tweak the solution to increase its throughput and help it cope with hotspots better. More on this later.

COST

With EventBridge, cron jobs are free, but we have to pay for the Lambda invocations even when there are no tasks to run. You can minimize the Lambda cost if you use a moderate memory size for the cron job. After all, it's not doing anything CPU-intensive and shouldn't need a lot of memory (and therefore CPU).

In our scenario, the main cost for this solution is the DynamoDB read and write requests. For every task, you need one write request (when scheduling the task) and one read request (when the cron job retrieves it). This access pattern makes it a good fit for DynamoDB's on-demand pricing and allows the cost of the solution to grow linearly with its scale. At $1.25 per million write units and $0.25 per million read units, the cost per million scheduled tasks can be as low as $1.50. That's just the DynamoDB cost, and even that depends on the size of the items you need to store for each task as DynamoDB read/write units are calculated based on payload size. You also have to factor in the Lambda costs too, which also depend on a number of factors such as memory size and execution duration.

Nonetheless, this is still a cost-effective solution, even when you scale to millions of scheduled tasks per day. And, hence, why we gave it a score of 7. Overall, this is a good solution for applications that don't have to deal with hotspots, and it is also easy to implement. As we mentioned earlier, we can also tweak the architecture slightly to address its problem with hotspots.

7.2.3 *Tweaking the solution*

Earlier, we mentioned that we can increase the throughput of this solution by allowing multiple concurrent executions of the Lambda to run in parallel. We can do this by duplicating the Lambda function target in the EventBridge rule. Because there's a limit of five targets per EventBridge rule, we can only hope for a fivefold increase at best. Beyond that, we can also duplicate the EventBridge rule itself as many times as we need.

But even with these tricks, Lambda's 15 minutes execution time limit is still looming over our head. We also have to shard the reads so that the concurrent executions don't process the same tasks. Doing that, we also incur higher operational cost and complexity as well. There are more resources to configure and manage, and there are more Lambda invocations and database reads, even though most of the time they're not necessary. Essentially, we have "provisioned" (for lack of a better term) our application for peak throughput all the time.

Increasing throughput this way is ineffective. A much better alternative is to fan-out the processing logic based on the number of tasks that need to run. Lambda's burst capacity limit allows up to 3,000 concurrent executions to be created instantly (see https://amzn.to/2BxRuVG). This allows for a huge potential for parallel processing even if we use just a fraction of it. For this to work, we need to move the business logic to fetch and run tasks into another Lambda function. From here, we can invoke as many instances of this new function as we deem necessary when faced with a large batch of tasks (figure 7.6 shows this approach).

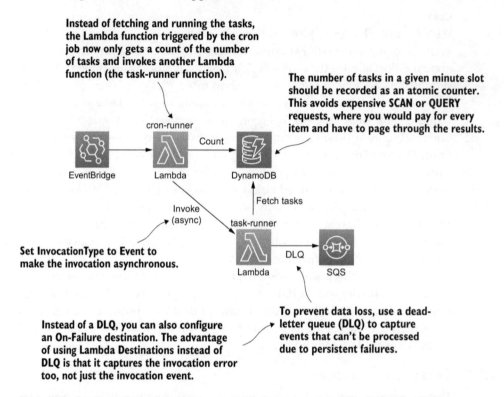

Instead of fetching and running the tasks, the Lambda function triggered by the cron job now only gets a count of the number of tasks and invokes another Lambda function (the task-runner function).

The number of tasks in a given minute slot should be recorded as an atomic counter. This avoids expensive SCAN or QUERY requests, where you would pay for every item and have to page through the results.

Set InvocationType to Event to make the invocation asynchronous.

Instead of a DLQ, you can also configure an On-Failure destination. The advantage of using Lambda Destinations instead of DLQ is that it captures the invocation error too, not just the invocation event.

To prevent data loss, use a dead-letter queue (DLQ) to capture events that can't be processed due to persistent failures.

Figure 7.6   An alternative architecture as a solution to our cron job. The solution fans out the processing logic to another function.

Once we know the number of tasks that needs to run, we can calculate the number of concurrent executions we need. To alleviate the time pressure and minimize the danger of timeouts, we can add some headroom into our calculation.

For example, if the throughput for the processing function is 10,000 tasks per minute, then we can start a new concurrent execution for every 5,000 tasks. If there are 1,000,000 tasks, then we need 200 concurrent executions. This is well below the burst capacity limit of 3,000 concurrent executions in the region.

> **Exercise: Score the modified solution**
> Consider how the proposed changes would affect the nonfunctional requirements of precision, scalability (number of open tasks), scalability (hotspots), and costs. How would you score this modified solution?

Exercise: Other alternatives

While keeping to the same general approach of using cron jobs, are there any modifications to the basic design that can compensate for its shortcomings in precision and scaling for hotspots?

7.2.4 Final thoughts

Cron jobs can be a simple and yet effective solution. As you saw, with some small tweaks it can also be scaled to support even large hotspots. However, it tends to push a lot of the load onto the database. In the aforementioned scenario of 1,000,000 tasks that need to be run in a single minute, it would require 1,000,000 reads from DynamoDB. Luckily for us, DynamoDB can handle this level of traffic, although we need to be careful with the throughput limits that are in place. For example, DynamoDB has a default limit of 40,000 read units per table for on-demand tables (https://amzn.to/3eH0THZ).

What if there's a way to implement the scheduling service without having to read from the DynamoDB table at all? It turns out we can do that by taking advantage of DynamoDB's time-to-live (TTL) feature (https://amzn.to/2NRgARU).

7.3 DynamoDB TTL

DynamoDB lets you specify a TTL value on items, and it deletes the items after the TTL has passed. This is a fully managed process, so you don't have to do anything yourself besides specifying a TTL value for each item.

You can use the TTL value to schedule a task that needs to run at a specific time. When the item is deleted from the table, a REMOVE event is published to the corresponding DynamoDB stream. You can subscribe a Lambda function to this stream and run the task when it's removed from the table (figure 7.7).

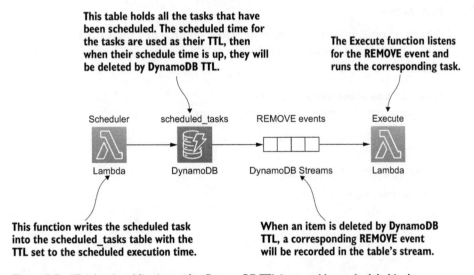

Figure 7.7 High-level architecture using DynamoDB TTL to run ad hoc scheduled tasks.

There are a couple of things to keep in mind about this solution. The first, and most important, is that DynamoDB TTL doesn't offer any guarantee on how quickly it deletes expired items from the table. In fact, the official documentation (https://amzn.to/2NRgARU) only goes as far as to say, "TTL typically deletes expired items within 48 hours of expiration" (see figure 7.8). In practice, the actual timing is usually not as bleak. Based on empirical data that we collected, items are usually deleted within 30 minutes of expiration. But as figure 7.8 shows, it can vary greatly depending on the size and activity level of the table.

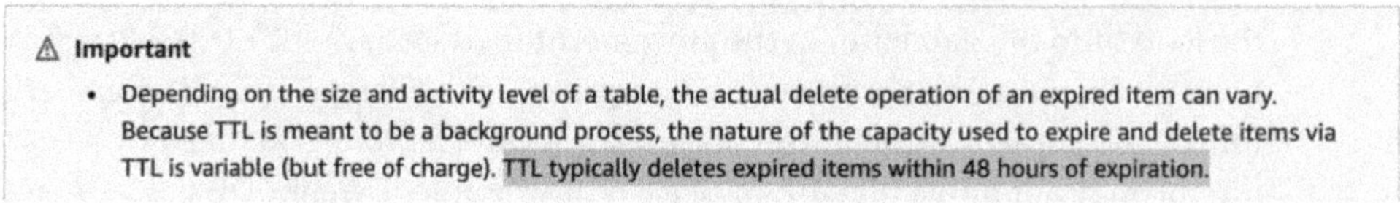

⚠ **Important**
  - Depending on the size and activity level of a table, the actual delete operation of an expired item can vary. Because TTL is meant to be a background process, the nature of the capacity used to expire and delete items via TTL is variable (but free of charge). TTL typically deletes expired items within 48 hours of expiration.

Figure 7.8 DynamoDB TLL's notification regarding its ability to delete expired items in tables

The second thing to consider is that the throughput of the DynamoDB stream is constrained by the number of shards in the stream. The number of shards is, in turn, determined by the number of partitions in the DynamoDB table. However, there's no way for you to directly control the number of partitions. It's entirely managed by DynamoDB, based on the number of items in the table and its read and write throughputs.

We know we're throwing a lot of information at you about DynamoDB, including some of its internal mechanics such as how it partitions data. Don't worry if these are all new to you, you can learn a lot about how DynamoDB works under the hood by watching this session from AWS re:invent 2018: https://www.youtube.com/watch?v=yvBR71D0nAQ.

7.3.1 *Your scores*

What do you think of this solution? How would you rate it on a scale of 1 to 10 for each of the nonfunctional requirements? As before, write your scores in the empty spaces in table 7.3.

Table 7.3 Your scores for DynamoDB TTL

	Score
Precision	
Scalability (number of open tasks)	
Scalability (hotspots)	
Cost	

7.3.2 *Our scores*

The biggest problem with this solution is that DynamoDB TTL does not delete the scheduled items reliably. This limitation means it's not suitable for any application that is remotely time sensitive. With that said, here are our scores in table 7.4. Again, we present how we arrived at these scores in the following subsections.

Table 7.4 Our scores for DynamoDB TTL

	Score
Precision	1
Scalability (number of open tasks)	10
Scalability (hotspots)	6
Cost	10

PRECISION

Scheduled tasks would be run within 48 hours of their scheduled time. A score of 1 might be considered a flattering score here.

SCALABILITY (NUMBER OF OPEN TASKS)

We gave this solution a perfect 10 because the number of open tasks equals the number of items in the scheduled_tasks table. Because DynamoDB has no limit on the total number of items you can have in a table, this solution can scale to millions of open tasks. Unlike relational databases, whose performance can degrade quickly as the database gets bigger, DynamoDB offers consistent and fast performance no matter how big it gets. Figure 7.9 provides a testimony to its performance.

SCALABILITY (HOTSPOTS)

We gave this solution a 6 because it can still face throughput-related problems because it's constrained by the throughput of the DynamoDB stream. But the tasks would be simply queued up in the stream and would run slightly later than scheduled.

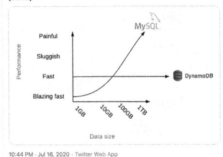

Alex DeBrie
@alexbdebrie

I have a new chart I've been showing in my DynamoDB training and talks recently.

It's about DynamoDB performance, and there are two key points I want folks to understand:

1. DynamoDB is fast (not blazing fast! but definitely not slow)

2. DynamoDB perf is consistent

(cont.)

10:44 PM · Jul 16, 2020 · Twitter Web App

Figure 7.9 A satisfied customer's statement regarding DynamoDB's scalability and number of opened tasks

Let's drill into this throughput constraint some more as that is useful for you to understand. As mentioned previously, the number of shards in the DynamoDB stream is managed by DynamoDB. For every shard the Lambda service would have a dedicated concurrent execution of the execute function. You can read more about how Lambda works with DynamoDB and Kinesis streams in the official documentation at https://amzn.to/2ZIu3Cx.

When a large number of tasks are deleted from DynamoDB at the same time, the REMOVE events are queued in the DynamoDB stream for the execute function to process. These events stay in the stream for up to 24 hours. As long as the execute function is able to eventually catch up, then we won't lose any data.

Although there is no scalability concern with hotspots per se, we do need to consider the factors that affect the throughput of this solution. Ultimately, these throughput limitations will affect the precision of this solution:

- *How quickly the hotspots are processed depends on how quickly DynamoDB TTL deletes those items.* DynamoDB TTL deletes items in batches, and we have no control over how often it runs and how many items are deleted in each batch.
- *How quickly the* execute *function processes all the tasks in a hotspot is constrained by how many instances of it runs in parallel.* Unfortunately, we can't control the number of partitions in the scheduled_tasks table, which ultimately determines the number of concurrent executions of the execute function. However, we can override the Concurrent Batches Per Shard configuration setting (https://amzn.to/2YUGE59), which allows us to increase the parallelism factor tenfold (see figure 7.10).

▼ Additional settings

On-failure destination
Lambda discards records that are expired or fail all retry attempts. You can send discarded records from a stream to an Amazon SQS queue or an Amazon SNS topic.

Queue or topic ARN

Retry attempts
The maximum number of times to retry when the function returns an error.

10000

Maximum age of record
The maximum age of a record that Lambda sends to a function for processing. The age can be up to 604,800 seconds (7 days).

604800

Split batch on error
If the function returns an error, split the batch into two and retry.

☐

Concurrent batches per shard
Process multiple batches from the same shard concurrently.

1	⬍

Figure 7.10   You can find the Concurrent Batches Per Shard setting under Additional Settings for Kinesis and DynamoDB Stream functions.

COST

This solution requires no DynamoDB reads. The deleted item is included in the REMOVE events in the DynamoDB stream. Because events in the DynamoDB stream are received in batches, they are efficient to process and require fewer Lambda invocations. Furthermore, DynamoDB Streams are usually charged by the number of read requests, but it's free when you process events with Lambda. Because of these characteristics, this solution is extremely cost effective even when it's scaled to many millions of scheduled tasks. Hence, this is why we gave it a perfect 10 for Cost.

7.3.3 Final thoughts

This solution makes creative use of the TTL feature in DynamoDB and gives you an extremely cost-effective solution for running scheduled tasks. However, because DynamoDB TTL doesn't offer any reasonable guarantee on how quickly tasks are deleted, it's ill-fitted for many applications. In fact, neither cron jobs nor DynamoDB TTL are well-suited for applications where tasks need to be run within a few seconds of their scheduled time. For these applications, our next solution might be the best fit as it offers unparalleled precision at the expense of other nonfunctional requirements.

7.4 Step Functions

Step Functions is an orchestration service that lets you model complex workflows as state machines. It can invoke Lambda functions or integrate directly with other AWS services such as DynamoDB, SNS, and SQS when the state machine transitions to a new state.

One of the understated superpowers of Step Functions is the Wait state (https://amzn.to/38po884). It lets you pause a workflow for up to an entire year! Normally, idle waiting is difficult to do with Lambda. But with Step Functions, it's as easy as a few lines of JSON:

```
"wait_ten_seconds": {
  "Type": "Wait",
  "Seconds": 10,
  "Next": "NextState"
}
```

You can also wait until a specific UTC timestamp:

```
"wait_until": {
  "Type": "Wait",
  "Timestamp": "2016-03-14T01:59:00Z",
  "Next": "NextState"
}
```

And using `TimestampPath`, you can parameterize the `Timestamp` value using data that is passed into the execution:

```
"wait_until": {
  "Type": "Wait",
  "TimestampPath": "$.scheduledTime",
  "Next": "NextState"
}
```

To schedule an ad hoc task, you can start a state machine execution and use a Wait state to pause the workflow until the specified date and time. This solution is precise. Based on the data we have collected, tasks are run within 0.01 second of the scheduled time in the 90th percentile. However, there are several service limits to keep in mind (see https://amzn.to/2C4fGPD):

- *There are limits to the StartExecution API.* This API limits the rate at which you can schedule new tasks because every task has its own state machine execution (see figure 7.11).

Quotas Related to API Action Throttling

Some Step Functions API actions are throttled using a token bucket scheme to maintain service bandwidth.

> ① **Note**
> Throttling quotas are per account, per AWS Region. AWS Step Functions may increase both the bucket size and refill rate at any time. Do not rely on these throttling rates to limit your costs.

Quotas In US East (N. Virginia), US West (Oregon), and Europe (Ireland)

API Name	Bucket Size	Refill Rate per Second
StartExecution	1,300	300

Quotas In All Other Regions

API Name	Bucket Size	Refill Rate per Second
StartExecution	800	150

Figure 7.11   StartExecution API limit for AWS Step Functions

- *There are limits to the number of state transitions per second.* When the Wait state expires, the scheduled task runs. However, when there are large hotspots where many tasks all run simultaneously, these can be throttled because of this limitation (see figure 7.12).

Quotas Related to State Throttling

Step Functions state transitions are throttled using a token bucket scheme to maintain service bandwidth.

> ① **Note**
> Throttling on the StateTransition service metric is reported as ExecutionThrottled in Amazon CloudWatch. For more information, see the ExecutionThrottled CloudWatch metric.

Service Metric	Bucket Size	Refill Rate per Second
StateTransition — *In US East (N. Virginia), US West (Oregon), and Europe (Ireland)*	5,000	1,500
StateTransition — *All other regions*	800	500

Figure 7.12   State transition limit for AWS Step Functions

- *There is a default limit of 1,000,000 open executions.* Because there is one open execution per scheduled task, this is the maximum number of open tasks the system can support.

Thankfully, all of these limits are *soft limits*, which means you can increase them with a service limit raise. However, given that the default limits for some of these are pretty low, it might not be possible to raise to a level that can support running a million scheduled tasks in a single hotspot.

There is also the *hard limit* on how long an execution can run, which is one year. This limits the system to schedule tasks that are no further than a year away. For most use cases, this would likely be sufficient. If not, we can tweak the solution to support tasks that are scheduled for more than a year away (more on this later).

7.4.1 Your scores

What do you think of this solution? How would you rate it on a scale of 1 to 10 against each of the nonfunctional requirements? As before, write down your scores in the empty spaces provided by table 7.5.

Table 7.5   Your solution scores for Step Functions

	Score
Precision	
Scalability (number of open tasks)	
Scalability (hotspots)	
Cost	

7.4.2 Our scores

Step Functions gives us a simple and elegant solution for the problem at hand. However, it's hampered by several service limits that makes it difficult to scale. We will dive into these limitations, but first, table 7.6 shows our scores for this solution.

Table 7.6   Our scores for Step Functions

	Score
Precision	10
Scalability (number of open tasks)	7
Scalability (hotspots)	4
Cost	2

PRECISION

As we mentioned before, Step Functions is able to run tasks within 0.01 s precision at the 90th percentile. It just doesn't get more precise than that!

SCALABILITY (NUMBER OF OPEN TASKS)

We gave this solution a 7 because the StartExecution API limit restricts how many scheduled tasks we can create per second. Whereas solutions that store scheduled tasks in DynamoDB can easily scale to scheduling tens of thousands of tasks per second, here we have to contend with a default refill rate of just 300 per second in the larger AWS regions. Luckily, it is a soft limit, so technically we can raise it to whatever we need. But the onus is on us to constantly monitor its usage against the current limit to prevent us from being throttled.

The same applies to the limit on the number of open executions. While the default limit of 1,000,000 is generous, we still need to keep an eye on the usage level. Once we reach the limit, no new tasks can be scheduled until existing tasks are run. User behavior would have a big impact here. The more uniformly the tasks are distributed over time, the less likely this limit would be an issue.

SCALABILITY (HOTSPOTS)

We gave this solution a 4 because the limit on StateTransition per second is problematic if a large cluster of tasks needs to run during the same time. Because the limit applies to all state transitions, even the initial Wait states could be throttled and affect our ability to schedule new tasks.

We can increase both the bucket size (think of it as the burst limit) as well as the refill rate per second. But raising these limits alone might not be enough to scale this solution to support large hotspots with, say, 1,000,000 tasks. Thankfully, there are tweaks we can make to this solution to help it handle large hotspots better, but we need to trade off some precision (more on this later).

COST

We gave this solution a 2 because Step Functions is one of the most expensive services on AWS. We are charged based on the number of state transitions. For a state machine that waits until the scheduled time and runs the task, there are four states (see figure 7.13), and every execution charges for these state transitions (http://mng.bz/ZxGm).

At $0.025 per 1,000 state transitions, the cost for scheduling 1,000,000 tasks would be $100 plus the Lambda cost associated with executing the tasks. This is nearly two orders of magnitude higher than the other solutions considered so far.

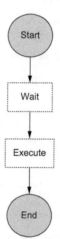

7.4.3   Tweaking the solution

So far, we have discussed several problems with this solution: not being able to schedule tasks for more than a year and having trouble with hotspots. Fortunately, there are simple modifications we can make to address these problems.

Figure 7.13   A simple state machine that waits until the scheduled time to run its task

EXTEND THE SCHEDULED TIME BEYOND ONE YEAR

The maximum time a state machine execution can run for is one year. As such, the maximum amount of time a Wait state can wait for is also one year. However, we can extend this limitation by borrowing the idea of tail recursion (https://www.geeksforgeeks.org/tail-recursion/) from functional programming. Essentially, at the end of a Wait state, we can check if we need to wait for even more time. If so, the state machine starts another execution of itself and waits for another year, and so on. Until eventually, we arrive at the task's scheduled time and run the task.

This is similar to a tail recursion because the first execution does not need to wait for the recursion to finish. It simply starts the second execution and then proceeds to complete itself. See figure 7.14 for how this revised state machine might look.

SCALING FOR HOTSPOTS

Sometimes, just raising the soft limits on the number of `StateTransitions` per second alone is not going to be enough. Because the default limits have a bucket size of 5,000 (the initial burst limit) and a refill rate of 1,500 per second, if we are to support running 1,000,000 tasks

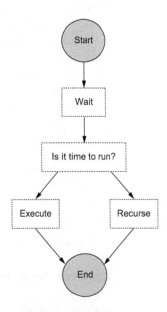

Figure 7.14 A revised state machine design that can support scheduled tasks that are more than one year away

around the same time, we will need to raise these limits by multiple orders of magnitude. AWS will be unlikely to oblige such a request, and we will be politely reminded that Step Functions is not designed for such use cases.

Fortunately, we can make small tweaks to the solution to make it far more scalable when it comes to dealing with hotspots. Unfortunately, we will need to trade off some of the precision of this solution for the new found scalability.

For example, instead of running every task scheduled for 00:00 UTC at exactly 00:00 UTC, we can spread them across a 1-minute window. We can do this by adding some random delay to the scheduled time. Following this simple change, some of the aforementioned tasks would be run at 00:00:12 UTC, and some would be run at 00:00:47 UTC, for instance. This allows us to make the most of the available throughput. With the default limit of 5,000 bucket size and refill rate of 1,500 per second, the maximum number of state transitions per minute is 93,500:

- Uses all 5,000 state transitions in the first second
- Uses the 1,500 refill per second for the remaining 59 seconds

Doing this would reduce the precision to "run within a minute," but we wouldn't need to raise the default limits by nearly as much. It'll be a trivial change to inject a variable amount of delay (0–59 s) to the scheduled time so that tasks are uniformly distributed across the minute window. With this simple tweak, Step Functions is no longer the scalability bottleneck. Instead, we will need to worry about the rate limits on the Lambda function that will run the task.

Another alternative would be to have each state machine execution run all the tasks that are scheduled for the same minute in batches and in parallel. For example, when scheduling a task, add the task with the scheduled time in a DynamoDB table as the HASH key and a unique task ID as the RANGE key. At the same time, atomically increment a counter for the number of tasks scheduled for this timestamp. Both of these updates can be performed in a single DynamoDB transaction. Figure 7.15 shows how the table might look.

timestamp ❶	sk	count	task
2020-07-04T21:53:22	item_count	2	
2020-07-04T21:53:22	item_3013a975-163e-45f6-89c0-357c161bb76c		{ "message": "world" }
2020-07-04T21:53:22	item_3aa4e344-5faf-4fd7-934a-c11f653e5730		{ "message": "hello" }

Figure 7.15   Set the scheduled task as well as the count in the same DynamoDB table.

We would start a state machine execution with the timestamp as the execution name. Because execution names have to be unique, the StartExecution request will fail if there's an existing execution already. This ensures that only one execution is responsible for running all the tasks scheduled for that minute (2020-07-04T21:53:22).

Instead of executing the scheduled tasks immediately after the Wait state, we could get a count of the number of tasks that need to run. From here, we would use a Map state to dynamically generate parallel branches to run these tasks in parallel. See figure 7.16 for how this alternative design might look.

Making these changes would not affect the precision by too much, but it would reduce the number of state machine executions and Lambda invocations required. Essentially, we would need one state machine execution for every minute when we need to run some scheduled tasks. There is a total of 525,600 minutes in a 365 days calendar year, so this also removes the need to increase the limit on the number of open executions (again, the default limit is 1,000,000). That's the beauty of these composable architecture components! Because there are so many ways to compose them, it gives you lots of different options and trade-offs.

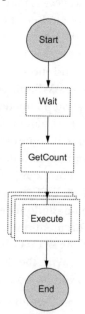

Figure 7.16   An alternative design for the state machine that can run tasks in batches in parallel

> **Exercise: Score the modified solutions**
> Repeat the same scoring exercise against the modified solutions we proposed.
>
> - How much would it impact the system's ability to handle a large number of open tasks or hotspots?
> - Is there any additional cost impact (e.g., one of the proposed tweaks uses a DynamoDB table) that needs to be considered?

7.4.4 *Final thoughts*

Step Functions offers a simple and elegant solution that can run tasks at great precision. The big drawback are its costs and the various service limits that you need to look out for, which hampers its scalability. But as you can see, if we are willing to make tradeoffs against precision, we can modify the solution to make it much more scalable.

We looked at a couple of possible modifications, including taking some elements of the cron job solution and turning this solution into a more flexible cron job that only runs when there are tasks that need to run. We also looked at a modification that allows us to work around the 1-year limit by applying tail recursion to the state machine design. In the next solution, we'll apply the same technique to SQS as it is bound by an even tighter constraint on how long a task can stay open.

7.5 SQS

The Amazon Simple Queue Service (SQS) is a fully managed queuing service. You can send messages to and receive messages from the queue. Once a message has been received by a consumer, the message is then hidden from all other consumers for a period of time, which is known as the *visibility timeout.* You can configure the visibility timeout value on the queue, but the setting can also be overridden for individual messages.

When you send a message to SQS, you can also use the `DelaySeconds` attribute to make the message become visible at the right time. You can implement the scheduling service by using these two settings to hide a message until its scheduled time. However, the maximum `DelaySeconds` is a measly 15 minutes, and the maximum visibility timeout is only 12 hours. But all is not lost.

When the `execute` function receives the message after the initial `DelaySeconds`, it can inspect the message and see if it's time to run the task (see figure 7.17). If not, it can call `ChangeMessageVisibility` on the message to hide the message for up to another 12 hours (https://amzn.to/3e1GVY6). It can do this repeatedly until it's finally time to run the scheduled task.

Before you score this solution, consider that there is a limit of 120,000 inflight messages. Unfortunately, this is a hard limit and cannot be raised. This limit has a profound implication that can mean it's not suitable for some use cases at all!

Once a message is inflight, this solution would keep it inflight by continuously extending its visibility timeout until its scheduled time. In this case, the number of inflight messages equates to the number of open tasks. However, once you reach the

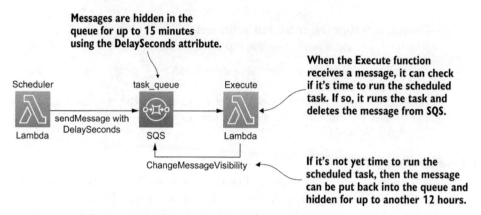

Figure 7.17   **High-level architecture of using SQS to schedule ad hoc tasks**

120,000 inflight messages limit, then newer messages would stay in the queue's back-log, even if some of the newer messages might need to run sooner than the messages that are already inflight. Priority is given to tasks based on when they were scheduled, not by their execution time.

This is not a desirable characteristic for a scheduling service. In fact, it's the opposite of what we want. Tasks that are scheduled to execute soon should be given the priority to ensure they're executed on time. That being said, this is a problem that would only arise when you have reached the 120,000 inflight messages limit. The further away tasks can be scheduled, the more open tasks you would have, and the more likely you would run into this problem.

7.5.1   *Your scores*

With this severe limitation in mind, how would you score this solution? Write down your scores in the empty spaces in table 7.7.

Table 7.7   **Your solution scores for SQS**

	Score
Precision	
Scalability (number of open tasks)	
Scalability (hotspots)	
Cost	

7.5.2   *Our scores*

This solution is best suited for scenarios where tasks are not scheduled too far away in time. Otherwise, we face the prospect of accumulating a large number of open tasks and running into the limit on inflight messages. Also, we would need to call Change-MessageVisibility on the message every 12 hours for a long time. If a task is scheduled to execute in a year, then that's a total of 730 times. Multiplied that by 1,000,000 tasks and that's a total of 730 million API requests or $292 for keeping 1,000,000 tasks open for a whole year. With these in mind, table 7.8 shows our scores.

Table 7.8 Our solution scores for SQS

	Score
Precision	9
Scalability (number of open tasks)	2
Scalability (hotspots)	8
Cost	5

PRECISION

Under normal conditions, SQS messages that are delayed or hidden are run no more than a few seconds after their scheduled times. Not as precise as Step Functions, but still very good. This is why we gave this solution a score of 9.

SCALABILITY (NUMBER OF OPEN TASKS)

We gave this solution a low score because the hard limit of 120,000 inflight messages severely limits this solution's ability to support a large number of open tasks. Even though the tasks can still be scheduled, they cannot run until the number of inflight messages drops below 120,000. This is a serious hinderance and, in the worst cases, can render the system completely unusable. For example, if 120,000 tasks are scheduled to run in one year, then nothing else that's scheduled after that can run until those first 120,000 tasks have been run.

SCALABILITY (HOTSPOTS)

The Lambda service uses long polling to poll SQS queues and only invokes our function when there are messages (http://mng.bz/Rqyj). These pollers are an invisible layer between SQS and our function, and we do not pay for them. But we do pay for the SQS `ReceiveMessage` requests they make. According to this blog post by Randall Hunt (https://amzn.to/31MfVtl)

> *The Lambda service monitors the number of inflight messages, and when it detects that this number is trending up, it will increase the polling frequency by 20 ReceiveMessage requests per minute and the function concurrency by 60 calls per minute. As long as the queue remains busy it will continue to scale until it hits the function concurrency limits. As the number of inflight messages trends down Lambda will reduce the polling frequency by 10 ReceiveMessage requests per minute and decrease the concurrency used to invoke our function by 30 calls per-minute.*

By keeping the queue artificially busy with a high number of inflight messages, we are artificially raising Lambda's polling frequency and function concurrency. This is useful for dealing with hotspots.

Because of the way this solution works, all open tasks are kept as inflight messages. This means the Lambda service would likely be running a high number of concurrent pollers all the time. When a cluster of messages become available at the same time, they will likely be processed by the `execute` function with a high degree of parallelism. And Lambda scales up the number of concurrent executions as more messages become available. We can, therefore, use the autoscaling capability that Lambda offers.

Because of this, we gave this solution a really good score. But, on the other hand, this behavior generates a lot of redundant SQS `ReceiveMessage` requests, which can have a noticeable impact on cost when running at scale.

COST

Between the many `ReceiveMessage` requests Lambda makes on our behalf and the cost of calling `ChangeMessageVisibility` on every message every 12 hours, most of the cost for this solution will likely be attributed to SQS. While SQS is not an expensive service, at $0.40 per million API requests, the cost can accumulate quickly because this solution is capable of generating many millions of requests at scale. As such, we gave this solution a 5, which is to say that it's not great but also unlikely to cause you too much trouble.

7.5.3   Final thoughts

If you put the scores for this solution side-by-side with DynamoDB TTL, you can see that they perfectly complement each other. Where one is strong, the other is weak. Table 7.9 shows the ratings for both services.

Table 7.9   Our ratings for SQS vs. DynamoDB TTL

	Score (SQS)	Score (DynamoDB TTL)
Precision	9	1
Scalability (number of open tasks)	2	10
Scalability (hotspots)	8	6
Cost	5	10

What if we can combine these two solutions to create a solution that offers the best of both worlds? Let's look at that next.

7.6   Combining DynamoDB TTL with SQS

So far, we have seen that the DynamoDB TTL solution is great at dealing with a large number of open tasks, but lacks the precision required for most use cases. Conversely, the SQS solution is great at providing good precision and dealing with hotspots but can't handle a large number of open tasks. The two rather complement each other and can be combined to great effect.

For example, what if long-term tasks are stored in DynamoDB until two days before their scheduled time? Why two days? Because it's the only soft guarantee that DynamoDB TTL gives:

TTL typically deletes expired items within 48 hours of expiration (https://amzn.to/ 2NRgARU).

Once the tasks are deleted from the DynamoDB table, they are moved to SQS where they are kept inflight until the scheduled time (using the ChangeMessageVisibility API as discussed earlier). For tasks that are scheduled to execute in less than two days, they are added to the SQS queue straight away. See figure 7.18 for how this solution might look.

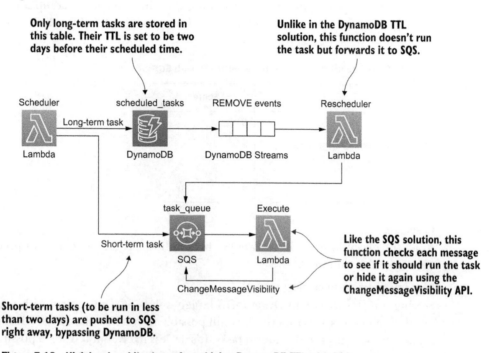

Figure 7.18 High-level architecture of combining DynamoDB TTL with SQS

7.6.1 *Your scores*

How would you score this solution? Again, write your scores in the empty spaces in table 7.10.

Table 7.10 Your solution scores for DynamoDB TTL with SQS

	Score
Precision	
Scalability (number of open tasks)	
Scalability (hotspots)	
Cost	

7.6.2   *Our scores*

According to "The Fundamental theorem of software engineering" (https://dzone .com/articles/why-fundamental-theorem):

> *We can solve any problem by introducing an extra level of indirection.*

Like the other alternative solutions we saw earlier in this chapter, this solution solves the problems with an existing solution by introducing an extra level of indirection. It does so by composing different services together in order to make up for the short-comings of each. Take a look at table 7.11 for our scores for this solution, then we'll discuss how we arrived at these scores.

Table 7.11   Our solution scores for DynamoDB TTL with SQS

	Score
Precision	9
Scalability (number of open tasks)	8
Scalability (hotspots)	8
Cost	7

PRECISION

As all the executions go through SQS, this solution has the same level of precision as the SQS-only solution, 9.

SCALABILITY (NUMBER OF OPEN TASKS)

Storing long-term tasks in DynamoDB largely solves SQS's problem with scaling the number of open tasks. However, it is still possible to run into the 120,000 inflight messages limit with just the short-term tasks. It's far less likely, but it is still a possibility that needs to be considered. Hence, we marked this solution as an 8.

SCALABILITY (HOTSPOTS)

As all the executions go through SQS, this solution has the same score as the SQS-only solution, 8.

COST

This solution eliminates most of the ChangeMessageVisibility requests because all the long-term tasks are stored in DynamoDB. This cuts out a large chunk of the cost associated with the SQS solution. However, in return, it adds additional costs for DynamoDB usage and Lambda invocations for the reschedule function. Overall, the costs this solution takes away are greater than the new costs it adds. Hence, we gave it a 7, improving on the original score of 5 for the SQS solution.

7.6.3 Final thoughts

This is just one example of how different solutions or aspects of them can be combined to make a more effective answer. This combinatory effect is one of the things that makes cloud architectures so interesting and fascinating, but also, so complex and confusing at times. There are so many different ways to achieve the same goal, and depending on what your application needs, there's usually no one-size-fits-all solution that offers the best results for all applications.

So far, we have only looked at the supply side of the equation and what each solution can offer. We haven't looked at the demand side yet or what application needs what. After all, depending on the application, you might put a different weight behind each of the nonfunctional requirements. Let's try to match our solutions to the right application next.

7.7 Choosing the right solution for your application

Table 7.12 shows our scores for the five solutions that we considered in this chapter. The solutions in this table do not include the proposed tweaks. Depending on the application, some of these requirements might be more important than others.

Table 7.12 Our scores for all five solutions

	Cron job	DynamoDB TTL	Step Functions	SQS	SQS + DynamoDB TTL
Precision	6	1	10	9	9
Scalability (number of open tasks)	10	10	7	2	8
Scalability (hotspots)	2	6	4	8	8
Cost	7	10	2	5	7

7.8 The applications

Let's consider three applications that might use the ad hoc scheduling service:

- Application 1 is a reminder app, which we'll call RemindMe.
- Application 2 is a multi-player app for a mobile game, which we'll call TournamentsRUs.
- Application 3 is a healthcare app that digitizes and manages your consent for sharing your medical data with care providers, which we'll call iConsent.

In the reminder app, RemindMe, users can create reminders for future events, and the system will send SMS/push notifications to the users 10 minutes before the event. While reminders are usually distributed evenly over time, there are hotspots around public holidays and major sporting events such as the Super Bowl. During these hotspots, the application might need to notify millions of users. Fortunately, because the reminders are sent 10 minutes before the event, the system gives us some slack in terms of timing.

In application 2, the multi-player mobile app called TournamentsRUs, players compete in user-generated tournaments that are 15–30 minutes long. As soon as the final whistle blows, the tournament ends and all participants wait for a winner to be announced via an in-game popup. TournamentsRUs currently has 1.5 million daily active users (DAU) and hopes to double that number in 12 months' time. At peak, the number of concurrent users is around 5% of its DAU, and tournaments typically consist of 10–15 players each.

In application 3, the healthcare app iConsent, users fill in digital forms that allow care providers to access their medical data. Each consent has an expiration date, and the app needs to change its status to expired when the expiration date passes. iConsent currently has millions of registered users, and users have an average of three consents.

Each of these applications need to use a scheduling service to run ad hoc tasks at specific times, but their use cases are drastically different. Some deal with tasks that are short-lived, while others allow tasks to be scheduled for any future point in time. Some are prone to hotspots around real-world events; others can accumulate large numbers of open tasks because there is no limit to how far away tasks can be scheduled.

To help us better understand which solution is the best for each application, we can apply a weight against each of the nonfunctional requirements. For example, TournamentsRUs cares a lot about precision because users will be waiting for their results at the end of a tournament. If the tasks to finalize tournaments are delayed, then it can negatively impact the users' experience with the app.

7.8.1 *Your weights*

For each of the applications, write a weight between 1 ("I don't care") and 10 ("This is critical") for each of the nonfunctional requirements in table 7.13. Remember, there are no right or wrong answers here! Use your best judgement based on the limited amount of information you know about each app.

Table 7.13   Your ratings for RemindMe, TournamentsRUs, and iConsent

	RemindMe	TournamentsRUs	iConsent
Precision			
Scalability (number of open tasks)			
Scalability (hotspots)			
Cost			

7.8.2 *Our weights*

Table 7.14 shows our weightings. Are these scores similar to yours? We'll go through each application and talk about how we arrived at these weights in the sections following the table.

Table 7.14 Our scores for RemindMe, TournamentsRUs, and iConsent

	RemindMe	TournamentsRUs	iConsent
Precision	5	10	4
Scalability (number of open tasks)	10	6	10
Scalability (hotspots)	8	3	1
Cost	3	3	3

REMINDME

We gave Precision a weight of 5 for this app because reminders are sent 10 minutes before the event. This gives us a lot of slack. Even if the reminder is sent 5 minutes late, it's still OK.

Scalability (number of open tasks) gets a weight of 10 because there are no upper bounds on how far out the events can be scheduled. At any moment, there can be millions of open reminders. This makes scaling the number of open tasks an absolutely critical requirement for this application. For Scalability (hotspots), we gave a weight of 8 because large hotspots would likely form around public holidays (for example, mother's day) and sporting events (for example, the Super Bowl or the Olympics).

Finally, for Cost, we gave it a weight of 3. This perhaps reflects our general attitude towards the cost of serverless technologies. Their pay-per-use pricing allows our cost to grow linearly when scaling. Generally speaking, we don't want to optimize for cost unless the solution is going to burn down the house!

TOURNAMENTSRUS

For TournamentsRUs, Precision gets a weight of 10 because when a tournament finishes, players will all be waiting for the announcement of the winner. If the scheduled task (to finalize the tournament and calculate the winner) is delayed for even a few seconds, it would provide a bad user experience.

We gave Scalability (number of open tasks) a weight of 6 because only a small percentage of its DAUs are online at once and because of the short duration of its tournaments. At 1.5 M DAU, 5% concurrent users at peak and an average of 10–15 players in each tournament, these numbers translate to approximately 5,000–7,500 open tournaments during peak times.

For Scalability (hotspots), it received a lowly 3 because the tournaments are user-generated and have different lengths of time (between 15–30 minutes). It's unlikely for large hotspots to form under these conditions. And, as with RemindMe, we gave Cost a weight of 3 (just don't burn my house down!).

ICONSENT

Lastly, for iConsent, Precision received a weight of 4. When a consent expires, it should be shown in the UI with the correct status. However, because the user is probably not going to check the app every few minutes for updates, it's OK if the status is updated a few minutes (or maybe even an hour) later.

We gave a weight of 10 for Scalability (number of open tasks). This is because medical consents can be valid for a year or sometimes even longer: all of these active consents are open tasks, so the system would have millions of open tasks at any moment. For Scalability (hotspots) on the other hand, we gave it a weight of 1 because there is just no natural clustering that can lead to hotspots. And finally, cost gets a weight of 3 because that's just how we generally feel about cost for serverless applications.

7.8.3   Scoring the solutions for each application

So far, we have scored each solution based on its own merits. But this says nothing about how well suited a solution is to an application because, as we have seen, applications have different requirements. By combining a solution's scores with an application's weights, we can arrive at something of an indicative score of how well they are suited for each other. Let's show you how this can be done and then you can do this exercise yourself. If you recall, the following table shows our scores for the cron job solution:

	Score (cron job)
Precision	6
Scalability (number of open tasks)	10
Scalability (hotspots)	2
Cost	7

For RemindMe, we gave the following weights:

	Weight (RemindMe)
Precision	5
Scalability (number of open tasks)	10
Scalability (hotspots)	8
Cost	3

Now, if we multiple the score with the weight for each nonfunctional requirement, we will arrive at the scores in the following table:

	Weighted Score (Cron job × RemindMe)
Precision	6 × 5 = 30
Scalability (number of open tasks)	10 × 10 = 100
Scalability (hotspots)	2 × 8 = 16
Cost	7 × 3 = 21

This adds up to a grand total of 30 + 100 + 16 + 21 = 167. On its own, this score means very little. But if we repeat the exercise and score each of the solutions for RemindMe, then we can see how well they compare with each other. This would help us pick the most appropriate solution for RemindMe, which might be different than the solution you would use for TournamentsRUs or iConsent.

With that in mind, use the whitespace in table 7.15 to calculate your weighted scores for each of the five solutions that we have discussed so far for RemindMe. Then do the same for TournamentsRUs and IConsent in tables 7.16 and 7.17, respectively.

Table 7.15   Weighted scores for the app RemindMe

	Cron job	DynamoDB TTL	Step Functions	SQS	SQS + DynamoDB TTL
Precision					
Scalability (number of open tasks)					
Scalability (hotspots)					
Cost					
Total score					

Table 7.16   Weighted scores for the app TournamentsRUs

	Cron job	DynamoDB TTL	Step Functions	SQS	SQS + DynamoDB TTL
Precision					
Scalability (number of open tasks)					
Scalability (hotspots)					
Cost					
Total score					

Table 7.17   Weighted scores for the app iConsent

	Cron job	DynamoDB TTL	Step Functions	SQS	SQS + DynamoDB TTL
Precision					
Scalability (number of open tasks)					
Scalability (hotspots)					
Cost					
Total score					

Did the scores align with your gut instinct for which solution is best for each application? Did you find something unexpected in the process? Did some solutions not fare as well as you thought they might?

If you find any uncomfortable outcomes as a result of these exercises, then they have done their job. The purpose of defining requirements up front and putting a weight against each requirement is to help us remain objective and combat cognitive biases. Table 7.18 shows our total weighted scores for each solution and application.

Table 7.18   Our total weighted scores for RemindMe, TournamentsRUs, and iConsent

	RemindMe	TournamentsRUs	iConsent
Cron job	167	147	147
DynamoDB TTL	180	115	137
Step Functions	158	160	120
SQS	144	141	79
DynamoDB TTL with SQS	210	183	145

These scores give you a sense as to which solutions are best suited for each application. But they don't give you definitive answers and you shouldn't follow them blindly. For instance, there are often factors that aren't included in the scoring scheme but need to be taken into account nonetheless. Factors such as complexity, resource constraints, and familiarity with the technologies are usually important for real-world projects.

Summary

In this chapter, we analyzed five different ways to implement a service for executing ad hoc tasks, and we judged these solutions on the nonfunctional requirements we set out at the start of the chapter. Throughout the chapter we asked you to think critically about how well each solution would perform for these nonfunctional requirements and asked you to rate them. And we shared our scores with you and our rationale for these scores. We hope through these exercises you have gained some insights into how we approach problem solving and the considerations that goes into evaluating a potential solution:

- What are the relevant service limits and how do they affect the scalability requirements of the application?
- What are the performance characteristics of the services in question and do they match up with the application's needs?
- How are the services charged? Project the cost of the application by thinking through how the application would need to use these AWS services and applying the services' billing model to that usage pattern.

These points are a lot easier said than done and it takes practice to become proficient at them. The AWS services are always evolving and new services and features become available all the time so you also have to continuously educate yourself as new options and techniques emerge. Despite having worked with AWS for over a decade, we are still learning ourselves and having to constantly update our own understanding of how different AWS services operate.

Furthermore, AWS do not publish the performance characteristics for many of its services. For example, how soon does Step Functions execute a Wait state after the specific timestamp. If your solution depends on assumptions about these unknown performance characteristics, then you should design small experiments to test your assumptions. In the course of writing this chapter, we conducted several experiments to find out how soon Step Functions and SQS executes delayed tasks. Failing to validate these assumptions early can have devastating consequences. Months of engineering work might go to waste if an entire solution was built on false assumptions.

At the end of the chapter we also asked you to do an exercise of finding the best solution for a given problem and gave you three example applications, each with a different set of needs. The scoring method we asked you to apply is not fool-proof but helps you make objective decisions and combat confirmation biases.

As you brainstormed and evaluated the solutions that have been put in front of you in this chapter, I hope you picked up on the even more important lessons here: that all architecture decisions have inherit tradeoffs and not all application requirements are created equally. The fact that different applications care about the characteristics of its architecture to different degrees gives us a lot of room to make smart tradeoffs.

There are so many different AWS services to choose from, each offering a different set of characteristics and tradeoffs. When you use different services together, they can often create interesting synergies. All of these give us a wealth of options to mix and match different architectural approaches and to engage in a creative problem-solving process, and that's beautiful!

Architecting serverless parallel computing

There's a secret about AWS Lambda that we like to tell people: it's a supercomputer that can perform faster than the largest EC2 instance. The trick is to think about Lambda in terms of parallel computation. If you can divide your problem into hundreds or thousands of smaller problems and solve them in parallel, you will get to a result faster than if you try to solve the same problem by moving through it sequentially.

Parallel computing is an important topic in computer science and is often talked about in the undergraduate computer science curriculum. Interestingly, Lambda, by its very nature, predisposes us to think and apply concepts from parallel computing. Services like Step Functions and DynamoDB make it easier to build parallel applications.

In this chapter, we'll illustrate how to build a serverless video transcoder in Lambda that outperforms bigger and more expensive EC2 servers.

8.1 Introduction to MapReduce

MapReduce is a popular and well-known programming model that's often used to process large data sets. It was originally created at Google by developers who were themselves inspired by two well-known functional programming primitives (higher-order functions): map and reduce. MapReduce works by splitting up a large data set into many smaller subsets, performing an operation on each subset and then combining or summing up to get the result.

Imagine that you want to find out how many times a character's name is mentioned in Tolstoy's *War and Peace*. You can sequentially look through every page, one by one, and count the occurrences (but that's slow). If you apply a MapReduce approach, however, you can do it much quicker:

1. You split the data into many independent subsets. In the case of *War and Peace*, it could be individual pages or paragraphs.
2. You apply the map function to each subset. The map function in this case scans the page (or paragraph) and emits how many times a character's name is mentioned.
3. There could be an optional step here to combine some of the data. That can help make the computation a little easier to perform in the next step.
4. The reduce function performs a summary operation. It counts the number of times the map function has emitted the character's name and produces the overall result.

NOTE It's important to understand that the power of MapReduce in the *War and Peace* example comes from the fact that the map step can run in parallel on thousands of pages or paragraphs. If this wasn't the case, then this program would be no different from a sequential count.

Figure 8.1 shows what a theoretical MapReduce architecture looks like. We'll build something like this soon.

As you may have already guessed, real-world MapReduce applications are often more complex. In a lot of cases, there are intermediary steps between map and reduce that combine or simplify data, and considerations such as locality of data become important in order to minimize overhead. Nevertheless, we can take the idea of splitting a problem into smaller chunks, processing them in parallel, and then combining and reducing them to achieve the outcome you need, and we can do that with Lambda.

A split procedure splits the data set into multiple chunks.

A reduce procedure performs summary options.

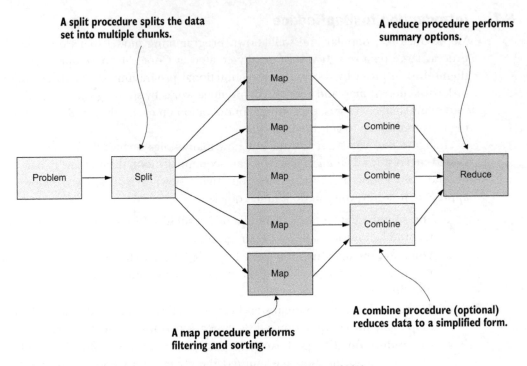

A map procedure performs filtering and sorting.

A combine procedure (optional) reduces data to a simplified form.

Figure 8.1   These are the steps a fictional MapReduce algorithm could take.

8.1.1   How to transcode a video

In the second chapter of this book, you built a serverless pipeline that converted video from one format to another. To do this, you used an AWS service called AWS Elemental MediaConvert. This service takes a video uploaded to an S3 bucket and transcodes it to a range of different formats specified by you. Our goal in this chapter is to do something crazy and implement our own video transcoder service using Lambda. Note that this is just an experiment and an opportunity to explore highly parallelized serverless architectures. Our major requirements for our serverless encoding service are as follows:

- Build a transcoder that takes a video file and produces a transcoded version in a different format or bit rate. We want complete control over the transcoding process.
- Use only serverless services in AWS, such as Lambda and S3. Obviously, we are not allowed to use an EC2 or a managed service to do transcoding for us.
- Build a product that is robust and fast. It should be able to beat a large EC2 instance most of the time.
- Learn about parallel computing and how to think about solving these problems.

The solution we are about to present works, but it's not something we recommend running in a production environment. Unless your core business is video transcoding, you should outsource as much of the undifferentiated heavy lifting as possible in order to focus on your own unique problem. In most cases, a managed service like AWS Elemental MediaConvert is better; you don't have to worry about keeping it running. Take this as just an exercise and an opportunity to learn about MapReduce and parallel computation (you never know when you might face a big problem that requires the skill you may pick up here).

> ### How would you do video transcoding in Lambda?
> Take a moment and think about how you would build a video transcoder using AWS Lambda. All guesses are good, and we'd love to know how you would approach the problem (twitter.com/sbarski). Can you build it yourself without reading the rest of the chapter?

8.1.2 Architecture overview

To transcode a file using Lambda, we need to apply principles of MapReduce. We are not implementing classical MapReduce here; instead, we are taking inspiration from this algorithm to build our transcoder.

An interesting thing about Lambda (that we've mentioned before) is that it forces us to think *parallel*. It's impossible to process large video files in a Lambda function if you treat a single function like a traditional computer. You'd run out of memory and timeout quickly. If the video file is large enough, the function would either stop after 15 minutes of processing or exhaust all available RAM and crash.

To get around this, we decompose the problem into smaller problems that can be processed within Lambda's constraints. The implication is that we can try the following to process a large video file:

1. Divide the video file into a lot of tiny segments.
2. Transcode these segments in parallel.
3. Combine these small segments together to produce a new video file.

We need to parallelize as much as possible to get the most out of our serverless supercomputer. For example, if some segments are ready to be combined while others are still processing, we should combine the ones that are ready. Performance is the name of the game here. So, with that in mind, here's an outline for our serverless transcoding algorithm that, let's say, is designed to transcode a video from one bit rate to another:

1. A user uploads a video file to S3 that invokes a Lambda function.
2. The Lambda function analyzes the file and figures out how to cut up the source file to produce smaller video files (segments) for transcoding.
3. To make things go a little bit faster, we strip away the audio from video and save it to another file. Not having to worry about the audio makes executing steps 4–6 faster.

4. This step performs the split process that creates small video segments for transcoding.

5. Now comes the map process that transcodes segments to the desired format or bit rate. The system can transcode a bunch of these segments in parallel.

6. The map process is followed by a combine step that begins to merge these small video files together.

7. The final step merges audio and video together and presents the file to the user. We have reduced our work to its final output.

8. As the kids say, the real final step is profit.

Here are the main AWS services and software that we will use to build the transcoder:

- *FFmpeg*—In the first edition of our book, we briefly used FFmpeg, a cross-platform library/application created for recording, converting, and streaming audio and video. This is a powerhouse of an application that is used by everyone and anyone ranging from hobbyists to commercial TV channels.

  We'll use ffmpeg in this chapter to do the transcoding, splitting, and merging of video files. We'll also use a utility called ffprobe to analyze the video file and figure out how to cut it up on keyframes. The ffmpeg and ffprobe binaries are shipped as a Lambda layer (http://mng.bz/N4MN), which allow other Lambda functions to access and run them. You don't necessarily have to use Lambda layers (you can upload the ffmpeg binary with each function that will use it), but that is redundant, inconvenient, and takes a long time to deploy. Therefore, making ffmpeg available via a Lambda layer is the recommended and preferred approach.

DEFINITION   A *keyframe* stores the complete image in the video stream, while a regular frame stores an incremental change from the previous frame. Cutting on keyframes prevents us from losing information in the video.

- *AWS Lambda*—It goes without saying that we'll use Lambda for nearly everything. Lambda runs ffmpeg and executes most of the logic. We'll write six functions to analyze the video, extract audio, split the original file, convert segments, merge video segments, and then merge video and audio in the final step.

- *Step Functions*—To help us orchestrate this workflow, we'll rely on Step Functions. This service helps us to define how and in what order our execution steps happen, makes the entire workflow robust, and provides additional visibility into the execution.

- *S3*—We'll use Simple Storage Service (S3) for storing the initial and the final video. We could also use it to store the temporary video chunks, but we'll use EFS for that. The reason why we chose EFS is because it is easy to mount and access as a filesystem from Lambda. We'll provide an alternative implementation that uses S3, but it is slightly harder to get right.

- *EFS*—We'll use the Elastic File System (EFS) for our serverless transcoder to store the temporary files that we generate. There will be a lot of small video files. Luckily, EFS can grow and shrink as needed.
- *DynamoDB*—Although Step Functions help to manage the overall workflow and execution of Lambda functions, we still need to maintain some state. We need to know whether certain video chunks were created or can be merged. We'll use DynamoDB to store this information. Everything that's stored is ephemeral and will be deleted using DynamoDB's Time to Live (TTL) feature.

Figure 8.2 shows a high-level overview of the system we are about to build. We will jump into individual components in the next section.

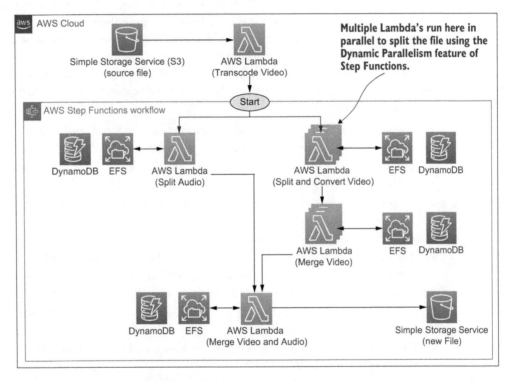

Figure 8.2 **This is a simplified view of the serverless transcoder. There are a few more components to it, but we've avoided including them in this figure to focus on the essential elements of the architecture.**

8.2 Architecture deep dive

Let's explore the architecture in more detail. There's nuance to the implementation and how things work. To avoid dealing with some pain later, let's plan how we will design, build, and deploy the serverless transcoder. Before going any further, recall that the entire idea is to split a giant video file into many small segments, transcode these segments in parallel, and then merge them together into a new file.

8.2.1 Maintaining state

We'll use DynamoDB to maintain state across the entire operation of the serverless pipeline. It'll keep track of which videos have been created and which haven't. To simplify the pipeline and, in particular, to simplify the code that monitors which segments have been created or transcoded, we are going to use a trick. (Before going any further, think about how you would keep track of all small video segments that have been created, transcoded, and merged given that segments will be created and processed in parallel.)

The trick is to create n^2 smaller video segments. Out of one large video file, we should generate 2, or 4, or 8, or 256, or 512, or more segments. Just remember to keep the number of segments at n^2. Why is this? The idea is that once we've created and transcoded our video segments, we can begin merging them in any order. Having n^2 segments easily allows us to identify which two neighbor segments can be merged. And, we can keep track of this information in the database.

We'll create a basic binary tree that helps to make the logic around this algorithm a little easier to manage. Let's imagine that we have 8 segments. Here's how the process could take place:

1. Segments 3 and 4 are transcoded quicker than the rest and can be merged together (they are neighbors) into a new segment called 3-4.
2. Then segment 7 is created, but segment 8 is not yet available. The system waits for segment 8 to become ready before merging 7 and 8 together.
3. Segment 8 is created and segments 7 and 8 can be merged together into a new segment 7-8.
4. Then segments 1 and 2 finish transcoding and are merged into a segment 1-2.
5. The good news is that a neighboring segment 3-4 is already available. Therefore, segments 3-4 and 1-2 can be merged together into a new segment called 1-4.
6. Segments 5 and 6 are transcoded and are merged into a segment 5-6.
7. Segment 5-6 has a neighboring segment 7-8. These two segments are merged together to create segment 5-8.
8. Finally, segments 1-4 and 5-8 can be merged together to create the final video that consists of segments 1 to 8.

Because we have n^2 segments, we can keep track of neighboring segments and merge them as soon as both neighbors (the left and the right) become available. Another interesting aspect is that segments themselves can figure out who their neighbors are for merging. A segment with an index that is cleanly divisible by 2 is always on the right, whereas a segment that is not cleanly divisible by 2 is on the left. For example, a segment with an index of 6 is divisible by 2, therefore, we can figure that it's on the right, and the neighbor it needs to merge with (when it becomes available) has an index of 5. Figure 8.3 illustrates how blocks can be merged together.

DynamoDB is an excellent tool for keeping track of which segments have been created and merged. In fact, we will precompute all possible segments and add them to

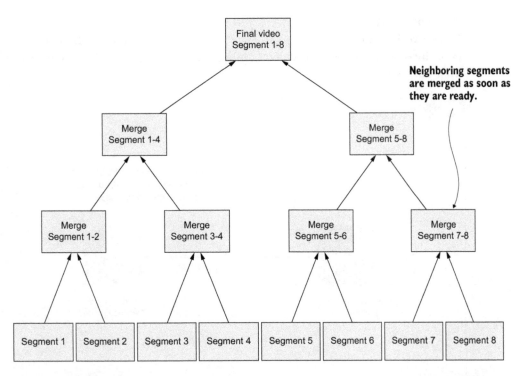

Figure 8.3 Segments are merged together into a new video. The beauty of our engine is that neighboring segments can be merged as soon as they are ready. There's no need to wait for other, nonrelated, segments to finish processing.

DynamoDB. Then we will atomically increment counters in DynamoDB to have a record of when segments have been created and merged. This allows the processing engine to figure out which blocks haven't been merged yet and which need to be done next.

This is an important part of the algorithm, so it's worth restating it again. Each record in DynamoDB represents two neighboring segments (for example, segment 1 and segment 2). The split-and-convert operation increments a confirmation counter each time a segment is created. When the confirmation counter equals 2, our system knows that the two neighboring segments exist and that they can be merged together.

This information and logic are used in the Split and Convert function and in the Merge Video function. Our algorithm continues to merge segments and increment the confirmation counter in DynamoDB until there's nothing left to merge.

There are more ways than one to do it

Our use of a binary tree is just one approach to solving this problem, keeping track of segments and ultimately merging them together. There are myriad other ways this can be done. How would you do it if you had to come up with a different approach?

TRANSCODE VIDEO

Our serverless transcoder kicks off once we upload a file into an S3 bucket. An S3 event invokes the Transcode Video Lambda and the process begins. Figure 8.4 shows what this looks like.

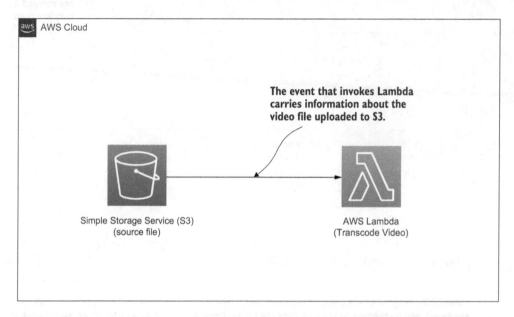

Figure 8.4   This is a basic and common serverless architecture. Invoking code from S3 is the bread and butter of Lambda functions.

The Transcode Video function performs the following steps:

1. Downloads the file from S3 to a local directory on EFS.
2. Analyzes the downloaded video file and extracts metadata from it. Video keyframes are provided in this metadata.
3. Creates the necessary directories in EFS for all future segments that are going to be created.
4. Works out how many segments need to be created based on the number of keyframes.

   Remember that we are always creating n^2 segments. This means that we may have to create some *fake* segments in DynamoDB. These will not really do anything. They are considered as segments that have already been created, so they don't need to be processed.
5. Creates the necessary records in DynamoDB including any fake records that are needed.
6. Runs a Step Functions workflow with two different inputs. The first parameter tells Step Functions to run a Lambda to extract and save the audio to EFS. The

second parameter is an array of objects that specify the start and end times of all segments that need to be created. Step Functions takes this array and applies the Map procedure. It fans out and creates a Lambda function for each object in the array, thus causing the original file to be split up by many Lambda functions in parallel.

The Transcode Video function is an example of a monolithic or "fat" Lambda function because it does a lot of different things. It may not be a bad idea to split it up, but that also comes with its own set of tradeoffs. In the end, whether you think this function should be kept together or not may depend on your personal taste and philosophy. We think that this function is a pragmatic solution for what we need to do, but we wouldn't be aghast if you decided to split it.

8.2.2 Step Functions

Step Functions plays a central role in our system. This service orchestrates and runs the main workflow that splits the video file into segments, transcodes them, and then merges them. Step Functions also run a function that extracts the audio from the video file and saves it to EFS for safekeeping. The Lambda functions that Step Functions invoke include:

- *Split Audio*—Extracts the audio from the video and saves it as a separate file in EFS.
- *Split and Convert Video*—Splits the video file from a particular start point (for example, 5 minutes and 25 seconds) to an end point (such as 6 minutes and 25 seconds) and then encodes the new segment to a different format or bit rate.
- *Merge Video*—Merges segments together after they have been transcoded. Multiple Merge Video functions will run to merge segments until one final video file is produced.
- *Merge Video and Audio*—Merges the newly created video file and the audio file to create the final output. This function uploads the new file back to S3.

> **TIP** You don't have to extract the audio from the video and then transcode just the video file separately. We decided to do that because in our tests, our system ran a bit faster when the video was processed on its own and then recombined with the audio. However, your mileage may vary, so we recommend that you test video transcoding with and without extracting the audio first.

Step Functions is a workflow engine that is fairly customizable. It supports different states like Task (this invokes a Lambda function or passes a parameter to the API of another service) or Choice (this adds branching logic).

The one important state that we'll use is Map. This state takes in an array and executes the same steps for each entry in that array. Therefore, if we pass in an array with information on how to cut up a video into segments, Map runs enough Lambda functions to process all of those arguments in parallel. This is exactly what we are going to build. We will pass an array to a Split and Convert Lambda function using the Map type. Step Functions will create as many functions as necessary to cut the original video into segments.

Here comes the more interesting part. As soon as the segments are created, Step Functions begins calling the Merge Video function until all segments are merged into a new video. We'll add some logic to the Step Functions execution workflow to figure out if Merge Video needs to be called. Once all Merge Video tasks are called and processed, Step Functions will take the result from Split Audio and from Merge Video and invoke the final Merge Video and Audio function. Figure 8.5 shows what this process looks like.

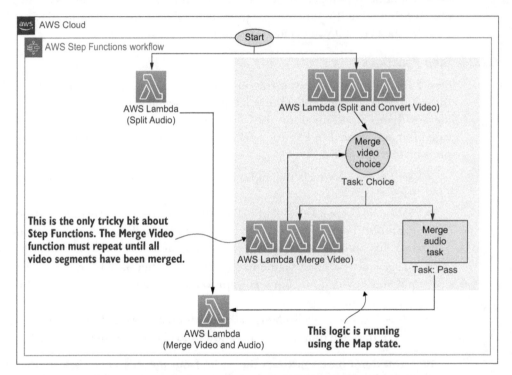

Figure 8.5   The Step Functions execution workflow does all the work in our transcoder. The video is split, converted, and merged again using two main functions and a bit of logic.

Now that you know what the Step Functions workflow does, let's discuss each of the Lambda functions in more detail.

SPLIT AUDIO

Step Functions runs the Split Audio Lambda function to extract audio from the video file. As we've mentioned, this step is done to accelerate the overall workflow because, from there on, the audio portion of the file isn't considered, and only the video portion is transcoded to another bit rate. We don't have to do this. We can leave audio and video together, but in our case, our testing showed that doing this improved the overall performance. The Split Audio function executes the following steps:

1. Extracts audio using ffmpeg and saves it to a folder in EFS.
2. Updates the relevant DynamoDB record to record that this was done.
3. Returns a Success message and additional parameters (like the location of the audio file) to the Step Functions orchestrator.

At a later stage, Step Functions invokes the Merge Video Audio function with the parameters that were returned by the Split Audio and Merge Video functions.

SPLIT AND CONVERT VIDEO

The Split and Convert Video function splits the original video file into a segment and converts that segment to a new bit rate or encoding. The original video file doesn't get changed in this process; instead, the function merely extracts a segment between a start time and an end time, specified in the parameters that are passed to it. These parameters are worked out by the Transcode Video function.

Many hundreds of Split and Convert Video functions can run in parallel. Here are the main actions that it performs:

1. Using ffmpeg, the function creates a new video file from the original one.
2. It increments a confirmation counter in the appropriate DynamoDB record to specify that the segment exists.
3. If the confirmation counter is equal to 2, it then returns to the Step Functions workflow with a Merge message. Otherwise, it returns with a Success message, which stops the execution of that particular Step Functions parallel execution.

You may recall from the previous section that, with DynamoDB, each record represents two neighboring segments. When a record counter is incremented to 2, the function knows that the two neighboring segments exist. The function returns a Merge message to Step Functions, and Step Functions knows that it can begin calling the Merge Video for these segments.

MERGE VIDEO

Step Functions calls the Merge Video function when two neighboring segments are ready to be merged into a new single segment. The merge operation happens using ffmpeg, and the new segment is saved to EFS. Here's what happens in a little more detail:

1. The Merge Video function is invoked with a number of parameters passed to it by Step Functions. These parameters include the left and the right segments.
2. Using ffmpeg, the left and right segments are merged to create a new segment. This new segment is saved to EFS.
3. DynamoDB confirmation is incremented. If there are two confirmations, then the function returns to the workflow with a Merge message.
4. However, if there are two confirmations and the last two remaining segments have been merged, the function returns with a MergeAudio message to the workflow.

As you can see, the Merge Video function creates a bit of a loop. It continues to merge segments, returns the Merge message, and causes Step Functions to invoke itself again. This happens until the last two segments are merged, then the return type is changed to MergeAudio. This is when Step Functions knows that it's time to combine audio and video and invokes the Merge Video and Audio function.

MERGE VIDEO AND AUDIO

The final function is Merge Video and Audio. It takes input from the Split Audio and Merge Video functions and merges the audio and the new video files together using ffmpeg. The new file is saved somewhere else (in another directory) on EFS. The function can also upload the new file to an S3 bucket for easier access.

8.3   An alternative architecture

You can build this serverless transcoder without using EFS (or Step Functions for that matter). In fact, our first iteration used only S3 and SNS to perform fan-out. We wanted to present you with an alternative architecture that shows that you don't necessarily have to use Step Functions or EFS if you don't want to. This section demonstrates that you can use SNS and S3 instead to achieve the same outcome. It's nice that AWS provides so many building blocks that we can build our desired architecture in different ways.

> **TIP**   One reason for adopting a different architecture could be because you don't want to pay for Step Functions and EFS. That is a reasonable concern. Using S3 is likely going to be much cheaper than using EFS and will probably perform just as well. Once you get the code working, using S3 is straightforward, and we don't have a reason not to recommend it. Whether you should use SNS instead of Step Functions is a tougher proposition. SNS is cheaper, but you will lose a lot of the robustness and observability that you get with Step Functions. Perhaps the best solution is to use Step Functions with S3? We'll leave it to you as an exercise to achieve.

This alternative implementation closely resembles what we created in the previous section except, as we mentioned, we'll replace Step Functions with SNS and EFS with S3. Figure 8.6 shows what this architecture looks like.

This architecture works well, but there are some improvements that can be made to it. For one, the implementation should be improved in case of errors such as the split or merge operation failing. Luckily, there is the Dead Letter Queue (DLQ) feature of Lambda that allows us to save, review, and even replay failed invocations. If you want a challenge, we invite you to implement DLQ for this architecture to make it more resilient to errors.

The second issue is observability and knowing what's happening with the system. Step Functions provides some level of visibility, but things get a little bit harder with SNS. One tool you can use to help yourself is AWS X-Ray. This AWS service can help you understand the interactions of different services within your system. It goes without saying that CloudWatch is essential too.

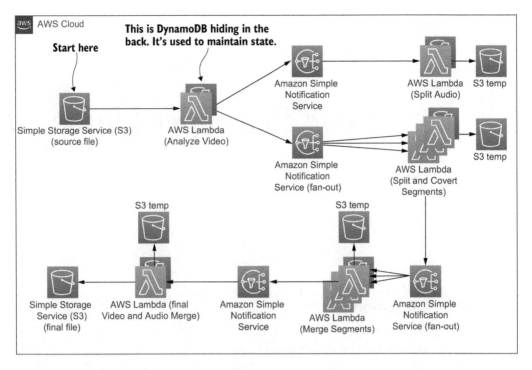

Figure 8.6 The SNS and S3 architecture for the serverless transcoder

Summary

- MapReduce can work really well with a serverless approach. Lambda invites you to think about parallelization from the start so take advantage of that.
- You can solve a lot of problems in Lambda and process vast amounts of data by splitting it up into smaller chunks and parallelizing the operations.
- Step Functions is an excellent service for defining workflows. It allows you to fan-out and fan-in operations.
- EFS for Lambda is an endless local disk—it grows as much as you need. You can run applications with EFS and Lambda that you couldn't have run before. Having said that, S3 is still likely to be cheaper so make sure to do your calculations and analysis before choosing EFS.
- You can solve problems in different ways:
  - You don't have to use Step Functions because you can use SNS (although Step Functions adds an additional level of robustness and visibility).
  - You don't need to use EFS because you can use S3.
- When coming up with an architecture for your system, explore the available options because there will be different alternatives with different tradeoffs.

Code Developer University

This chapter covers

- AWS Glue and Amazon Athena
- Using EventBridge to connect system components
- Using Kinesis Firehose and Lambda for at-scale data processing

One idea that we've been mulling for a while has been a web app designed to help developers learn programming skills in a fun way with gamification and useful analytics. Our idea, let's call it Code Developer University (CDU), evolved into a proof-of-concept website with a collection of interesting programming challenges for budding developers to solve and to build skills.

Each challenge would pose a problem. The student would have space to type in their solution and then submit it to our system for processing. The system would run the solution through a battery of tests and decide whether the solution passed or failed. If the solution failed, the user would have a chance to update their code and resubmit again. If the solution passed, the user would advance to the next challenge, receiving between 50 and 500 experience points (XP) based on the difficulty of the problem.

To make the entire experience more interesting and exciting, there would be elements of gamification baked-in throughout the system. For instance, experience points would be used to create various leaderboards. That way, users interested in a friendly competition would be able to compete for a top 10 position. The more challenges solved, the higher the score. These leaderboards would show the overall top 10 performers and then the best performers for each language like Python or JavaScript.

If a student wanted to dig into more data and perhaps see, search, and filter more advanced reports, that would be supported too. A student could, for example, look at the most common mistakes that other users make (anonymized, of course) and learn from that as well.

The original idea was lofty but doable. The key to building this project would be to lean on as many different AWS services as possible. That way we could focus on the unique aspects of the system and leave the rest of the undifferentiated heavy lifting, like authentication, to AWS. At the end, and as you will see, we used the following services to put everything together:

- EventBridge (messaging)
- Glue (data preparation and transformation)
- Athena (data querying)
- DynamoDB (database)
- QuickSight (reporting)
- S3 (storage)
- Lambda and API Gateway

In this chapter, we focus specifically on data, leaderboards, and reporting for CDU. It's a fascinating part of the system because it uses so many parts of the AWS ecosystem and because you can build something similar just as rapidly yourself. Other features of CDU are quite standard for a web app. There are user accounts, an HTML5 user interface, and all the basic bolts and bits you would expect. If you want to learn how to build such a system yourself, take a look at the first edition of this book, which describes a similar, albeit video-focused web application.

9.1 Solution overview

The leaderboard and reporting aspect of CDU is interesting because it is serverless, scalable, and, frankly, fun to implement. There are many serverless AWS services that make data collection, aggregation, and analysis possible without resorting to traditional reporting and data-warehousing products of yesteryear. Let's take a look first at the requirements and then the overall solution.

9.1.1 Requirements listed

CDU is a website with user registration and account features, and the ability for users to access and try code exercises and receive points if they are successful in implementing and solving a coding challenge. To that end, the following sections provide a list of high-level requirements for CDU.

GENERAL

- The user must be able to run their code solution and determine if it passes or fails the tests.
- If the tests pass, then the solution is considered to be correct.
- A correct solution awards the user some number of points, which are saved to the user's profile.
- There should be leaderboards and advanced reports for users to view.
- The entire system must be serverless, event-driven, and as automated as much as possible (no intervention from the administrator should be needed to update leaderboards and reports).

USERS AND EXPERIENCE POINTS

- Points are awarded for the programming language that is used to solve the challenge. For example, if the user codes in Python, then they get points allocated toward Python. If they use JavaScript, then points are allocated to their JavaScript score.
- The user's profile should show the overall score (sum of all previous points for all programming languages) and scores for each programming language individually. The user's profile and scores should be updated in near real time.
- The user shouldn't receive points for the same challenge more than once.

LEADERBOARDS

- CDU should feature a leaderboard that shows the top scorers across different programming languages (e.g., Python and JavaScript).
- An overall leaderboard should show the top performers (regardless of the programming language) for last month, last year, and all time.
- Leaderboards don't need to be updated in real time, however, but they should refresh at least every 60 minutes. There should also be a way to refresh them on demand by the administrator.

REPORTS

- Apart from the leaderboard, users should also have access to more in-depth reports that they can search and filter.
- The exact implementation of the reports can be left to the data team; however, a basic report could show the best performers, similar to the leaderboard.
- Reports should be refreshed at least every 60 minutes but could also be refreshed sooner (if needed) by the administrator.
- Any user, not just the administrator, should have access to the leaderboard.

9.1.2   *Solution architecture*

Let's now take a look at a possible architecture that ought to address our major requirements. Figure 9.1 shows most of the major architectural pieces. These include the following three main microservices:

- Code Scoring Service
- Student Profile Service
- Analytics Service

We will break down the solution in the coming sections, but let's take a look at the high-level architecture shown in figure 9.1. The Code Scoring Service runs a Lambda function that processes submitted code. If it passes the test, information is sent across to the EventBridge, which invokes two other microservices:

- The Student Profile Service updates the student's profile in the database and adds to the student's overall score.
- The Analytics Service processes and stores the user's test data in S3, which later enables the creation of the QuickSight dashboards.

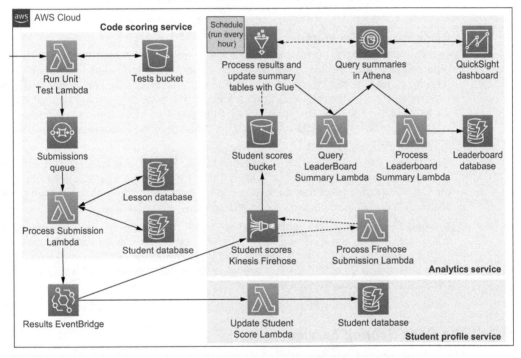

Figure 9.1   **The architecture of Code Developer University (CDU) that's responsible for scoring and leaderboards**

There's actually quite a bit that happens in the Analytics Service. It is covered in detail in section 9.4, but here's a high-level overview of what actually takes place in this microservice:

- The message (with the user's solution) is pushed into Kinesis Firehose, which uses a Lambda function to modify the format of the message so that it can be processed later by other AWS services.

- Kinesis then stores the newly processed message (as a JSON file) in an S3 bucket.
- AWS Glue runs on schedule, which is set to trigger every 60 minutes. When that happens, Glue processes the aforementioned S3 bucket and updates a Glue Data Catalog (think: a table with metadata) that points to the data stored in S3.
- Glue then triggers a Lambda function, which uses Amazon Athena to query the data stored in S3 via the Glue Data Catalog.
- Once Athena finishes, it triggers another Lambda function that gets the result of the query and updates the appropriate leaderboards saved in DynamoDB.
- Finally, there's an Amazon QuickSight report that uses Athena to query the data in the S3 bucket when a user wants to see more information.

There's a little more detail to all the services, and you may have other questions, which should be cleared up in coming sections. Read on!

QuickSight vs. DynamoDB

One question you may be asking yourself is why are we using Amazon QuickSight for reporting and also storing leaderboards in DynamoDB? Isn't that redundant? The reason is that QuickSight is heavy, powerful, but also slow. You can integrate it into your website (in an iFrame), but it takes a long time to load. If you are committed to using QuickSight to explore data in detail, then you'll wait for 10 or 20 seconds. But if you want to see results quickly, waiting for it can be unbearable (AWS, please look at performance!).

This is why we store important leaderboard results in DynamoDB, which can be loaded and displayed to the user quickly. Then it's up to the user to choose to see the QuickSight version of this data, especially if they need more detail. You can think of our DynamoDB leaderboards as an informal cache for QuickSight.

The negative aspect of this implementation is that the DynamoDB table and the data in QuickSight must be synchronized. If the Student Profile Service updates the student's score, but the Analytics Service fails, DynamoDB may end up showing something different to QuickSight. There are ways to fix this though. What would you do? We will discuss this in section 9.3.

9.2 The Code Scoring Service

The purpose of the Code Scoring Service is to receive submitted code from the user and run it against a set of tests. If tests pass, the Run Unit Test Lambda creates a submission, which it puts into the submissions queue. The submission is picked up from the queue by the Process Submission Lambda and is enriched with data from a couple of DynamoDB tables. Finally, the Process Submission Lambda pushes the newly enriched message on to Amazon EventBridge for consumption by other services in our system.

The actual design of the Code Scoring Service is fairly straightforward, but let's take a look at its design in more detail. Figure 9.2 shows a closeup of the architecture beginning with the Run Unit Test Lambda. This Run Unit Test Lambda function is invoked via HTTPS (via the API Gateway) and receives a zip payload as part of the request body. The zip payload contains the user's code submission and metadata, such as what challenge the user is attempting and what programming language is being used. The Lambda function looks up the appropriate test in the Tests bucket (it knows which test to grab based on the lesson name) and downloads that test file from S3.

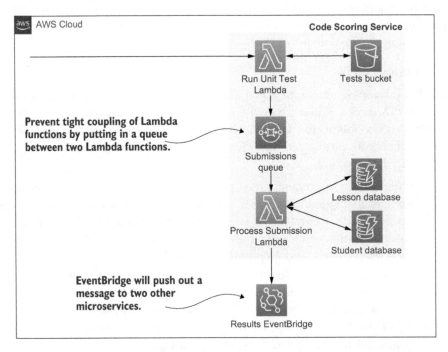

Figure 9.2   The Code Scoring Service runs the user's code and, if it's successful, kicks of the rest of the chain of events in our system.

Now the Lambda function can execute the appropriate interpreter or compiler, run the unit test, and test the user's submission.

Lambda layers

If you want to support multiple languages like Python, JavaScript, C++, C#, Java, and so on, use Lambda layers. A *layer* is a zip file that can contain additional libraries or custom runtimes.

You can have a Lambda layer with a Python interpreter or a layer with a C compiler. Moreover, you deploy layers separately from Lambda functions, thus keeping your actual Lambda functions small. At run time, as long as it's configured correctly, your Lambda functions can access the contents of your layers (which are extracted to the /opt directory in the function execution environment). You can deploy as many layers as you like, but know that Lambda can only use up to five layers at a time. You can read more about them at http://mng.bz/doJO.

The Run Unit Test Lambda by itself is not particularly complex. It needs to know how to run a unit test and then parse the result to figure out if it passed successfully or not. If the test failed, then the function sends back an HTTP response with the output from the interpreter or the compiler. Thus, the user can see the error message, fix the code issue, and resubmit. Otherwise, if it passes, the function sends back a celebratory message to the user and places a message containing the user's submission on the Submissions SQS queue for further processing.

9.2.1 *Submissions Queue*

The Submissions Queue is an SQS queue that sits between the only two Lambda functions in this service. When a message is placed in the queue, it leads to an invocation of the Process Submission Lambda that retrieves the message and enriches it with more data before pushing it to the EventBridge. There are a few reasons we do this, including the following:

- One of the requirements is to prevent the user from receiving points for the same challenge multiple times. The Process Submission Lambda needs to look up the Student DynamoDB table to figure out whether the user has already completed this challenge. If the user has already completed that challenge, then that is noted, and no points are earned.
- Assuming that the student has solved the challenge for the first time and is supposed to receive points, the Process Submission Lambda also looks up how many points should be awarded from the Lesson database.
- All of this information, including the message that came from the queue, is combined and pushed to Amazon EventBridge.

By now you might be thinking, "Why not do everything in the initial Run Unit Test Lambda?" The reason is to separate responsibility. The Run Unit Test function is intended to run code and figure out if it passes a test. The second Process Submission Lambda function has to perform database lookups and evaluate whether the student should be awarded points. As a rule of thumb, you should use multiple Lambda functions when you are dealing with different concerns rather than having everything lumped into one. Hence, this is the reason we created two functions and introduced a message queue between them.

Another question you may have is why we used SQS rather than have functions call one another directly. Our recommendation is never to have functions call each other directly unless you are using a feature called Lambda Destinations (which adds a hidden queue between two functions anyway). Lambda Destinations, however, only works for asynchronous invocations, so it wouldn't have been possible in our case. The Run Unit Test Lambda was invoked synchronously via HTTP. The reason for having a queue between two functions is to reduce coupling (e.g., the two functions have no direct knowledge of one another) and to have an easier time handling errors and retries.

We also could have chosen to use Amazon EventBridge instead, but SQS was acceptable in this scenario. And, if we ever wanted to enable First-In First-Out (FIFO) queues at a later stage, we'd need to use SQS because EventBridge doesn't support this feature, so that further weighed our decision.

The last action performed by the Process Submission Lambda is to push the message to Amazon EventBridge. As you may recall, this message contains the original submission made by the user together with additional details that consists of information on whether the experience points should be awarded to the user and the amount of those points (this information was obtained by looking up a couple of tables in the Process Submission Lambda function).

Amazon EventBridge

Amazon EventBridge is a serverless event bus that can *connect* different AWS (and non-AWS) services. It has a few great features that services like SQS, SNS, and Kinesis do not possess. Chief among them is the ability to use more than 90 AWS services as event sources and 17 services as targets, automated scaling, content-based filtering, schema discovery, and input transformation. But like any other technology, it has certain deficiencies like no guarantee on ordering of events or buffering. As always, what you end up choosing should depend on your requirements and the capabilities of the product you are using.

9.2.2 Code Scoring Service summary

The Code Scoring Service is a relatively trivial service apart, perhaps, from running the code provided by the user. Even then it's not too difficult to unzip a file and run an interpreter (or a compiler) within Lambda. One important thing to mention is security. If you are running someone else's code in a function, you must be prepared that someone will try to subvert it, find a vulnerability to exploit, and do something bad. Therefore, you must follow the principle of least privilege and disallow anything that isn't critical to the running of your function. This should be a rule for all Lambda functions, but in this instance, you should be doubly careful and vigilant.

9.3 Student Profile Service

The Student Profile Service is small. Its purpose is to increment the number of experience points in the student record in the DynamoDB table. That way, the student can immediately see the cumulative score added to their tally and feel good about their achievement. This service consists of a single Lambda function that communicates with DynamoDB. This function receives an event from EventBridge, reads it, and updates the user profile if the user has received any points. Figure 9.3 shows what this basic service looks like.

You may remember that earlier (in section 9.1), we posed a question about keeping different tables in sync. Given that the Student Profile Service and the Analytics

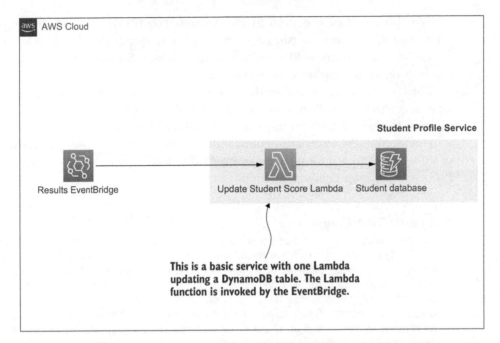

Figure 9.3   The Student Profile Service is the simplest one in this entire architecture. It's a Lambda function that writes to a Dynamo table.

Service store similar data (namely the user's score), what happens if one of the services goes down and falls out of sync with the other service? In other words, if there's a fault in a service that causes a data mismatch, what can we do about it? There are a number of solutions you can think about implementing to address this problem:

- *Serial invocation*—One approach is to make the Analytics Service and the Student Profile Service run in serial rather than parallel. That way your system would update the Student Profile Service first and then run through the update procedure in the Analytics Service (invoking it via another EventBridge). If the Analytics Service fails, the system would roll back the change in the Student Profile Service, and both services would continue operating in sync.
- *One source of truth*—Alternatively, you could make the Analytics Service your source of truth and then simply copy the data over to the Student Profile Service. That way you could even delete all data in the Student Profile Service and regenerate it as many times as necessary from the Analytics Service.
- *Share the database*—Both services could read and write to the same database. That would avoid some problems, but then, we no longer have a microservices architecture in which each service is responsible for its own view of the world. We would end up with a distributed monolith. It must be mentioned that in many circumstances having a distributed monolith is a fine and acceptable solution.

- *Orchestrator*—Another approach is to have an orchestrator sit above the two services and monitor what is happening. If there is an error, the orchestrator could run additional actions to compensate for the issue (for example, retry or roll back).

Quite frankly, this is a common situation with a microservices-based approach. How do you keep services in sync without having all microservices coupled to a central database? There are different solutions to this problem but, as with anything in software engineering, they all have different trade-offs. In the case of CDU, we decided to update both services in parallel. If an issue were to occur, we would use the Analytics Service as our source of truth and regenerate the data needed by the Student Profile Service.

9.3.1 Update Student Scores function

The Update Student Score function is shown in listing 9.1. It performs three primary actions:

- It parses the event received from the EventBridge that has the scores/data.
- Updates the amount of XP gained for the topic like JavaScript or Python.
- Updates the total amount of XP earned by the user.

Listing 9.1 Updating the Student Score Lambda

```
'use strict';

const AWS = require('aws-sdk');
const sns = new AWS.SNS();

const dynamoDB = require('aws-sdk/clients/dynamodb');
const doc = new dynamoDB.DocumentClient();

const updateTotalXP = (record, lessons) => {
    const date = new Date(Date.now()).toISOString();

    const xp = lessons.filter(m => m.xp)
        .map(m => m.xp)
        .reduce((a, b) => a+b);

    const params = {
        TableName: process.env.USER_DATABASE,
        Key: {
            userId: record.username
        },
        UpdateExpression: `set \
                        modified = :date, \
                        xp.#total = :xp`,
        ExpressionAttributeNames: {
            '#total': 'total'
        },
        ExpressionAttributeValues: {
            ':date': date,
            ':xp': xp
        },
```

Calculates the total XP for a user by summing up the XP for all of the lessons. This is woefully inefficient to do each time but OK for an example. Can you think of a better way?

This params object has all the necessary attributes needed to update the relevant DynamoDB table. Note the 'total' in the ExpressionAttributeNames. It's a reserved keyword so it has to be specified using ExpressionAttributeNames.

```
                    ReturnValues: 'ALL_NEW'
        };

        return doc.update(params).promise();
    }

const updateTopicXP = (record) => {
    const date = new Date(Date.now()).toISOString();

    const lesson = {
        lesson: record.lesson,
        topic: record.topic,
        modified: date,
        xp: record.xp,
        isCompleted: record.isCompleted
    };

    const params = {
        TableName: process.env.USER_DATABASE,
        Key: {
            userId: record.username
        },
        UpdateExpression: `set \
                    modified = :date, \
                    lessons = list_append(if_not_exists(lessons,
            :empty_list), :lesson), \
                    xp.${record.topic} =
        if_not_exists(xp.${record.topic}, :zero) + :xp`,
        ExpressionAttributeValues: {
            ':lesson': [ lesson ],
            ':empty_list': [],
            ':zero': 0,
            ':date': date,
            ':xp': parseInt(record.xp, 10)
        },
        ReturnValues: 'ALL_NEW'
    };

    return doc.update(params).promise();
}

exports.handler = async (event, context) => {
    try {
        const record = event.detail;

        if (record.isCompleted) {
            const user = await updateTopicXP(record);

            if (user.Attributes.lessons.length > 0) {
                await updateTotalXP(record, user.Attributes.lessons);
            }
        }
    } catch (error) {
        console.log(error);
    }
}
```

> This update expression appends a lesson to a list of lessons in DynamoDB. Otherwise, if a list doesn't exist, a new and empty one is created.

> This function is invoked via the EventBridge. The parameter event.detail contains the information that was sent over from the Process Submission Lambda function in the previous section.

The Student Profile Service is a small microservice with a single Lambda function. Its purpose is to update a DynamoDB table and that's pretty much as basic as you can get. The next service, however, is not as straightforward. Let's take a look at it now.

9.4 *Analytics Service*

This is going to be a big one, so grab yourself a tea or a coffee before jumping in. If you recall, the purpose of the Analytics Service is twofold:

- Enable the creation and display of QuickSight dashboards.
- Maintain leaderboards in DynamoDB that could be *quickly* accessed and read.

The data collected and processed by the Analytics Service must enable us to achieve those two aims. Let's take a look at the architecture in figure 9.4. The steps that the Analytics Service takes are as follows:

1. The EventBridge service pushes a message from the Code Scoring Service on to the Student Scores Kinesis Firehose.
2. The Firehose runs a Lambda that processes and transforms each incoming message into a format that is palatable for Amazon Glue to work on later.
3. After the message is transformed by Lambda, Firehose stores it in an S3 bucket.
4. Every hour (or on demand) AWS Glue runs and crawls the messages stored in the S3 bucket. It updates a table within the AWS Glue Data Catalog with the metadata based on the crawl.
5. Once Glue is finished processing, the Query Leaderboard Summary function is run. The Lambda function invokes Athena that runs a query to work out the leaderboard.
6. Athena accesses Glue and S3 and extracts the relevant data for the query. Once the query is complete, the Process Leaderboard Summary Lambda is invoked.
7. This Process Leaderboard Summary Lambda function receives the result of the query from Athena, reads it, and updates the Leaderboard DynamoDB table.
8. Finally, the QuickSight Dashboard component uses Athena to execute queries based on what the user is trying to see in a QuickSight report.

You may agree that this is quite a lot to take in one go, so let's break down the most interesting components. We'll do that in the following sections.

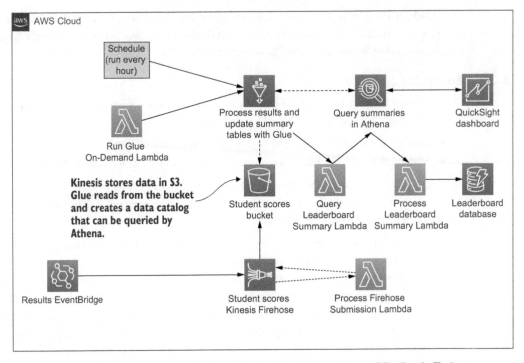

Figure 9.4   The Analytics Service architecture includes Glue, Athena, DynamoDB, Kinesis Firehose, QuickSight, and Lambda.

9.4.1   *Kinesis Firehose*

Kinesis Firehose provides a way to capture and stream data into Elasticsearch, Redshift, and S3. AWS says that it's the ". . . easiest way to reliably load streaming data into data lakes, data stores, and analytics services" (https://aws.amazon.com/kinesis/data -firehose/), which sounds perfect for our use case. Kinesis Firehose, unlike other Kinesis services, is serverless, meaning that you don't need to worry about scaling partitions or sharding as is the case with, say, Kinesis Data Stream. It is all done for you automatically. Another nice feature of Firehose is that it can run Lambda for messages as they are ingested. Lambda can be used to convert raw streaming data to other, more useful, formats and this is exactly what we would do. In our use case, we can use a Lambda function to convert the messages to a JSON format that would later be read by the AWS Glue service before storing them in S3.

Listing 9.2 shows a Kinesis Firehose processing function that takes a message, processes it, creates a new record with a different set of fields, and pushes it back to Firehose for storage in S3. In this listing, we are extracting only a few properties from the original message because we don't want to keep everything. For example, we may discard the user's submitted source code because we care only if they've passed the test or not. There are a few things to keep in mind in this listing:

- All transformed records must contain a `recordId`, `result`, and `data`. Otherwise, Kinesis Firehose rejects the entire record and treats it as a "transformation failure."
- The property called `recordId` is passed from Firehose to Lambda. The transformed record has to contain the same `recordId` as the original. A mismatch results in transformation failure (so, don't make your own or append anything to it).
- The property `result` must either be `Ok` (record transformed) or `Dropped` (record was dropped intentionally). The only other allowed value is `ProcessingFailed` if you want to flag that the transformation couldn't take place.
- The property `data` is your base-64 encoded transformed record.

Listing 9.2   Kinesis Firehose processing function

```
'use strict';

exports.handler = (event, context) => {
    let records = [];

    for (let i = 0; i < event.records.length; i++) {
        const payload = Buffer.from(
            event.records[i].data, 'base64')
            .toString('utf-8');
        const data = JSON.parse(payload);

        const record = {
            username: data.detail.username,
            name: data.detail.user.name,
            lesson: data.detail.lesson,
            topic: data.detail.topic,
            xp: data.detail.xp,
            hasPassedTests: (data.detail.hasPassedTests || false),
            runTests: (data.detail.runTests || false),
            isCompleted: (data.detail.isCompleted || false),
            time: data.time,
        };

        records.push({
            recordId: event.records[i].recordId,
            result: 'Ok',
            data: Buffer.from(JSON.stringify(record)).toString('base64')
        });
    }

    console.log(`Return: ${ JSON.stringify({records}) }`);

    return Promise.resolve({
        records
    });
};
```

The original message that was pushed to Firehose. You can now extract the relevant bits you might want to save in S3.

The record you create here and store in S3 will be JSON.

All transformed records must contain a property called recordId, result, and data. Transformation is the ultimate goal for this Lambda.

Finally, you must ensure that your response doesn't exceed 6 MB. Otherwise, Firehose will refuse to play along.

9.4.2 *AWS Glue and Amazon Athena*

AWS Glue is a serverless ETL (extract, transform, and load) service that can scour an S3 bucket with a crawler and update a central metadata repository called the Glue Data Catalog. You and other services can then use this metadata repository to quickly search for relevant information among the records scattered in S3. Glue never actually moves or copies any data. The tables with metadata it creates in the Glue Data Catalog point to the data in S3 (or other sources like Amazon Redshift or RDS). This means that the Data Catalog can be recreated from the original data if necessary.

Amazon Athena is a serverless query service that can analyze data in S3 using standard SQL. If you haven't tried Athena, you have to give it a go. You simply point it to S3, define the schema, and begin querying using SQL. What's even nicer is that it integrates closely with Glue and its Data Catalog (which takes care of the schema). Once you have AWS Glue configured and the Data Catalog created, you can begin querying Athena immediately.

Listing 9.3 shows how to perform a query. An important thing to note is that the query is asynchronous. You will not get a response once you've run it. You have to start the query execution and then, using CloudWatch events, react to when you get the result. Luckily everything can be accomplished with two Lambda functions. Listing 9.3 shows how to execute a query and listing 9.4 shows how to process it if you have hooked up CloudWatch events to respond.

Listing 9.3 Query Leaderboard Summary Lambda

```
'use strict';

const AWS = require('aws-sdk');
const athena = new AWS.Athena();

const runQuery = (view) => {
    const params = {
        QueryString: `SELECT * FROM "${view}"`,        Views are supported by Athena
        QueryExecutionContext: {                        and are as useful as regular SQL.
            Catalog: process.env.ATHENA_DATA_SOURCE,
            Database: process.env.ATHENA_DATABASE        Parameters such as the Catalog,
        },                                               Database and WorkGroup are
        WorkGroup: process.env.ATHENA_WORKGROUP          set up in Athena when you
    };                                                   configure it.

    return athena.startQueryExecution(params).promise();
}

exports.handler = async (event) => {
    let promises = [];
```

```
        promises.push(runQuery(process.env
        ➥ .ATHENA_LEADERBOARD_VIEW_TOPICS));
        promises.push(runQuery(process.env
        ➥ .ATHENA_LEADERBOARD_VIEW_OVERALL));

        const query = await Promise.all(promises);

        console.log('Athena Query Id', query);
}
```

Views are supported by Athena and are as useful as regular SQL.

Listing 9.4 shows a Process Leaderboard Lambda function that responds to a Cloud-Watch event that contains information about the query performed in listing 9.3. Note that the actual result (meaning the data itself) must be retrieved from Athena using the GetQueryResults API call. When the Process Leaderboard Summary function is invoked, only queryExecutionId is passed into it, but that's enough to perform the GetQueryResults API call to get the data. The code in the following listing is quite lengthy because, apart from showing how to get a result out of Athena, it demonstrates how to update a DynamoDB table.

Listing 9.4 Process Leaderboard Summary Lambda

```
'use strict';

const AWS = require('aws-sdk');
const athena = new AWS.Athena();
const dynamodb = new AWS.DynamoDB.DocumentClient();

const getQueryResults = (queryExecutionId) => {
    const params = {
        QueryExecutionId: queryExecutionId
    };

    return athena.getQueryResults(params).promise();
}

const updateDynamoLeaderboard = (rows, index) => {
    let transactItems = [];
    const date = new Date(Date.now()).toISOString();

    //
    // Skip the first row because it's the label
    // Data: [
    //    { VarCharValue: 'topic' },
    //    { VarCharValue: 'username' },
    //    { VarCharValue: 'name' },
    //    { VarCharValue: 'score' },
    //    { VarCharValue: 'rn' }
    // ]
    //

    for (let i = 0; i < rows.length; i++) {
        const row = rows[i].Data;
```

You need the QueryExecutionId to run GetQueryResults, then the result of the query is yours.

```
        const params = {
            TableName: process.env.LEADERBOARD_DATABASE,
            Key: {
                uniqueId: row[1].VarCharValue, //username
                type: row[0].VarCharValue //topic
            },
            UpdateExpression: `set \
                                #name = :name, \
                                modified = :date, \
                                #rank = :rank,
                                score = :score`,
            ExpressionAttributeNames: {
                '#name': 'name',
                '#rank': 'rank'
            },
            ExpressionAttributeValues: {
                ':date': date,
                ':name': row[2].VarCharValue,
                ':score': parseInt(row[3].VarCharValue, 10),
                ':rank': parseInt(row[4].VarCharValue, 10)
            },
            ReturnValues: 'ALL_NEW'
        }

        transactItems.push({Update: params});
    }

    return dynamodb.transactWrite({TransactItems:transactItems}).promise();
}

exports.handler = async (event) => {

    try {
        if (event.detail
            ➥ .currentState === 'SUCCEEDED') {
            const queryExecutionId =
            ➥ event.detail.queryExecutionId;

            const result =
            ➥ await getQueryResults(queryExecutionId);

            result.ResultSet.Rows.shift();

            if (result.ResultSet.Rows.length > 0) {

                const maxItemsPerTransaction = 20;

                for (let i = 0; i <
        ➥ result.ResultSet.Rows.length/maxItemsPerTransaction; i++) {

                    const factor =
        ➥ result.ResultSet.Rows.length/maxItemsPerTransaction;
                    const remainder =
        ➥ result.ResultSet.Rows.length%maxItemsPerTransaction;
```

We only ever want to retrieve the results and save them if the query executes successfully. Luckily, this parameter checks if it's all good.

The first row in the array contains labels for the columns (e.g., topic, score, etc.). Shifting that row removes it because we are only interested in the values.

Updates in chunks of 20 items. DynamoDB can handle 25 items in a transaction, but we only do 20 here instead.

```
                  let data =
⇨ result.ResultSet.Rows.slice(i*maxItemsPerTransaction,
⇨ i*maxItemsPerTransaction + Math.max(maxItemsPerTransaction,
⇨ remainder));

                  const update = await updateDynamoLeaderboard(data,
⇨ i*maxItemsPerTransaction);

            }
        }

    } else {
        console.log('Query Unsuccessful');
    }

} catch (error) {
    console.log(error);
}
}
```

We use a little bit of math to retrieve the necessary records (slice) from the array. This formula gets 20 or fewer rows to store in DynamoDB at a time.

Serverless architectures are typically push-based and event-driven. You should try to avoid polling whenever you can. We could have polled for the status of the query and then called the Lambda function to process the result, but it would have been more complex and error prone. Instead, we rely on CloudWatch events to get notified about the query state transition. Interestingly, this feature wasn't always available, and people had to poll. There really was no other option, so it's good to see AWS adding the necessary support and enabling our serverless dream to continue.

9.4.3 *QuickSight*

Amazon QuickSight is AWS's Business Intelligence (BI) service in the vein of Tableau. You can use it to build dashboards of all kinds and embed them into your website. QuickSight has some really interesting features, like its ability to formulate answers using natural language (this is underpinned by machine learning).

Truth be told, however, at the time of writing, QuickSight is an underwhelming AWS service. It's slow, reasonably pricey, and weirdly different enough from other AWS services to necessitate a steeper learning curve. Nevertheless, it is also serverless, and it allows us to stay within the AWS environment, which is an advantage. We hope that AWS substantially improves QuickSight over the coming months and years. If you are looking for a BI solution, you should have a look at QuickSight but evaluate other options too.

We used QuickSight to create dashboards that read data straight from S3 via Athena for the CDU. Describing how to use QuickSight is out of scope for this chapter, but it does have a fairly intuitive interface that you can click through. QuickSight isn't supported by CloudFormation (at least at the time of writing this in the second half of 2021), so creating consistent, repeatable dashboards is challenging and that's a bummer. However, if your data is in S3 and can be queried with Athena, you can always recreate your dashboards. The main thing is having the data in the right format and place, which you will have with the tools described in this chapter.

In summary, to build an Analytics Service, AWS services such as Kinesis Firehose, Athena, and Glue can be what you need. These are serverless services, meaning that you don't have to think about scaling or managing them the same way that you'd need to think about Amazon Redshift. Nevertheless, if you decide to embark on a serverless journey with these services make sure to do your evaluation first.

- Are they capable of meeting all of your requirements?
- Is there a situation where, in your case, Amazon Redshift may be better?

Athena's charges are based on the amount of data scanned in each query; Redshift is priced based on the size of the instance. There could be circumstances where Athena is cheaper, but Redshift is faster, so you should spend a little bit of time with Excel projecting cost. Nevertheless, in many cases, especially for smaller data sets, the combination of Athena and Glue is more than enough for most needs.

Summary

- AWS has a variety of services and ways to capture, transform, analyze, and report on data relevant to your application.
- Capturing, processing, and reporting on data using services such as Event-Bridge, DynamoDB, Amazon Glue, Amazon Athena, and Amazon QuickSight to build a web application with three microservices leaves us with a few takeaways, including the following:
  - Amazon QuickSight is slow (and it can be expensive). If you need to show leaderboards, cache them in something like DynamoDB for quick retrieval.
  - Glue and Athena are fantastic tools. Glue can index the data stored in S3, and Athena can search across it using standard SQL. The result is less "lifting" and coding for you.
  - Kinesis Firehose has a fantastic feature that allows you to modify records before they get to whatever destination they are going to. This is a fantastic feature that's worth the price of admission.
  - Do not have Lambda functions call each directly unless you are using Lambda Destinations. Always use a queue like SQS or EventBridge if Lambda Destinations is not available.
  - EventBridge is an excellent message bus for use within AWS. Apart from not having FIFO functionality (this could change by the time you read this), it has a ton of excellent features, and we highly recommended it.

Part 4

The future

The last two chapters of this book are really fun. The next chapter is on the AWS Lambda internals and is fascinating for anyone wanting to know how Lambda works. The last chapter of this book is about emerging practices. It covers the usage of multiple AWS accounts, temporary CloudFormation stacks, management of sensitive data, and the use of EventBridge in event-driven architectures. These two chapters are some of our favorites. We hope you like reading them as much as we loved working on them.

Blackbelt Lambda

Performance (how fast your application responds) and availability (whether or not your application provides a valid response) are critical aspects of your end user experience. When using serverless architectures, your performance also has a direct impact on your costs; for example, AWS Lambda bills you for the duration your function runs, weighted by the memory you assign to it. Serverless architectures eliminate many of the common surface areas for performance optimizations, like scaling available servers or tweaking server configurations, which can make it challenging for new users to understand how to go about making these optimizations.

This chapter introduces you to key tools and approaches available to you to improve performance across the various services that make up your serverless application. We'll use relevant examples to demonstrate how these techniques work.

10.1 Where to optimize?

Before we delve into how we optimize serverless architectures, let's quickly recap how to think about them. Serverless architectures have multiple conceptual layers as figure 10.1 illustrates. *Endpoints* are responsible for secure interactions with your end users and devices, and for the ingress of requests or events to your application from the end user. Examples of endpoints you can use in your AWS Serverless architecture include API Gateway, AWS IoT, Amazon Alexa (if you were building an Alexa skill), or even just the AWS SDK.

The *compute layer* of your workload manages requests from external systems (received through the endpoints), while controlling access and ensuring requests are appropriately authorized. It contains the run-time environment that deploys and runs your business logic embodied as Lambda functions (we'll delve into this shortly).

The *data layer* of your workload manages persistent storage from within a system. It provides a secure mechanism to store states that your business logic will need. It also provides a mechanism to trigger events in response to data changes, which in turn can feed into other parts of your business logic. As you can imagine, this is a broad surface area to discuss optimizations across, so we'll focus on the following points, highlighted in figure 10.1:

- Functions
- Invocations of these functions (either via requests from endpoints or events from backend systems)
- Interactions the functions have with downstream resources

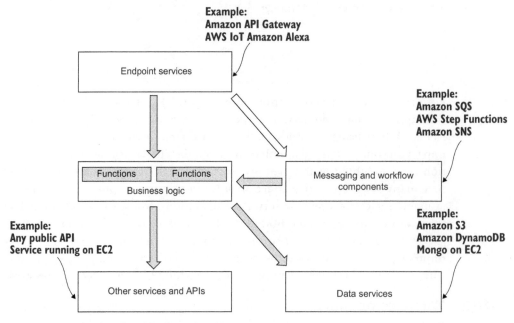

Figure 10.1   Conceptual architecture of a serverless application

Now that you have a conceptual understanding of the various points of optimization, let's look at the tools available to do so. We'll discuss those in the following sections.

10.2   Before we get started

To effectively optimize applications, there are certain tools and concepts we must be familiar with. In this section, we will recap what happens when a Lambda function executes and how it impacts latency, how to observe the latency and contributors to it, and how to generate load to a function to get enough sample data.

10.2.1   How a Lambda function handles requests

To understand how to optimize functions, we need to have a shared understanding of how Lambda goes about executing our functions. Let's use an example to illustrate what happens when a function is deployed. We'll use the image-resizer-service application from the Serverless Application Repository (http://mng.bz/WBy4) for reference. This serverless application deploys a Lambda function (written in Node.js) and an API Gateway to your AWS account in the US East (N. Virginia)east-1 region that reads images from a S3 bucket (whose name is defined at deployment) and serves them through the API Gateway. The function uses the ImageMagick library to process the image.

> **NOTE**   You need to specify a new bucket name for the application to use. Use the name "image-resizer-service-demo" for this example.

Once deployed, click the Test App button on the page, and it will take you to the Applications list view on the Lambda console, where you'll see the newly deployed application. In figure 10.2 these are marked as (1) and (2), respectively.

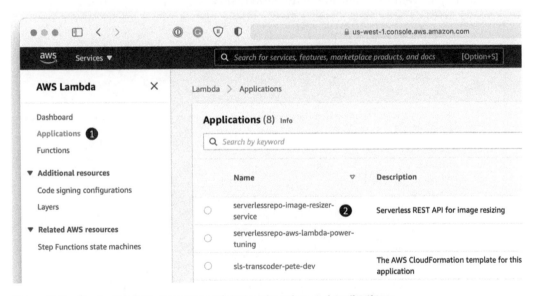

Figure 10.2   The Applications view shows all deployed services and applications.

To test the application, you need to navigate to the main function. Click the application and on the detailed view (figure 10.3); click the image's ResizeFunction (1) to access the function.

Figure 10.3   Application detail view of the image resizer service

Once you select the function, you are taken to the Function Overview page (figure 10.4). Here you can test the function by selecting Test (1), but you need to configure a sample event to supply to the function first (2).

Figure 10.4   The Function Overview page lets you customize and execute the function.

You can use the test event in listing 10.1 to test the function. However, first upload a file from https://commons.wikimedia.org/wiki/File:Happy_smiley_face.png to the image-resizer-service-demo bucket. If you chose to upload a different image, be sure to change the object name in the key field in this listing. You need to do this so that the function doesn't error out looking for an object that doesn't exist!

Listing 10.1 Adding a sample event

```
{
"Records": [
  {
   "eventVersion": "2.0",
   "eventTime": "1970-01-01T00:00:00.000Z",
   "requestParameters": {
    "sourceIPAddress": "127.0.0.1"
   },
   "s3": {
    "configurationId": "testConfigRule",
    "object": {
     "eTag": "0123456789abcdef0123456789abcdef",
     "sequencer": "0A1B2C3D4E5F678901",
     "key": "Happy_smiley_face.png",
     "size": 1024
    },
    "bucket": {
     "arn": "arn:aws:s3::: image-resizer-service-demo ",
     "name": " image-resizer-service-demo ",
     "ownerIdentity": {
      "principalId": "EXAMPLE"
     }
    },
    "s3SchemaVersion": "1.0"
   },
   "responseElements": {
    "x-amz-id-2": "EXAMPLE123/5678abcdefghijklambdaisawesome/mnopqrstuv
    ➥ wxyzABCDEFGH",
    "x-amz-request-id": "EXAMPLE123456789"
   },
   "awsRegion": "us-east-1",
   "eventName": "ObjectCreated:Put",
   "userIdentity": {
    "principalId": "EXAMPLE"
   },
   "eventSource": "aws:s3"
  }
 ]
}
```

Invoke the function a few times to evaluate the behavior; we will use this function to discuss the various optimizations that follow. When you invoke this function, there are different layers in play—the Lambda compute substrate, the execution environment, and the function code (figure 10.5). The substrate is invisible to you; the execution

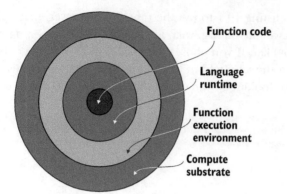

Figure 10.5   Layers involved in executing a function

environment is instantiated on demand for scale events (like a burst of requests); the function code is instantiated for every request.

When the first request or event arrives for your function, the AWS Lambda service performs a series of steps. Once the environment exists, Lambda runs the code inside your function handler. Figure 10.6 shows the steps as follows:

1. Downloads your Lambda function Node.js code onto the part of the compute substrate where your code will run.
2. Instantiates a new execution environment (size is based on your function allocation) with a Node.js runtime.
3. Instantiates your nonfunction dependencies (in this case, ImageMagick).
4. Runs the parts of your function written outside the handler (we don't have any in this example).

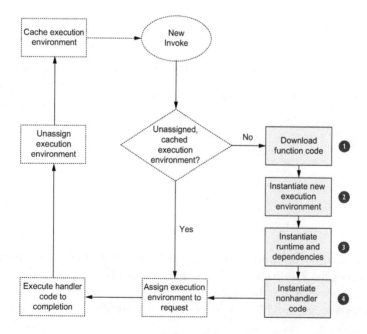

Figure 10.6   The Lambda request lifecycle

In our ResizeFunction example, when your function handler runs, it processes the image and returns the image metadata. Lambda considers the function as done processing the request when the handler logic (and any threads spawned from within the function handler) finishes executing. When the request is complete, however, AWS Lambda does not discard the execution environment (with the run time and code initialized). Instead, it caches the execution environment, where all processes inside the execution environment are paused. AWS does not publish any official guidance on how long the environment is retained in this state, but various published experiments (https://www.usenix.org/conference/atc18/presentation/wang-liang) show this ranging from 5 to 20 minutes.

When a subsequent request arrives during this time and a cached execution environment is available, AWS Lambda will reuse that execution environment to service the request. On the other hand, if a cached execution environment is not available, AWS Lambda will repeat all the steps to serve the request. This has significant implications to both the performance of your function and how you write your function; we'll discuss this further later in this chapter. One important behavior to remember is that AWS Lambda always runs only one request per execution environment. This means that if all execution environments are processing requests and a new one comes in, AWS Lambda will instantiate a new execution environment.

10.2.2 *Latency: Cold vs. warm*

The latency incurred due to steps 1 through 4 in this example (figure 10.6) is referred to commonly as the *cold start penalty*. We refer to the request latency for a request incurring a cold start as *cold latency*, and we refer to the actual function execution latency as the *warm latency*. As a reminder, you incur the cold start penalty only in two situations. First, you'll see cold starts if your function has never been invoked before or is being invoked after an extended period (such that all cached execution environments are removed). Second, you'll see cold starts if there is an increase in the incoming request rate such that AWS Lambda needs to spawn new execution environments because all available ones are servicing requests.

For most production scenarios, cold starts impact less than 0.5% of requests, but cold starts disproportionally impact functions that are invoked infrequently and functions having a burst of traffic (specifically for the requests that first lead to the increased traffic). Requests that experience cold starts may also experience timeouts because the AWS Lambda timeout setting is applied to the total request latency.

10.2.3 *Load generation on your function and application*

As you go about optimizing your application, you want to do so at a load representative of real-life usage. As you can see, your latency characteristics may vary based on load as well. Serverless-artillery is a Nordstrom open source project. It builds on artillery.io and serverless.com by using the horizontal scalability and pay-as-you-go nature of AWS Lambda to instantly and inexpensively throw arbitrary load at your services and report results to an InfluxDB time-series database (other reporting plugins are available). This capability gives you performance and load testing on every commit early in your CI/CD pipeline, so performance bugs can be caught and fixed immediately. https://github.com/Nordstrom/serverless-artillery-workshop presents a detailed walk through on using and setting up the tool.

10.2.4 *Tracking performance and availability*

You can't optimize what you can't measure. Before you go about figuring out how to reduce the latency and improve the availability of your serverless application, you must have a consistent approach to monitor this information. AWS offers a variety of both native and third-party tools for this task. To see what's available, pick any of your functions on the AWS Lambda console, click the function in the function list in the AWS Lambda console, and navigate to the Monitor tab (figure 10.7). You'll see three tools available to you out of the box: CloudWatch metrics (1) on the selected page, CloudWatch logs (2), and AWS X-Ray (3).

The Monitor tab has access to all the metrics and insights you will need. You'll also be able to access relevant CloudWatch logs and X-Ray traces from here.

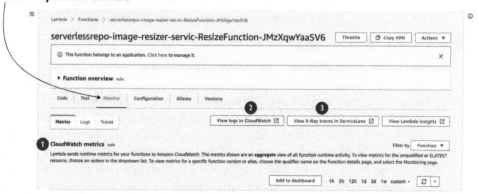

Figure 10.7   Monitoring tab for AWS Lambda functions showing three tools for monitoring

In this chapter, we'll use CloudWatch metrics and X-Ray as the two primary tools to observe the latency characteristics of the application.

CLOUDWATCH METRICS

Each serverless service (like AWS Lambda and API Gateway) emits standard metrics that help you understand the performance and availability characteristics. For Lambda, AWS offers the following metrics among others:

- *Invocations*—Total number of requests received by the given function. This is inclusive of all requests, independent of whether they were processed successfully, throttled, or resulted in an error. This also includes any requests that were retried due to Lambda's built-in retry policy (more on this later).

- *Duration*—Measures the elapsed wall clock time from when the function code starts executing (because of an invocation) to when it stops executing. This is a reasonable proxy for what your function will be billed, although not exact, because AWS Lambda rounds your billed duration to the nearest 1 milliseconds.

- *Errors*—Measures the number of invocations that failed due to errors in the function. Note that this does *not* measure errors due to problems in the AWS Lambda service or due to throttling.

- *Throttles*—Measures the number of invocations that did not result in your function code executing because your function hit either its concurrency limit or caused the account to hit its concurrency limit (1,000 concurrent executions is the default limit but it can be raised by contacting AWS).

AWS X-RAY

AWS X-Ray is a service that allows you to detect, analyze, and optimize performance issues with your AWS Lambda functions and trace requests across multiple services within your serverless architecture. X-Ray generates traces for a sample of requests that each function receives, where a trace consists of segments for each service that the request traverses. A segment may further contain subsegments that detail what particular aspect of the service added to the latency of the request. To turn on X-Ray, you must enable Active tracing under the Monitoring and Operations tools on the function's Configuration tab.

As an example, figure 10.8 shows the trace for a simple sample application. You can see the total time spent in Lambda (1), the time your function took to execute (2), as well as the time spent in a cold start (3). X-Ray can be a useful tool to determine where the bottlenecks in your function execution are, including whether the top contributor is a cold start.

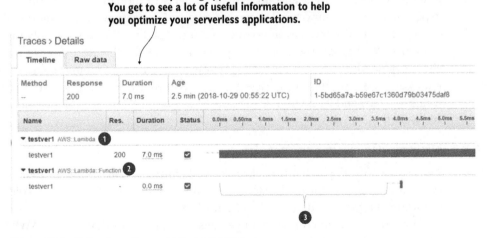

Figure 10.8   X-Ray trace for a sample application

THIRD-PARTY TOOLS

There's a growing ecosystem of non-AWS tools that can also be used for performance and availability monitoring from well established companies like NewRelic (https://newrelic.com/) and serverless-first companies like Epsagon (https://epsagon.com/). We won't dive deep into these tools in this chapter, but we encourage you to explore all options and choose what works best for you from https://aws.amazon.com/lambda/partners/ (the AWS Lambda partner page).

A note on CloudWatch logs

As discussed in earlier chapters, CloudWatch logs capture any log activity specified within a Lambda function. CloudWatch logs can also be used in two additional ways:

- As a *data source for custom metrics*—For example, you can emit data points for the time spent within a specific method of your Lambda function and visualize and alarm on that information as a custom metric in CloudWatch metrics.
- As a *bridge to surface data to third-party tools*—CloudWatch logs makes it easy to send data to third-party tools like NewRelic, which in turn can provide additional visualization and tracing. While Lambda does support the inclusion of third-party agents directly via AWS Lambda Extensions, CloudWatch logs remains an easy way to surface operational information to other services.

10.3   *Optimizing latency*

You now have an understanding of what contributes to your application latency, how to generate load to your application to observe the latency, and what tools to observe the latency. In this section, we'll discuss how to improve it.

Your best return on effort at optimizing latency is within individual functions. As the core glue and logic component of your application, any changes made to the function can have direct and immediate impacts to the latency that your customers experience and to your overall application costs. For example, reducing function execution time by 10% reduces the cost of the function by 10%, which can be significant at high scale. The decision on what percentile and number to optimize for is your choice, depending on your customers. For example, if you are building a website, you want your response time to be less than 2 seconds at the 99th percentile; if you are running a backend API, you may be able to tolerate 10's of seconds of response time at the 99th percentile.

10.3.1   *Minimize deployment artifact size*

The size of your deployment package directly impacts your cold start penalty in two ways. As a reminder, one of the steps that AWS Lambda undertakes on a "cold" invoke is downloading your code (step 1 in figure 10.9).

The larger your function, the longer this step takes—it's that simple! AWS Lambda enforces a limit of 250 MB for your functions' deployment package, so there's a natural

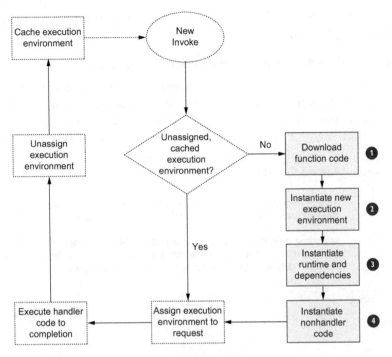

Figure 10.9 Lambda execution request lifecycle

"worst case" impact for your deployment package. Second, for functions written in com-
piled languages like Java and C#, larger deployment packages with many dependencies
take longer to instantiate when there are many classes to load into the CLASSPATH. As
an example, a simple "hello world" on Java loads only 429 classes in the JVM in about
0.1 seconds, while doing the same "hello world" using Clojure loads 1,988 classes: three
times as much and taking about 1 second.

A best practice to follow is to audit any function dependencies. Are there any
heavyweight library dependencies that could be removed or lightweight versions that
can be used? Especially look for libraries that act as HTTP servers or agents; they have
no use inside Lambda functions because Lambda acts as the server for you. For example, instead of using the default Java Spring library, you can use the streamlined
https://github.com/awslabs/aws-serverless-java-container library, which is approximately 30% faster in experiments. In our example, instead of packaging the entire
AWS SDK, you could include only the SDK required for accessing S3. You can audit
your dependencies for Node.js using tools like https://npm.anvaka.com/, for Python
using https://pypi.org/project/modulegraph/, or for Java using the Maven dependency tree.

Languages also offer specific tools to reduce deployment package sizes. For example, you can use minify for Node.js (https://www.npmjs.com/package/node-minify)
to reduce the overall size of your Node.js function package. You can also use

ProGuard (https://www.guardsquare.com/en/products/proguard) to reduce the size of your Java deployment package (JAR files).

10.3.2 *Allocate sufficient resources to your execution environment*

Your code requires compute resources (CPU, memory) to run. AWS Lambda provides a single dial to set the resources required by your function: the memory setting. You can change this setting by opening a Lambda function in the AWS console, selecting the Configuration tab, and then selecting Edit next to General Configuration. You can then experiment with different memory allocations (1 in figure 10.10). You can also set the same value via the API and CLI.

Around December of 2020, AWS Lambda began supporting 10,240 MB of memory (and 6 vCPUs) for new existing Lambda functions.

According to AWS, Lambda functions with 10 GB of memory and 6 vCPUs can be particularly useful for machine learning, modeling, genomics, as well as more traditional ETL and media-processing applications.

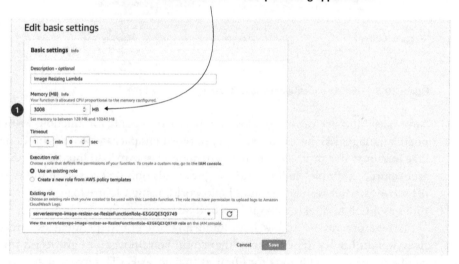

Figure 10.10   In Edit Basic Settings, you can adjust the amount of memory allocated to the function.

AWS Lambda allocates CPU power proportional to the memory by using the same ratio as a general-purpose Amazon EC2 instance type such as an M3 type. For example, if you allocate 256 MB memory, your Lambda function will receive twice the CPU share than if you allocate only 128 MB. You can update the configuration and request additional memory in 64 MB increments from 128 MB to 10240 MB. This change is not free: AWS Lambda pricing weights the billed duration for your function by its memory setting: 1 second of function execution time at 1024 MB costs the same as 8 seconds of execution at 128 MB.

Let's experiment with the memory setting on the image-resizer-service function you created so you can see the impact (if you haven't, see section 10.2.1 earlier in this chapter). Set the memory to 128 MB, 256 MB, 512 MB, and 1024 MB and run a few test invokes using the console (we recommend at least 10). Now note the average execution time for those invocations from CloudWatch metrics. You should see results similar to that in table 10.1. The estimated costs are based on AWS Lambda public pricing for 1,000 requests to the function.

Table 10.1   Estimated costs for 1,000 requests

Memory	Duration	Estimated cost for 1,000 requests
128 MB	11.722965s	$0.024628
256 MB	6.678945s	$0.028035
512 MB	3.194954s	$0.026830
1024 MB	1.465984s	$0.024638

We see that increasing the memory in this case keeps the cost relatively flat, while increasing the performance ~10x. You'll typically see these kind of gains for CPU-bound functions like image processing; more resources can help the function run faster without changing the costs. For I/O-bound operations (such as those waiting for a downstream service to respond), you'll see no benefit in increasing the resource allocation. For lightweight run times like Node.js and Go, you may be able to reduce the setting to the lowest (128 MB); for run times like Java and C#, going lower than 256 MB can have detrimental effects to how the run time loads your function code.

Finding the right resource allocation for your function requires some experimentation. The easiest path is to start with a high setting and reduce it until you see a change in performance characteristics. You can use the popular tuning tool at https://github.com/alexcasalboni/aws-lambda-power-tuning to help estimate your function's resource usage.

Resource allocation during cold starts

AWS Lambda respects the resource allocation while executing your function but will attempt to "boost" the CPU available while loading and initializing your function dependencies. This means that increasing the resource allocation will not really make a difference to your cold starts.

10.3.3   *Optimize function logic*

AWS Lambda bills your usage based on the time your function starts executing to the time it stops executing, not by CPU cycles spent or any other time-based metrics. This implies that what your function does during that time is important. Consider the image-resizer-service function. When you are downloading the S3 object, your code is simply waiting for S3 service to respond, and you are paying for that wait time. In this function's case, the time spent is negligible, but this wait time can get excessive for services that have long response times (for example, waiting on an EC2 instance being provisioned) or wait times (such as downloading a very large file). There are two options to minimize this idle time:

- *Minimize orchestration in code*—Instead of waiting on an operation inside your function, use AWS Step functions to separate the "before" and "after" logic as two separate functions. For example, if you have logic that needs to run before and after an API call is made, sequence them as two separate functions and use an AWS Step function to orchestrate between them.
- *Use threads for I/O intensive operations*—You can use multiple threads within a Lambda function (if the programming language supports it), just like code running in any compute environment. However, unlike conventional programs, the best use for multi-threading isn't for parallelizing computations. This is because Lambda does not allocate multiple cores to Lambda functions running with memory less than 1.8 GB, so you need to allocate more resources to get the parallelization benefit. Instead, you can use threads as a way to parallelize I/O operations. For example, a Python version of the image_resizer function could act on multiple functions by executing the S3 download on a separate thread to thumbnailing.

By following these best practices, you can significantly reduce the latency (and cost!) of your serverless application. Finally, let's look at concurrency, and we'll do that in the following section.

10.4   Concurrency

Another important concept to understand for AWS Lambda functions is concurrency. *Concurrency* is the unit of scale for a Lambda function. Underneath the covers, it maps to the number of execution environments assigned to requests. You can estimate the concurrency of your function at any time with the following formula:

```
Concurrency = Requests per second (TPS) * Function duration
```

Using peak values will give you peak concurrency; using average values will give you average concurrency. You can monitor the concurrency for any given function (and for the overall account) using the ConcurrentExecutions CloudWatch metric. AWS Lambda enforces two limits to the concurrency of a function:

- *There is an account-wide soft limit on the total concurrent executions of all functions within the account.* This is set by default to 1,000 at the time of writing, and it can be raised to desired values through a support case. You can view the account-level setting by using the GetAccountSettings API and viewing the AccountLimit object.

- *There is also an account-wide limit on the rate at which you can scale up your concurrent executions.* In larger AWS regions, you are allowed to scale instantly to 3,000 concurrent and then add 500 concurrent executions every subsequent minute; this limit is lower in smaller regions. These limits may change, so be sure to refer to the latest values listed in http://mng.bz/80PZ.

This makes it important to always estimate what your peak and average concurrency needs will be, how quickly you'll need to ramp up, and to file a request to raise limits as needed.

10.4.1 *Correlation between requests, latency, and concurrency*

For most functions, concurrency increases as a function of requests and function duration, subject to the concurrency limits on the function and account. However, for functions used to process stream data (Kinesis and DynamoDB streams), the concurrency is determined by the number of shards on the stream being processed. Given that latency is determined by the function itself, this means for stream-processing functions, you may see variable request rate or throughput. To put it another way,

```
Effective processing rate = Effective concurrency / average duration (events
➥ per second)
```

Consider a function that takes 1 second to process a stream with 5 shards and with a batch size of 100. This means the maximum number of requests (each with 100 records) that the function can process would be 5, and the maximum number of records processed at any given time would be 5 * 100 = 500. On the other hand, if the same stream had 10 shards, the throughput would double as well.

10.4.2 *Managing concurrency*

AWS offers two settings for managing concurrency. The first one is the account level concurrency limit that is enforced on the total concurrency across all functions within your account. This limit is set to 1,000 by default and can be raised through a service limit increase ticket: you cannot "self-service" this increase at the time of writing. The second is a per function concurrency control, which you can use to control the concurrency of an individual function. You only use the per function concurrency control if you have a function that you want to "reserve" concurrency for or a function that needs to be limited in its concurrency (because of a downstream resource).

For example, you may want to restrict how high a Lambda function scales because it calls an API that can only handle a certain load. If this was left unchecked, then your function could cause the downstream API to be overloaded, causing an availability for your overall application. This makes monitoring concurrency and managing it an important step to follow. You can learn more about the limits and the controls here: http://mng.bz/v4mq.

Summary

- Serverless applications do not require conventional application performance monitoring steps. Instead, optimizing the performance of your function code gives you the most gain.
- Use the toolsets (like X-Ray) and configurations (like the memory setting) to easily locate and optimize performance.
- Concurrency for Lambda functions can affect your function latency (and vice versa), so ensure you monitor and manage it for your critical functions.

Emerging practices

This chapter covers

- Using multiple AWS accounts
- Using temporary stacks
- Avoiding keeping sensitive data in plain text in environment variables
- Using EventBridge in event-driven architectures

The term *serverless* came about after AWS released the Lambda service back in 2014. In that sense, the serverless paradigm (building applications using managed services, including for all your compute needs) is something of a new kid on the block.

New paradigms give us new ways to look at problems and solve them differently, perhaps more efficiently. This should be obvious by now as we have discussed several serverless architectures in this book, and you must admit they look very different than the equivalent serverful architectures; they are more event-driven, and they often involve many different services working together.

New paradigms also require us to think and work differently. For example, instead of thinking about cost as a function of the size of a fleet of virtual machines and how long you need them for, we need to think about cost in terms of request count and execution duration. The code we write and the way we deploy and monitor our applications also need to change to take full advantage of this new paradigm and mitigate some of its limitations.

The following emerging practices are used by teams that have successfully adopted serverless technologies in their organization. Many are useful outside of the context of serverless, such as using multiple AWS accounts and using EventBridge in an event-driven architecture. Although none of them are silver bullets (is anything?), they are useful in the right contexts and are ideas worth considering.

11.1 Using multiple AWS accounts

Every AWS employee you speak to nowadays will tell you that you should have multiple AWS accounts and manage them with AWS Organizations (https://aws.amazon .com/organizations). At the minimum, you should have at least one AWS account per environment. For larger organizations, you should go further and have at least one AWS account per team per environment. There are many reasons why this is considered a best practice—regardless of whether you're working with serverless technologies—including those discussed in the following sections.

11.1.1 Isolate security breaches

Imagine the nightmare scenario where an attacker has gained access into your AWS environment and is then able to access and steal your users' data. This nightmare scenario can happen in many ways, and here are three that jump to mind right away:

- *An EC2 instance is exposed publicly and the attacker is able to SSH into the instance using brute force.* Once inside, they can use the instance's IAM role to access other AWS resources.
- *A misconfigured web application firewall (WAF) allows the attacker to execute a server-side request forgery (SSRF) attack and trick the WAF to relay requests to the EC2 metadata service.* This allows the attacker to find out the temporary AWS credentials used by the WAF server. From here, the attacker is able to access other AWS resources in the account. This is what happened in the Capital One data breach in 2019.
- *An employee accidentally includes their AWS credentials in a Git commit in a public GitHub repo.* The attacker scans public GitHub repos for AWS credentials and finds this commit. The attacker is then able to access all the AWS resources that the employee had access to. AWS also scans public GitHub repos for active AWS credentials and warns its customers when it finds them. But the damage is often done already by the time the customer realizes it.

Using multiple accounts doesn't stop these attack vectors, but it limits the blast radius of a security breach to a single account (and hopefully not your production account!).

11.1.2 *Eliminate contention for shared service limits*

Throughout this book, we have talked about AWS service limits several times already. As your organization and your system grow, more engineers need to work on the system, and you will likely create more and more services that take care of specific domains within the larger system (think microservices). As this happens, you will likely run into those pesky service limits more frequently because there is more contention for the shared-service limits.

It gets worse from here. Because service limits apply at the region level and affect all the resources in a region, it means that one team or one service can exhaust all the available throughput (for example, Lambda concurrent executions) in the region and throttle everything else.

What's more, if all the environments are run from the same AWS account, then something happening in a non-production environment can also impact users in production. For example, a load test in staging can consume too many Lambda concurrent executions so that users are not able to access your APIs in production because those API functions are throttled.

Having separate accounts for each team and each environment eliminates the contention altogether. If a team makes mistakes or experiences a sudden traffic spike in their services, the extra throughput they consume will not impact other services. Any service limit-related throttling would be contained to that account and limit the blast radius of these incidents. Equally, you can safely run load tests in non-production environments knowing that they won't affect your users in production.

What if, within a team, the same contention exists between different services? Maybe one of the team's services handles much more traffic than the rest and occasionally causes other services to be throttled. Well, then you want to move that service into its own set of accounts of dev, test, staging, and production. This technique of using AWS accounts as bulkheads to isolate and contain the blast radius can go as far as you need. You don't have to stop at one account per team per environment. Make the techniques work for you, not the other way around.

11.1.3 *Better cost monitoring*

If everything runs from the same AWS account, then you will have a hard time attributing your AWS costs to different environments or teams or services. Having multiple accounts lets you see the cost for those accounts easily.

11.1.4 *Better autonomy for your teams*

From a security and access control point of view, if each team has its own set of AWS accounts, then you can afford to give them more autonomy and control of their own AWS accounts. If everyone shares the same AWS account and that account is used for both non-production as well as production environments, then the stakes are high. Mistakes have a large blast radius and teams can accidentally delete or update other teams' resources, or even delete users' data in production. That is why you need to be careful in terms of managing access. It creates a lot of complexity and stress for whomever must manage access (typically the security team or a cloud platform team).

In my experience, the high stakes and complexity invite gatekeeping and create friction between the various disciplines. Feature teams often have to suffer delays as they wait for an over-worked platform team to grant them the access they need. Resentment builds and harmony erodes, and soon it becomes an "us versus them" situation.

Giving every team their own AWS accounts limits the blast radius of any issues and lowers the stakes. You can then afford to give your teams more autonomy within their own accounts. The platform team/security team can instead focus on setting up guardrails and governance infrastructure so they can identify problems quickly. And they should work with the feature teams to ensure they follow organizational best practices and meet your security requirements.

11.1.5 *Infrastructure-as-code for AWS Organizations*

Having multiple AWS accounts means you need to have some way to manage them, especially as you scale your organization. The number of AWS accounts can grow, and as more engineers join the organization, it becomes more important to have strong governance and oversight of your AWS environment.

One of the shortcomings of AWS Organizations is that you can't update the configurations of your organization using infrastructure as code (IaC). For example, CloudFormation is a regional service and is limited to provisioning resources within a single account and region. At the time of writing, the only tool that allows you to apply IaC to AWS Organizations is org-formation (https://github.com/org-formation/org -formation-cli). It's an open source tool that lets you capture the configuration of your AWS accounts and the entire AWS organization using IaC. I have used it with several projects and I can't recommend it highly enough!

A topic related to using multiple AWS accounts is the use of temporary CloudFormation stacks for temporary environments, such as those for feature branches or to carry out end-to-end (e2e) tests. We discuss temporary stacks next.

11.2 *Using temporary stacks*

One of the benefits of serverless technologies is that you pay for them only when people use your application. When your code is not running, you aren't charged. Combine this with the fact that it's easy to deploy a serverless application using tools such as the Serverless Framework. Because it's so easy to create new environments and there is no uptime cost for having these environments, many teams create temporary environments for when they work on feature branches or to run their e2e tests.

11.2.1 *Common AWS account structure*

It's common for teams to have multiple AWS accounts, one for each environment. Though there doesn't seem to be a consensus on how to use these environments, we tend to follow these conventions:

- *The dev environment is shared by the team.* This is where the latest development changes are deployed to and tested end to end. This environment is unstable by nature and shouldn't be used by other teams.
- *The test environment is where other teams can integrate with your team's work.* This environment should be stable so it doesn't slow down other teams.
- *The staging environment should closely resemble the production environment and may often contain dumps of production data.* This is where you can stress test your release candidate in a production-like environment.
- *And then there's the production environment.*

As discussed earlier in this chapter, it's best practice to have multiple AWS accounts— at least one account per team per environment. In the dev account, you can also have more than one environment—one for each developer or each feature branch.

11.2.2 Use temporary stacks for feature branches

When we start work on a new feature, we still feel our way toward the best solution for the problem. The codebase is unstable and many bugs haven't been ironed out yet. Deploying our half-baked changes to the dev environment can be quite disruptive:

- It risks destabilizing the team's shared environment.
- It overwrites other features the team is working on.
- Team members may fight over who gets to deploy their feature branch to the shared environment.

Instead, we can deploy the feature branch to a temporary environment. Using the Serverless Framework is as easy as running the command `sls deploy -s my-feature`, where `my-feature` is both the name of the environment and the name of the Cloud-Formation stack. This deploys all the Lambda functions, API Gateway, and any other related resources such as DynamoDB tables in their own CloudFormation stack. We are able to test our work-in-progress feature in an AWS account without affecting other team members' work.

Having these temporary CloudFormation stacks for each feature branch has negligible cost overhead. When the developer is done with the feature, the temporary stack can be easily removed by running the command `sls remove -s my-feature`. However, because these temporary stacks are an extension of your feature branch, they exhibit the same problems when you have long-lived feature branches. Namely, they get out of sync with other systems they need to integrate with. This applies to the incoming events that trigger your Lambda functions (such as the payloads from SQS/SNS/Kinesis), as well as data your function depends on (such as the data schema in DynamoDB tables). We find teams that use serverless technologies tend to move faster, which makes the problems with long-lived feature branches more prominent and noticeable.

As a rule of thumb, don't leave feature branches hanging around for more than a week. If the work is large and takes longer to implement, then break it up into smaller features. When you're working on a feature branch, you should also integrate from the main development branch regularly—no less than once per day.

11.2.3 Use temporary stacks for e2e tests

Another common use of temporary CloudFormation stacks is for running e2e tests. One of the common problems with these tests is that you need to insert test data into a shared AWS environment. Over time, this adds a lot of junk data in those environments and can make it difficult for other team members. For example, testers often have to do manual tests on the mobile or web app, and all the test data left by your automated tests can create confusion and make their job more difficult than it needs to be. As a rule of thumb, we always do the following:

- Insert the data a test case needs before the test.
- Delete the data after the test finishes.

Using the Jest (https://jestjs.io) JavaScript framework, you can capture the before and after steps as part of your test suite. They help keep our tests robust and self-contained because they don't implicitly rely on data to exist. They also help reduce the amount of junk data in the shared dev environment.

But despite our best intentions, mistakes happen, and sometimes we deliberately cut corners to gain agility in the short term. Over time, these shared environments still end up with tons of test data. As a countermeasure, many teams employ cron jobs to wipe these environments from time to time.

An emerging practice to combat these challenges is to create a temporary Cloud-Formation stack during the CI/CD pipeline. The temporary stack is used to run the e2e tests and destroyed afterwards. This way, there is no need to clean up test data, either as part of your test fixture or with cron jobs. The drawbacks include the following:

- The CI/CD pipeline takes longer to run.
- You still leave test data in external systems, so it's not a complete solution.

You should weigh the benefits of this approach against the delay it adds to your CI/CD pipeline. Personally, we think it's a great approach, and we see more teams starting to adopt it. To make CI/CD pipelines go faster, some teams keep a number of these temporary stacks around and reuse them in a round-robin fashion. This way, you still enjoy the benefit of being able to run e2e tests against a temporary environment but shorten the time it takes to deploy the temporary environment (updating an existing CloudFormation stack is significantly faster than creating a new stack).

11.3 Avoid sensitive data in plain text in environment variables

One common mistake we have seen for both serverful and serverless applications is that sensitive data (such as API keys and credentials) is left in plain text in environment variables. When it comes to security, serverless applications are more secure because AWS takes care of the security of the operational environment of our application. This includes securing the virtual machines our code runs on as well as their network configurations, and it includes the security of the operating system itself.

Our Lambda functions run on bare-metal EC2 instances that AWS manages, and the EC2 instances reside in AWS-managed VPCs. There's no easy way for an attacker to find out information about the virtual machine itself, and there's no way for attackers to SSH into these virtual machines.

The operating systems are constantly updated and patched with the latest security patches, sometimes before the patch is even available to the general public. Such was the case during the Meltdown and Spectre debacle when all EC2 instances behind Lambda and Fargate were quickly patched against the vulnerabilities long before the rest of us were able to patch our container and EC2 images. Having AWS manage the operational environment of our code removes a huge class of attack vectors from our plate, but we are still responsible for the security of our application and its data.

11.3.1 Attackers can still get in

Even though the operational environment of our code is secured by AWS, it's still possible for attackers to get inside the execution environment of our functions via other means, including the following:

- *Attacker successfully executes a code injection attack.* For example, if your application or any of its dependencies use JavaScript's eval() function against a piece of user input, then you're vulnerable to these attacks.
- *Attacker compromises one of your dependencies and publishes a malicious version of the dependency that steals information from your application at run time.* Remember that time when a security researcher gained publish access to 14% of NPM packages (http://mng.bz/N4PN)? Or that time an attacker compromised the NPM account for one of EsLint's maintainers and published a malicious version of eslint-scope and eslint-config-eslint (http://mng.bz/DKPn)?
- *Attacker publishes a malicious NPM package with similar names to popular NPM packages and steals information from your application on initialization.* An example is the time when an attacker published a malicious package called crossenv using the popular NPM package cross-env as bait (http://mng.bz/l9d6).

Once inside, attackers often steal information from common, easily accessible places such as environment variables. This is why it's so important that we avoid putting sensitive data in plain text in environment variables.

11.3.2 Handle sensitive data securely

Sensitive data should be encrypted both in transit and at rest. This means it should be stored in an encrypted form; within AWS, you can use both the SSM Parameter Store and the Secrets Manager to store it. Both services support encryption at rest, integrate directly with AWS Key Management Service (KMS), and allow you to use Customer Managed Keys (CMKs). The same encrypted at-rest principle should be applied to how sensitive data is stored in your application. There are multiple ways to achieve this; for example:

- Store the sensitive data in encrypted form in environment variables and decrypt it using KMS during cold start.
- Keep the sensitive data in SSM Parameter Store or Secrets Manager, and during the Lambda function cold start, fetch it from SSM Parameter Store/Secrets Manager.

Once decrypted, the data can be kept in an application variable or closure where it can be easily accessed by your code. The important thing is that sensitive data should never be placed back into the environment variables in unencrypted form. Our personal preference is to fetch sensitive data from the SSM Parameter Store/Secrets Manager during cold start. We would use middy's SSM middleware (https://github.com/middyjs/middy/tree/main/packages/ssm) to inject the decrypted data into the `context` variable and cache it for some time.

This way, we can rotate these secrets at the source without having to redeploy the application. Once the cache expires, the middleware fetches the new values on the next Lambda invocation. It also makes it easier to manage shared secrets where multiple services need to access the same secret. Finally, this approach allows more granular control of permissions because the Lambda function requires permissions to access the secrets in SSM Parameter Store/Secrets Manager.

There are other variants of these two approaches; for example, instead of storing encrypted secrets in environment variables, you can store them in an encrypted file that is deployed as part of the application. During Lambda cold start, this file is decrypted with KMS, and the secrets it contains are then extracted and stored *away from the environment variables.*

11.4   Use EventBridge in event-driven architectures

Amazon SNS and SQS have long been the go-to option for AWS developers when it comes to service integration. However, since its rebranding, Amazon EventBridge (formerly Amazon CloudWatch Events) has become a popular alternative, and I would argue that it's actually a much better option as the event bus in an event-driven architecture.

11.4.1   Content-based filtering

SNS lets you filter messages via filtering policies. But you can't filter messages by their content, you can only filter by message attributes, and you can only have up to 10 attributes per message. If you require content-based filtering, then it has to be done in code. EventBridge, on the other hand, supports content-based filtering and lets you pattern match against an event's content. In addition, it supports advanced filtering rules such as these:

- Numeric comparison
- Prefix matching
- IP address matching
- Existence matching
- Anything-but matching

NOTE Check out the blog post at http://mng.bz/B1w0 on EventBridge's content-based filtering for more details on these advanced rules.

In an event-driven architecture, it's often desirable to have a centralized event bus. It makes it easy for subsystems to subscribe to events triggered by any other subsystem and for you to create an archive that captures everything happening in the whole application (for both audit and replay purposes).

With content-based filtering, it's possible to have a centralized event bus in Event-Bridge. Subscribers can freely subscribe to the exact events they want without having to negotiate with the event publishers on what attributes to include. This is usually not feasible with SNS, and you have to use multiple SNS topics.

11.4.2 Schema discovery

A common challenge with event-driven architectures is identifying and versioning event schemas. EventBridge deals with this challenge with its schema registry and provides a built-in mechanism for schema discovery.

EventBridge captures a wide range of events from AWS services (such as when an EC2 instance's state has changed) in the default event bus. It provides the schema for these AWS events in the default schema registry. You also can enable schema discovery on any event bus, and EventBridge samples the ingested events and generates and versions schema definitions for these events.

If you're programmatically generating schema definitions for your application events already, then you can also create a custom schema registry and publish your schema definitions there as part of your CI/CD pipeline. That way, your developers always have an up-to-date list of the events in circulation and what information they can find on these events.

Open-source tools such as the evb-cli (https://www.npmjs.com/package/@mhlabs/evb-cli) even let you generate EventBridge patterns using the schema definitions in a schema registry. This is handy, especially if you're new to EventBridge's pattern language!

11.4.3 Archive and replay events

Another common requirement for event-driven architectures is to be able to archive the ingested events and replay them later. The archive requirement is often part of a larger set of audit or compliance requirements and is therefore a must-have in many systems. Luckily, EventBridge offers archive and replay capabilities out of the box. When you create an archive, you can configure the retention period, which can be set to indefinite. You can optionally configure a filter so that only matching events are included in the archive.

When you need to replay events from the archive, you can choose a start and end time so that only the events captured in the specified time range will be replayed. One thing to keep in mind about event replays is that EventBridge does not preserve the original order of the events as they were received. Instead, EventBridge looks to replay these events as quickly as possible, which means you can expect a lot of concurrency and that most events will be replayed out of sequence.

If ordering is important to you when replaying events, then you should check out the evb-cli project mentioned earlier. Its `evb replay` command supports paced replays, which retains the ordering of events and lets you control how quickly events are replayed. For example, using a replay speed of 100 replays events in real time means replaying an hour's worth of events would take an hour.

11.4.4 *More targets*

Whereas SNS supports a handful of targets (such as HTTP, Email, SQS, Lambda, and SMS), EventBridge supports more than 15 AWS services (including SNS, SQS, Kinesis, and Lambda), and you can forward events to another EventBridge bus in another account.

This extensive reach helps to remove a lot of unnecessary glue code. For example, to start a Step Functions state machine, you would have needed a Lambda function between SNS and Step Functions. With EventBridge, you can connect the rule to the state machine directly.

11.4.5 *Topology*

There are different ways to arrange event buses in EventBridge. For example, you can have a centralized event bus, every service can publish events to their own event bus, or maybe you have a few domain-specific event buses that are shared by related services. There is no clear consensus on which approach is the best because everyone's context is different, and each approach has its pros and cons. However, we personally favor the centralized event bus approach because it has some great advantages including the following:

- You can implement an archive and a schema registry in one place.
- You can manage access and permissions in one place.
- All the events you need are available in one event bus.
- There are fewer resources to manage.

But it also has some shortcomings that you need to consider:

- There is a single point of failure. Having said that, EventBridge is already highly available, and the infrastructure that ingests, filters, and forwards events to configured targets is distributed across multiple availability zones.
- Service teams have less autonomy as they all depend on the centralized event bus.

There is also the question of AWS account topology. That is, which account do you deploy the event bus to if a given environment consists of multiple AWS accounts (such as when you have one account per team)? Should you deploy the centralized event bus in its own account or in the account that perhaps make the most sense? That is a wider topic that is outside the scope of this chapter, but I recommend you check this re:Invent 2020 session by Stephen Liedig: https://www.youtube.com/watch?v=Wk0FoXTUEjo. It goes into detail about the different configurations and the pros and cons of each.

Summary

And that's it for a list of emerging practices that you should seriously consider adopting in your projects. We call these *emerging practices* because they are not adopted ubiquitously but are gaining traction in the AWS community. As the AWS ecosystem and serverless technologies develop and mature, more practices emerge and take root. It's worth remembering that no practice should be considered *best* in its own right, and you must always consider the context and environment a practice is applied in.

As technology and your organization change, your context changes too. Many of the things that you might once consider as best practice can easily become anti-patterns. For example, monorepos work great when you are a small team, but by the time you grow to hundreds or perhaps thousands of engineers, monorepos present many challenges that require complex solutions to address.

The same goes for how we build, test, deploy, and operate software. What worked great in private data centers and server farms might not translate well to the cloud. And practices that serve us well when we have to manage both the infrastructure our code runs on as well as the code itself might work against us as we build applications with serverless technologies.

Best practices and design patterns should be the start of the conversation, not the end. After all, these so-called best practices and design patterns are collective documentations of things that others have done that worked for them to some degree at some time. There's no guarantee that they'll work for you today. And it's easy to see parallels from other industries. For example, did you know that lobotomies were part of mainstream mental healthcare from 1930s to 1950s before they were outlawed in the 1970s and considered outright barbaric by today's standards?

appendix A
Services for your serverless architecture

AWS is a giant playground of different services and products you can use to build serverless applications. Lambda is a key service that we discussed in this book, but other services and products can be just as useful, if not crucial, for solving certain problems. There are many excellent non-AWS products too, so don't feel obligated to use only what Amazon has to offer. Have a look at the offerings from Microsoft and Google too. The following sections provide a sample of services that we've found useful. You can use this appendix as a guide to various services and products we'll discuss throughout the book.

A.1   API Gateway

The Amazon API Gateway is a service that you can use to create an API layer between the frontend and backend services. The lifecycle management of the API Gateway allows multiple versions of the API to be run at the same time, and it supports multiple release stages such as development, staging, and production. API Gateway also comes with useful features like caching and throttling requests.

The API is defined around resources and methods. A *resource* is a logical entity such as a user or product. A *method* is a combination of an HTTP verb (such as GET, POST, PUT, or DELETE) and the resource path. API Gateway integrates with Lambda and other AWS services. It can be used as a proxy service and forward requests to regular HTTP endpoints.

A.2   Simple Notification Service (SNS)

Amazon Simple Notification Service (SNS) is a scalable pub/sub service designed to deliver messages. Producers or publishers create and send messages to a topic. Subscribers or consumers subscribe to a topic and receive messages over one of the supported protocols. SNS stores messages across multiple servers and data centers for redundancy and guarantees at-least-once delivery. At-least-once delivery stipulates that a message will be delivered at least once to a subscriber, but on rare occasions, due to the distributed nature of SNS, it may be delivered multiple times.

In cases where a message can't be delivered by SNS to HTTP endpoints, it can be configured to retry deliveries at a later time. SNS can also retry failed deliveries to Lambda when throttling is applied. SNS supports message payloads of up to 256 KB.

A.3   Simple Storage Service (S3)

Simple Storage Service (S3) is Amazon's scalable storage solution. Data in S3 is stored redundantly across multiple facilities and servers. The event notifications system allows S3 to send events to SNS, SQS, or Lambda when objects are created or deleted. S3 is secure, by default, with only owners having access to the resources they create, but it's possible to set more granular and flexible access permissions using access control lists and bucket policies.

S3 uses the concept of buckets and objects. *Buckets* are high-level directories or containers for objects. *Objects* are a combination of data, metadata, and a key. A *key* is a unique identifier for an object in a bucket.

S3 also supports the concept of a *folder* as a means of grouping objects in the S3 console. Folders work by using key name prefixes. A forward slash character (/) in the key name delineates a folder. For example, an object with the key name documents/personal/myfile.txt is represented as a folder called documents, containing a folder called personal, containing the file myfile.txt in the S3 console.

A.4   Simple Queue Service (SQS)

Simple Queue Service (SQS) is Amazon's distributed and fault-tolerant queuing service. It ensures at-least-once delivery of messages similar to SNS and supports message payloads of up to 256 KB. SQS allows multiple publishers and consumers to interact with the same queue, and it has a built-in message lifecycle that automatically expires and deletes messages after a preset retention period. As with most AWS products, there are access controls to help control access to the queue. SQS integrates with SNS to automatically receive and queue messages.

A.5   Simple Email Service (SES)

Simple Email Service (SES) is a service designed to send and receive email. SES handles email-receiving operations such as scanning for spam and viruses and rejection of email from untrusted sources. Incoming email can be delivered to an S3 bucket or used to invoke a Lambda notification, or create an SNS notification. These actions can be configured as part of the receipt rule, which tells SES what to do with the email once it arrives.

Sending emails with SES is straightforward, but there are limits that are in place to regulate the rate and the number of messages sent. SES automatically increases the quota as long as high-quality email, and not spam, is sent.

A.6 *Relational Database Service (RDS)*

Amazon Relational Database Service (RDS) is a web service that helps with the setup and operation of a relational database in the AWS infrastructure. RDS supports the Amazon Aurora, MySQL, MariaDB, Oracle, MS-SQL, and PostgreSQL database engines. It takes care of routine tasks such as provisioning, backup, patching, recovery, repair, and failure detection. Monitoring and metrics, database snapshots, and multiple availability zone (AZ) support are provided out of the box. RDS uses SNS to deliver notifications when an event occurs. This makes it easy to respond to database events such as creation, deletion, failover, recovery, and restoration when they happen.

A.7 *DynamoDB*

DynamoDB is Amazon's NoSQL database. Tables, items, and attributes are Dynamo's main concepts. A *table* stores a collection of items. An *item* is made up of a collection of attributes. Each *attribute* is a simple piece of data such as a person's name or phone number. Every item is uniquely identifiable. Lambda integrates with DynamoDB tables and can be triggered by a table update. Global tables is a notable feature of Dynamo that seamlessly replicates tables across different AWS regions and resolves any data conflicts (using "last writer wins" reconciliation to handle concurrent updates). It makes DynamoDB a good database for scalable, global applications. Finally, an in-memory cache (DAX) is available for DynamoDB. It shortens the response time but comes at a price.

A.8 *Algolia*

Algolia is a (non-AWS) managed search engine API. It can search through semi-structured data and has APIs to allow developers to integrate search directly into their websites and mobile applications. One of Algolia's outstanding capabilities is its speed. Algolia can distribute and synchronize data across 15 regions around the world and direct queries to the closest data center.

Algolia has a concept of *indices* (". . . an entity where you import the data you want to search . . . analogous to a table within a database . . ."), *records* (". . . a JSON schema-less object that you want to be searchable . . .") and *operations* (which are essentially atomic actions such as update or delete). These concepts are straightforward and make Algolia one of the easier search platforms to use. Paid plans begin from about $35 per month but can quickly grow in cost, depending on the number of records and operations performed by your application and users.

A.9 *Media Services*

AWS Media Services is a new product designed for developers to build video workflows. Media Services consist of the following products:

- MediaConvert is designed to transcode between different video formats at scale.
- MediaLive is a live video-processing service. It takes a live video source and compresses it into smaller versions for distribution.

- MediaPackage enables developers to implement video features such as pause and rewind. It can also be used to add Digital Right Management (DRM) to content.
- MediaStore is a storage service optimized for media. Its aim is to provide a low-latency storage system for live and on-demand video content.
- MediaTailor enables developers to insert individually targeted ads in to the video stream.

Media Services provide an advanced suite of services that are superior to Elastic Transcoder. Nevertheless, Elastic Transcoder has a few features (such as the ability to create WebM files and animated GIFs) that Media Services is missing.

A.10   *Kinesis Streams*

Kinesis Streams is a service for real-time processing of streaming big data. It's typically used for quick log and data intake, metrics, analytics, and reporting. It's different from SQS in that Amazon recommends that Kinesis Streams be used primarily for streaming big data, whereas SQS is used as a reliable hosted queue, especially if more fine-grained control over messages such as visibility timeouts or individual delays is required.

In Kinesis Streams, *shards* specify the throughput capacity of a stream. The number of shards needs to be stipulated when the stream is created, but resharding is possible if throughput needs to be increased or reduced. In comparison, SQS makes scaling much more transparent. Lambda can integrate with Kinesis to read batches of records from a stream as soon as they're detected.

A.11   *Athena*

AWS bills Athena as a serverless interactive query service. Essentially, this service allows you to query data placed into S3 using standard SQL. In a lot of cases, there's no need to run ETL (extract, transform, and load) jobs to transform your data before querying can take place (although you can combine Athena with AWS Glue if you needed to transform your data a certain way). As a user, you upload data to S3, prepare a schema, and begin querying almost immediately.

A.12   *AppSync*

AppSync is billed as allowing developers to create " . . . data driven apps with real-time and offline capabilities." In reality, AppSync is a managed GraphQL endpoint provided by AWS. It integrates with DynamoDB, Lambda, and Amazon Elasticsearch. If you are familiar with GraphQL and GraphQL schemas, you can get started with AppSync straight away. If you are not familiar with GraphQL, we recommend doing a bit of reading beforehand (http://graphql.org/learn/). GraphQL has certainly been finding its share of acclaim over the past few years, particularly among adopters of serverless technologies.

A.13 Cognito

Amazon Cognito is an identity management service. It integrates with public identity providers such as Google, Facebook, Twitter, and Amazon or with your own system. Cognito supports *user pools*, which allow you to create your own user directory. This lets you register and authenticate users without having to run a separate user database and authentication service. Cognito supports synchronization of user application data across different devices and has offline support that allows mobile devices to function even when there's no internet access.

A.14 Auth0

Auth0 (recently acquired by Okta) is a non-AWS identity management product that has a few features that Cognito doesn't. Auth0 integrates with more than 30 identity providers including Google, Facebook, Twitter, Amazon, LinkedIn, and Windows Live. It provides a way to register new users through the use of its own user database, without having to integrate with an identity provider. In addition, it has a facility to import users from other databases. As expected, Auth0 supports standard industry protocols including SAML, OpenID Connect, OAuth 2.0, OAuth 1.0, and JSON Web Token (JWT). It's simple to integrate with AWS Identity, Access Management, and Cognito.

A.15 Other services

The list of services provided in this section is a short sample of the different products you can use to build your application. There are many more services, including those provided by large cloud-focused companies such as Google and Microsoft and smaller, independent companies like Auth0. There are also auxiliary services that you need to be aware of. These can help you be more efficient and build software faster, improve performance, or achieve other goals. When building software, consider the following products and services:

- Content Delivery Networks (CloudFront, CloudFlare)
- DNS management (Route 53)
- Caching (ElastiCache)
- Source control (GitHub, GitLab)
- Continuous integration and deployment (GitHub Actions)

For every service suggestion, you can find alternatives that may be just as good or even better, depending on your circumstances. We urge you to do more research and explore the various services that are currently available.

appendix B
Setting up your cloud

Most of the architecture described in this book is built on top of AWS. This means you need a clear understanding of AWS from the perspectives of security, alerting, and costs. It doesn't matter whether you use Lambda alone or have a large mix of services. Being able to configure security, knowing how to set up alerts, and controlling cost are important. This appendix is designed so that you can understand these concerns and learn where to look for important information in AWS.

AWS security is a complex subject, but this appendix gives you an overview of the difference between users and roles and shows you how to create policies. This information is needed to configure a system in which services can communicate effectively and securely. Some of the time, you will not need to create or configure policies directly; tools like Serverless framework will do it for you. But it's still important to understand how the pieces fit together and where to look for help if things go wrong.

Cost is an important consideration when using a platform such as AWS and implementing serverless architecture. It's essential to understand the cost calculation of the services you're going to use. This is useful not only for avoiding bill shock but also for predicting next month's bill and beyond. We look at estimating the cost of services and discuss strategies for tracking costs and keeping them under control. This appendix is not an exhaustive guide to AWS. If you have further questions after reading this appendix, take a look at AWS documentation (https://aws.amazon.com/documentation).

B.1 Security model and identity management

In chapter 2, you created an Identity and Access Management (IAM) user and a number of roles in order to use Lambda, S3, and MediaConvert. In this section, you'll take your new-found knowledge and develop it further by learning about users, groups, roles, and policies in more detail.

B.1.1 *Creating and managing IAM users*

As you'll recall, an IAM user is an entity in AWS that identifies a human user, an application, or a service. A user normally has a set of credentials and permissions that can be used to access resources and services across AWS.

An IAM user typically has a friendly name to help you identify the user and an Amazon Resource Name (ARN) that uniquely identifies it across AWS. Figure B.1 shows a summary page and an ARN for a fictional user named Alfred. You can get to this summary in the AWS console by clicking IAM, clicking Users in the navigation pane, and then clicking the name of the user you want to view.

Figure B.1   The IAM console shows metadata such as the ARN, groups, and creation time for every IAM user in your account.

You can create IAM users to represent human users, applications, or services. IAM users created to work on behalf of an application or a service sometimes are referred to as *service accounts*. These types of IAM users can access AWS service APIs using an access key. An access key for an IAM user can be generated when the user is initially created, or you can create it later by clicking Users in the IAM console, clicking the required user name, selecting Security Credentials, and then clicking the Create Access Key button.

The two components of an access key are the Access Key ID and the Secret Access Key. The Access Key ID can be shared publicly, but the Secret Access Key must be kept hidden. If the Secret Access Key is revealed, the whole key must be immediately invalidated and recreated. An IAM user can have, at most, two active access keys.

If an IAM user is created for a real person, then that user should be assigned a password. This password allows a human user to log into the AWS console and use services and APIs directly. To create a password for an IAM user, follow these steps:

1. In the IAM console, click Users in the navigation pane.
2. Click the required username to open the user's settings.
3. Click the Security Credentials tab and then click Manage next to Console password (figure B.2).

Summary

User ARN	arn:aws:iam::571060592278:user/Alfred 📋
Path	/
Creation time	2021-09-27 11:41 UTC+1000

Permissions	Groups	Tags	Security credentials	Access Advisor

Sign-in credentials

Summary	• User does not have console management access
Console password	Disabled | Manage
Assigned MFA device	Not assigned | Manage
Signing certificates	None ✏️

The Manage option is available for any IAM user. Users with passwords can log into the AWS Console.

Figure B.2 IAM users have a number of options including being able to set a password, change access keys, and enable multifactor authentication.

4. In the popup, choose whether to enable or disable console access, type in a new custom password, or let the system autogenerate one. You can also force the user to create a new password at the next sign-in (figure B.3).

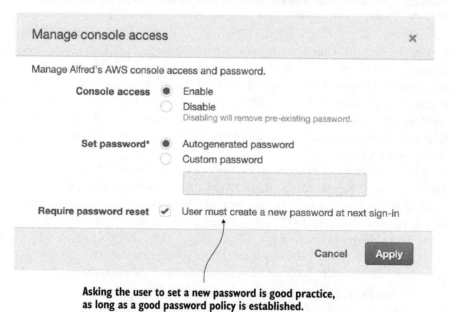

Manage console access   ✕

Manage Alfred's AWS console access and password.

Console access   ◉ Enable
                  ○ Disable
                    Disabling will remove pre-existing password.

Set password*   ◉ Autogenerated password
                  ○ Custom password

                    [   ]

Require password reset ☑ User must create a new password at next sign-in

                                            Cancel   **Apply**

Asking the user to set a new password is good practice, as long as a good password policy is established.

Figure B.3 Make sure to create a good password policy with a high degree of complexity if you allow users to log into the AWS console. Password policy can be set up in Account Settings of the IAM console.

After a user is assigned a password, they can log into the AWS console by navigating to https://<Account-ID>.signin.aws.amazon.com/console. To get the account ID, click Support in the upper-right navigation bar, and then click Support Center. The account ID (or account number) is shown at the top of the console. You may want to set up an alias for the account ID also so that your users don't have to remember it (for more information about aliases, see http://amzn.to/1MgvWvf).

Multi-factor authentication

Multi-factor authentication (MFA) adds another layer of security by prompting users to enter an authentication code from their MFA device when they try to sign into the console (this is in addition to the usual username and password). It makes it more difficult for an attacker to compromise an account. Any modern smartphone can act as a virtual MFA appliance using an application such as Google Authenticator or AWS Virtual MFA. It's recommended that you enable MFA for any user who might use the AWS console. You'll find the option Assign MFA Device in the Security Credentials tab when you click an IAM user in the console.

Temporary security credentials

At this time, there's a limit of 5,000 users per AWS account, but you can raise the limit if needed. An alternative to increasing the number of users is to use temporary security credentials. Temporary security credentials can be set up to expire after a short while and can be generated dynamically. See Amazon's online documentation at http://mng.bz/drnN for more information on temporary security credentials. You can find more information about IAM users at http://mng.bz/r6zB.

B.1.2 Groups

Groups represent a collection of IAM users. They provide an easy way to specify permissions for multiple users at once. For example, you may want to create a group for developers or testers in your organization or have a group called Lambda to allow all members of that group to execute Lambda functions. Amazon recommends using groups to assign permissions to IAM users rather than defining permissions individually. Any user who joins a group inherits permissions assigned to the group. Similarly, if a user leaves a group, the group's permissions are removed from the user. Furthermore, groups can contain only users, not other groups or entities such as roles.

B.1.3 Roles

A *role* is a set of permissions that a user, application, or a service can assume for a period of time. A role is not uniquely coupled to a specific user, nor does it have associated credentials such as passwords or access keys. It's designed to grant permissions to a user or a service that typically doesn't have access to the required resource.

Delegation is an important concept associated with roles. Put simply, *delegation* is concerned with the granting of permissions to a third party to allow access to a particular resource. It involves establishing a trust relationship between a trusting account that owns the resource and a trusted account that contains the users or applications that need to access the resource. Figure B.4 shows a role with a trust relationship established for a service called CloudCheckr.

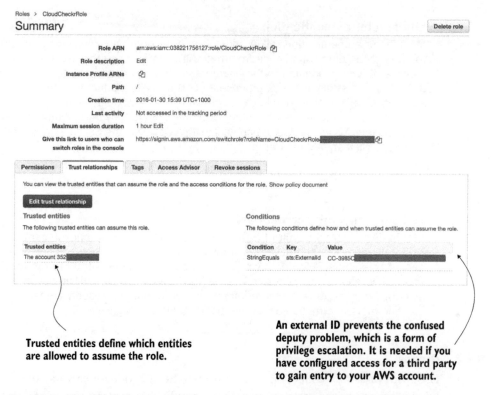

Trusted entities define which entities are allowed to assume the role.

An external ID prevents the confused deputy problem, which is a form of privilege escalation. It is needed if you have configured access for a third party to gain entry to your AWS account.

Figure B.4   This role grants CloudCheckr access to the AWS account to perform analysis of costs and recommend improvements.

Federation is another concept that's discussed often in the context of roles. *Federation* is the process of creating a trust relationship between an external identity provider such as Facebook, Google, or an enterprise identity system that supports Security Assertion Markup Language (SAML) 2.0 and AWS. It enables users to log in via one of those external identity providers and assume an IAM role with temporary credentials.

B.1.4   *Resources*

Permissions in AWS are either *identity-based* or *resource-based*. Identity-based permissions specify what an IAM user or a role can do. Resource-based permissions specify what an AWS resource such as an S3 bucket or an SNS topic is allowed to do or who can have access to it. A resource-based policy often specifies who has access to the given resource. This allows trusted users to access the resource without having to assume a role. The AWS user guide at http://mng.bz/VBJP states:

> Cross-account access with a resource-based policy has an advantage over a role. With a resource that is accessed through a resource-based policy, the user still works in the trusted account and does not have to give up his or her user permissions in place of the role permissions. In other words, the user continues to have access to resources in the trusted account at the same time as he or she has access to the resource in the trusting account.

Not all AWS services support resource-based policies (the user guide at http://mng.bz/xX8W lists all the services that do).

B.1.5   *Permissions and policies*

When you initially create an IAM user, it's not able to access or do anything in your account. You need to grant the user permissions by creating a policy that describes what the user is allowed to do. The same goes for a new group or role. A new group or a role needs to be assigned a policy to have any effect.

The scope of any policy can vary. You can give your user or role administrator access to the whole account or specify individual actions. It's better to be granular and specify only permissions that are needed to get the job done (least privilege access). Start with a minimum set of permissions and add additional permissions only if necessary.

There are two types of policies: *managed* and *inline*. Managed policies apply to users, groups, and roles but not to resources. Managed policies are standalone. Some managed policies are created and maintained by AWS. You also can also create and maintain customer-managed policies. Managed policies are great for reusability and change management. If you use a customer-managed policy and decide to modify it, all changes are automatically applied to all IAM users, roles, and groups that the policy is attached to. Managed policies allow for easier versioning and rollbacks.

Inline policies are created and attached directly to a specific user, group, or role. When an entity is deleted, the inline policies embedded within it are deleted also. Resource-based policies are always inline. To add an inline or a managed policy, click the required user, group, or role and then click the Permissions tab. You can attach, view, or detach a managed policy and similarly create, view, or remove an inline policy.

A policy is specified using JSON notation. The following listing shows a managed `AWSLambdaExecute` policy.

Listing B.1   `AWSLambdaExecute` policy

Version specifies the policy language version; the current version is 2012-10-17. If you're creating a custom policy, make sure to include the version and set it to 2012-10-17.

```
{
    "Version":"2012-10-17",
    "Statement":[          ◄─────  Contains one or more statements that specify
        {                          the actual permissions that make up the policy
            "Effect":"Allow",
```

```
        "Action": "logs:*",
        "Resource":"arn:aws:logs:*:*:*"
    },
    {
        "Effect":"Allow",            ◄─
        "Action":[                ◄─
            "s3:GetObject",
            "s3:PutObject"
        ],
        "Resource":"arn:aws:s3:::*"  ◄─
    }
  ]
}
```

> **The Effect element is required and specifies whether the statement allows or denies access to the resource. The only two available options are Allow and Deny.**

> **Specifies the specific actions on the resource that should be allowed or denied. The use of a wildcard (*) character is allowed (for example, "Action": "s3:*").**

> **The Resource element identifies the object or objects that the statement applies to. It can be specific or include a wildcard to refer to multiple entities.**

Many IAM policies contain additional elements such as `Principal`, `Sid`, and `Condition`. The `Principal` element specifies an IAM user, an account, or a service that's allowed or denied access to a resource. The `Principal` element isn't used in policies that are attached to IAM users or groups. Instead, it's used in roles to specify who can assume the role. It's also common to resource-based policies. Statement ID (`Sid`) is required in policies for certain AWS services, such as SNS. A condition allows you to specify rules that dictate when a policy should apply. An example of a condition is presented in the next listing.

Listing B.2   Policy condition

> **You can use a number of conditional elements, which include DateEquals, DateLessThan, DateMoreThan, StringEquals, StringLike, StringNotEquals, and ArnEquals.**

```
"Condition": {
    "DateLessThan": {
            "aws:CurrentTime": "2020-09-12T12:00:00Z"
        },
        "IpAddress": {
            "aws:SourceIp": "127.0.0.1"  ◄─
        }
    }
```

> **The condition keys represent values that come from the request issued by a user. Possible keys include SourceIp, CurrentTime, Referer, SourceArn, userid, and username. The value can be either a specific literal value such as "127.0.0.1" or a policy variable.**

Multiple conditions

The AWS documentation at http://amzn.to/21UofNi states "If there are multiple condition operators, or if there are multiple keys attached to a single condition operator, the conditions are evaluated using a logical AND. If a single condition operator includes multiple values for one key, that condition operator is evaluated using a logical OR." See http://amzn.to/21UofNi for great examples you can follow and a whole heap of useful documentation.

Amazon recommends using conditions to the extent that is practical for security. The next listing, for example, shows an S3 bucket policy that forces content to be served only over HTTPS/SSL. This policy refuses connections over unencrypted HTTP.

Listing B.3   Policy to enforce HTTPS/SSL

```
{
    "Version": "2012-10-17",
    "Id": "123",
    "Statement": [
        {
            "Effect": "Deny",
            "Principal": "*",
            "Action": "s3:*",
            "Resource": "arn:aws:s3:::my-bucket/*",
            "Condition": {
                "Bool": {
                    "aws:SecureTransport": false
                }
            }
        }
    ]
}
```

Explicitly denies access to s3 if the condition is met

The condition is met when requests are not sent using SSL. This forces the policy to block access to the bucket if a user tries to access it over regular, unencrypted HTTP.

B.2   Cost

Receiving an unpleasant surprise in the form of a large bill at the end of the month is disappointing and stressful. Amazon CloudWatch can create billing alarms that send notifications if total charges for the month exceed a predefined threshold. This is useful not only to avoid unexpectedly large bills but also to catch potential misconfigurations of your system.

For example, it's easy to misconfigure a Lambda function and inadvertently allocate 3.0 GB of RAM to it. The function might not do anything useful except wait for 15 s to receive a response from a database. In a heavy-duty environment, the system might perform 2 M invocations of the function a month, costing a little over $1,462. The same function with 128 MB of RAM would cost around $56 per month. If you perform cost calculations up front and have a sensible billing alarm, you'll quickly realize that something is going on when billing alerts begin to come through.

B.2.1   Creating billing alerts

Follow these steps to create a billing alert:

1. In the main AWS console, click your name (or the name of the IAM user that's representing you) and then click My Billing Dashboard.
2. Click Billing Preferences in the navigation pane and then enable the check box next to Receive Billing Alerts.
3. Click Save preferences, then go back to the main AWS console and find the CloudWatch service.

4. Open the CloudWatch service, click Alarms, and select All Alarms in the navigation pane. Click the Create alarm button and then click the Select metric button.

5. Under the Metrics heading, select Billing and click Total Estimated Charges. (If you don't see Billing it means you may not have enabled the Receive Billing Alerts option in step 2).

6. Tick the checkbox for EstimatedCharges and click Select metric to continue.

7. Make sure that the Threshold type is set to Static and that Whenever Estimated-Charges is set to Greater.

8. In the Define the threshold value, enter the amount that you'd like to trigger the alarm (for example, 200 as seen in figure B.5).

9. Click Next to continue to the next page.

   Here you can set or create a new SNS topic to notify you when the alarm is triggered. This is important! You need an SNS topic to receive emails to alert you what is happening.

10. Click the Add notification button.

11. Choose Create new topic, enter a name for it, and then type in your email address. Click Create topic button to save your SNS topic settings. When you are ready to proceed click Next.

12. Type in a name for your Alarm and click Next again.

13. Finally, at the bottom, click the Create alarm button to finish.

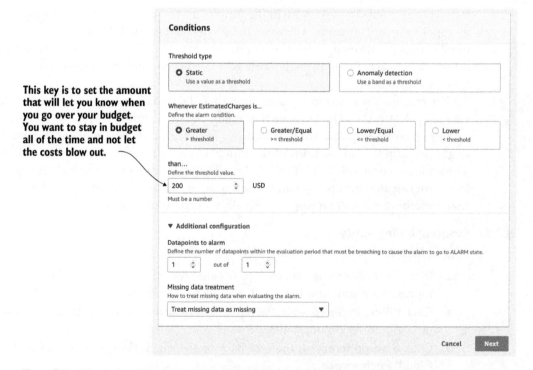

Figure B.5   It's good practice to create multiple billing alarms to keep you informed of ongoing costs.

B.2.2 *Monitoring and optimizing costs*

Services such as CloudCheckr (http://cloudcheckr.com) can help to track costs, send alerts, and even suggest savings by analyzing services and resources in use. CloudCheckr comprises several different AWS services including S3, CloudSearch, SES, SNS, and DynamoDB. It's richer in features and easier to use than some of the standard AWS features. It's worth considering for its recommendations and daily notifications.

AWS also has a service called Trusted Advisor that suggests improvements to performance, fault tolerance, security, and cost optimization. Unfortunately, the free version of Trusted Advisor is limited, so if you want to explore all of the features and recommendations it has to offer, you must upgrade to a paid monthly plan or access it through an AWS enterprise account.

Cost Explorer (figure B.6) is a useful, albeit high-level reporting and analytics tool built into AWS. You must activate it first by clicking your name (or the IAM username) in the top-right corner of the AWS console, selecting My Billing Dashboard, then clicking Cost Explorer from the navigation pane and enabling it. Cost Explorer analyzes your costs for the current month and the past four months. It then creates a forecast for the next three months. Initially, you may not see any information because it takes 24 hours for AWS to process data for the current month. Processing data for previous months make take even longer. More information about Cost Explorer is available at http://amzn.to/1KvN0g2.

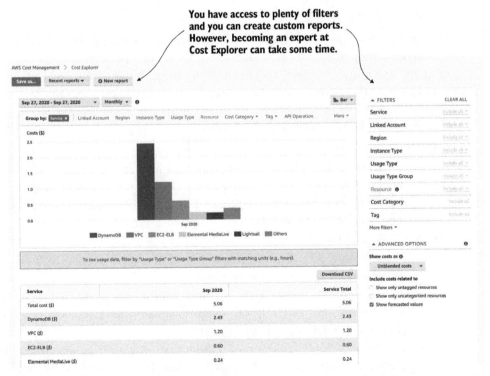

Figure B.6 Cost Explorer allows you to review historical costs and estimate what future costs may be.

B.2.3   *Using the Simple Monthly Calculator*

The AWS Pricing Calculator (https://calculator.aws) is a web application developed by Amazon to help model costs for many of its services. This tool allows you to select a service, enter information related to the consumption of that particular resource, and get an indicative cost.

B.2.4   *Calculating Lambda and API Gateway costs*

The cost of running serverless architecture often can be a lot less than running traditional infrastructure. Naturally, the cost of each service you might use will be different, but you can look at what it takes to run a serverless system with Lambda and the API Gateway.

Amazon's pricing for Lambda (https://aws.amazon.com/lambda/pricing/) is based on the number of requests, duration of execution, and the amount of memory allocated to the function. The first million requests are free with each subsequent million charged at $0.20. Duration is based on how long the function takes to execute measured to the millisecond (ms). Amazon charges in 1 ms increments, while also factoring in the amount of memory reserved for the function. A function created with 1 GB of memory will cost $0.000001667 per 100 ms of execution time, whereas a function created with 128 MB of memory will cost $0.000000208 per 100 ms.

> **NOTE**   Amazon prices may differ depending on the region and that they're subject to change at any time.

Amazon provides a perpetual free tier with 1M free requests and 400,000 GB-seconds of compute time per month. This means that a user can perform a million requests and spend an equivalent of 400,000 seconds running a function created with 1 GB of memory before they have to pay. As an example, consider a scenario where you have to run a 256 MB function, 5 million times a month. The function executes for 2 seconds each time. The cost calculation follows:

- Monthly request charge:
  - The free tier provides 1 million requests, which means that there are only 4 million billable requests (5M requests − 1M free requests = 4M requests).
  - Each million is priced at $0.20, which makes the request charge $0.80 (4M requests × $0.2/M = $0.80).
- Monthly compute charge:
  - The compute price for a function per GB-second is $0.00001667. The free tier provides 400,000 GB-seconds free.
  - In the compute price scenario, the function runs for 10 ms (5M × 2s).
  - 10M seconds at 256 MB of memory equates to 2,500,000 GB-seconds (10,000,000 × 256 MB / 1024 = 2,500,000).
  - The total billable amount of GB-seconds for the month is 2,100,000 (2,500,000 GB-seconds − 400,000 free tier GB-seconds = 2,100,000). The

compute charge is therefore $35.007 (2,100,000 GB-seconds $\times$ $0.00001667 = $35.007).

– The total cost of running Lambda in this example is $35.807.

The API Gateway pricing is based on the number of API calls received and the amount of data transferred out of AWS. In the eastern United States, Amazon charges $3.50 for each million API calls received and $0.09/GB for the first 10 TB transferred out. Given the previous example and assuming that monthly outbound data transfer is 100 GB a month, the API Gateway pricing is as follows:

- Monthly API charge:
  - The free tier includes 1M API calls per month but is valid for only 12 months. Given that it's not a perpetual free tier, it won't be included in this calculation.
  - The total API cost is $17.50 (5M requests $\times$ $3.50/M = $17.50).
- The monthly data charge is $9.00 (100 GB $\times$ $0.09/GB = $9).
- The API Gateway cost in this example is $26.50.
- The total cost of Lambda and the API Gateway is $62.307 per month.

It's worthwhile to attempt to model how many requests and operations you may have to handle on an ongoing basis. If you expect 2M invocations of a Lambda function that uses only 128 MB of memory and runs for 1 second, you'll pay approximately $0.20 month. If you expect 2M invocations of a function with 512 MB of RAM that runs for 5 seconds, you'll pay a little more than $75.00. With Lambda, you have an opportunity to assess costs, plan ahead, and pay for only what you actually use. Finally, don't forget to factor in other services such as S3 or SNS, no matter how insignificant their cost may seem to be.

appendix C
Deployment frameworks

Automation and continuous delivery are important if you're building anything on a cloud platform such as AWS. If you take a serverless approach, it becomes even more critical because you end up having more services, more functions, and more things to configure. You need to be able to script your entire application, run tests, and deploy it automatically. The only time you should deploy Lambda functions manually or self-configure API Gateway is while you learn. Once you begin working on real serverless applications, you need to have a repeatable, automated, and robust way of provisioning your system. Apart from Terraform, the other frameworks discussed in this appendix do not provision resources on their own. Instead, they rely on AWS CloudFormation (https://aws.amazon.com/cloudformation/) to provision resources and are therefore bound by CloudFormation's limitations. These include the following:

- A CloudFormation template can have no more than 500 resources. To go beyond this limit, you can use nested CloudFormation stacks.
- A CloudFormation template can have no more than 200 parameters or outputs.
- It's cumbersome to add existing resources to a CloudFormation stack.

Although Terraform alleviates these limitations, it has shortcomings of its own. The most notable of which is the lack of support for rollback. If there was a problem during a deployment, then your application can end up in a broken state if some resources are updated but others are not.

Some of the frameworks discussed in this appendix also provide additional utilities, such as the ability to invoke Lambda functions locally or even simulate API Gateway locally. With that said, let's go through some of the most popular deployment frameworks for serverless applications.

C.1   *Serverless Framework*

The Serverless Framework (https://serverless.com) is an open source framework and is easily one of the most popular and mature deployment frameworks out there. At its essence, it allows users to define an entire serverless application (including Lambda functions, API Gateway APIs, SNS topics, and any other CloudFormation resources) and then deploy it using a command-line interface (CLI). It helps you organize and structure serverless applications, which is of great benefit as you begin to build larger systems, and it's fully extensible via its plugin system.

C.1.1   *Getting started*

The Serverless Framework supports both JSON and YAML. It also lets you describe your application in a manifest file like that shown in the following listing.

> **Listing C.1   Describing a service in serverless.yml**

The name of the service. This would appear as part of the name for the generated CloudFormation stack as well as any provisioned API Gateway APIs and Lambda functions.

```
service: user-service

provider:              ◄──         Top level configuration for the project:
  name: aws                        the language runtime for the Lambda
  runtime: nodejs12.x              functions, the region, and the name of
  region: us-east-1                the deployment stage.
  stage: dev

functions:      ◄──── Your functions
  usersCreate:
    events:          ◄──           The events that trigger
      - http:                      these functions
          path: users/create
          method: post

  usersDelete:
    events:
      - http:
          path: users/delete
          method: delete
                                   The resource your functions use. Raw
                                   AWS CloudFormation syntax goes here.
resource:       ◄────
  Resources:
    UserTable:
      Type: AWS::DynamoDB::Table
      Properties:
        BillingMode: PAY_PER_REQUEST
        KeySchema:
          ...
```

To deploy the application, you only have to run a single command:

```
serverless deploy
```

The Serverless Framework packages your code, uploads it to S3, and provisions the resources specified in the serverless.yml through CloudFormation. You can also override the default region and stage name with CLI options as the following shows (http://mng.bz/AOJz):

```
serverless deploy -s prod -r eu-west-1
```

C.1.2   Language support

The Serverless Framework supports a number of language runtimes: Node.js, Python, Java, Golang, C#, and Scala to name a few. You have a lot of control over how the Serverless Framework packages your functions. By default, it uses the same packaged artifact for all the functions you have configured in the serverless.yml. But you can optionally package each function separately and include or exclude specific folders or files.

Through the `serverless-webpack` plugin (https://bit.ly/sls-webpack), you can also incorporate webpack into the packaging process to tree shake and bundle Java-Script functions. Doing so can produce much smaller artifacts, which helps with both deployment time as well as cold-start performance.

For Python functions, it can be challenging to include third-party libraries into the deployment artifact. The `serverless-python-requirements` plugin (http://bit.ly/sls-python-reqs) handles this for you transparently and lets you use your existing requirements.txt file.

C.1.3   Invoking functions locally

Besides packaging and deploying serverless applications, the Serverless Framework also has a number of useful utilities. The most notable is the ability to invoke functions locally using the `invoke local` command:

```
serverless invoke local -f functionName -d "{}"
```

The `invoke local` command is useful for quickly testing a function locally. It gives you fast feedback without having to deploy the function to AWS first. You can also attach a debugger and step through the code line by line (for more information, see this post http://bit.ly/sls-debug-vscode for how to do it with VS Code).

But what if you want to emulate API Gateway locally? The `serverless-offline` plugin (http://bit.ly/sls-offline) lets you do exactly that and emulates API Gateway on a localhost post. We find this useful when doing server-side rendering with Lambda. Although we can use `invoke local` to test a function locally and inspect its output, we can't render HTML in our heads! Having a local endpoint lets us point a browser to it and inspect the server-side rendered HTML in all its CSS glory.

C.1.4   Plugins

The Serverless Framework has a rich ecosystem of plugins that extend its capability far and beyond what the framework is capable of out-of-the-box. Some plugins modify the CloudFormation template the Serverless Framework generates. For example, whereas the Serverless Framework generates a shared identity and access management (IAM) role for all the functions in a project, the popular `serverless-iam-roles-per-function` plugin lets you configure IAM roles for each function.

Some plugins add support for services that the Serverless Framework does not support natively. For example, the Serverless Framework does not support AppSync out of the box. You can still configure an AppSync API in the serverless.yml using raw CloudFormation syntax (in the resources section of the serverless.yml), but this is tedious and laborious. The `serverless-appsync-plugin` plugin extends the Serverless Framework to support AppSync and lets you configure AppSync APIs with a much more succinct syntax. Similarly, the `serverless-step-functions` plugin adds support for Step Functions.

Some plugins can add additional commands to the Serverless Framework's CLI. For example, the `serverless-offline` plugin adds an `offline` command that starts a local instance of API Gateway. Similarly, the `serverless-export-env` plugin adds an `export-env` command that captures the environment variables referenced by the Lambda functions and exports them to a .env file.

The Serverless Framework has a flexible plugin architecture and lets you customize just about everything the framework does. This flexibility allows you to disagree with framework defaults and tailor its behavior to suit your needs. Its rich ecosystem of available plugins is also what sets it apart from AWS SAM.

C.2   Serverless Application Model (SAM)

The Serverless Application Model (https://aws.amazon.com/serverless/sam) (SAM), is AWS's answer to the Serverless Framework and shares many similarities with the Serverless Framework. Like the Serverless Framework, SAM uses CloudFormation to provision resources and lets you use a simpler (compared with CloudFormation) syntax to define serverless applications in terms of Lambda functions, API Gateway, and so on. It also has a number of CLI commands that let you invoke Lambda functions locally or start a local instance of API Gateway too. The biggest difference between SAM and the Serverless Framework is that SAM's syntax is much closer to the raw CloudFormation syntax, and it doesn't have a plugin system.

The former is often held as a reason why one should favor SAM over the Serverless Framework, but it's a question of personal preference. Ultimately, the CloudFormation syntax is verbose, and that's one reason why we prefer to use these frameworks that offer a simpler syntax and more productive abstraction level to work with. So why should one favor a framework because its syntax is closer to the thing that you try to get away from? It doesn't make sense.

The lack of a plugin system, on the other hand, is often a deal breaker. It means you're limited by what the framework supports and have no easy way to override the framework defaults (unless the framework makes it a configurable option, of course). For example, although SAM added support for Step Functions in May 2020 (which is more than three years after the `serverless-step-functions` plugin did the same for the Serverless Framework), it still has no support for AppSync at the time of writing (April 2021).

And while the Serverless Framework's plugin system offers an escape hatch for when you need to disagree with the framework's defaults, the lack of a plugin system restricts you to what the framework allows you to configure with SAM. In order to disagree with the choices that SAM makes for you, you'd have to work around it with CloudFormation macros and use those macros to modify the SAM-generated CloudFormation template at deployment time. If this sounds like a tedious solution, it's because it is as we learned the hard way two years ago (http://mng.bz/ZxJP).

Having said that, SAM does certain things very well. For example, it lets you define IAM roles for individual functions out of the box. And the way it provisions API Gateway resources is also more efficient (compared with the Serverless Framework) in terms of the number of CloudFormation resources. Whereas the Serverless Framework would provision the API resources and methods as individual resources, SAM encodes all of them in the `Body` attribute of the `AWS::ApiGateway::RestApi` resource. This approach minimizes the number of resources in the CloudFormation stack and helps mitigate the risk of hitting the 500 resource limit in a CloudFormation stack. This comes in handy in large API projects. With the Serverless Framework, these large projects often have to rely on plugins such as the `serverless-plugin-split-stacks` plugin to work around the 500 resources limit.

C.3   *Terraform*

Terraform (https://www.terraform.io) is a popular infrastructure-as-code (IaC) tool by HashiCorp. It is by far the least opinionated framework in this appendix. True to its motto of "Write, Plan, and Create Infrastructure as Code," Terraform has long been favored by infrastructure engineers and is not designed with Lambda as its focus. Instead, it treats Lambda functions as AWS resources: nothing more, nothing less. As such, you have the utmost control and can configure Lambda, API Gateway, and any other resources however you like. But this exposes you to all the underlying complexities of those resources; complexities that the other tools try hard to manage for you.

For example, you need to understand how API Gateway resources are organized, which we find is one of the most laborious aspects of using Terraform for Lambda. A single line of human-readable URL in the Serverless Framework or SAM can easily translate to 50 lines of Terraform code (figure C.1).

Because Terraform is designed to give you a way to describe and create your infrastructure, it doesn't offer any value-add services for serverless applications. There's no

Serverless framework

```
lookup:
  handler: functions/lookup.handler
  description: handles the lookup/country/zipcode endpiont
  events:
    - http:
        path: lookup/{country}/{zipcode}
        method: get
```

Terraform

```
1   resource "aws_api_gateway_rest_api" "rest_api" {
2     name = "${var.stage}-${var.feature_name}"
3     description = "REST API for zipcode lookup"
4   }
5
6   resource "aws_api_gateway_resource" "lookup" {
7     rest_api_id = "${aws_api_gateway_rest_api.rest_api.id}"
8     parent_id = "${aws_api_gateway_rest_api. rest_api.root_resource_id}"
9     path_part = "Lookup"
10  }
11
12  resource "aws_api_gateway_resource" "country" {
13    rest_api_id = "${aws_api_gateway_rest_api.rest_api.id}"
14    parent_id = "${aws_api_gateway_resource.lookup.id}"
15    path_part = "{country}"
16  }
17
17  resource "aws_api_gateway_resource" "zipcode" {
19    rest_api_id = "${aws_api_gateway_rest_api.rest_api.id}"
20    parent_id = "${aws_api_gateway_resource.country.id}"
21    path_part = "{zipcode}"
22  }
23
24  resource "aws_api_gateway_method" "get_zipcode" {
25    rest_api_id = "${aws_api_gateway_rest_api.rest_api.id}"
26    resource_id = "${aws_api_gateway_resource.zipcode.id}"
27    http_method = "GET"
28    authorization = "NONE"
29  }
30
31  resource "aws_api_gateway_integration" "zipcode_lookup" {
32    rest_api_id = "${aws_api_gateway_rest_api.rest_api.id}"
33    resource_id = "${aws_api_gateway_resource.zipcode.id}"
34    type = "AWS_PROXY"
35
36    http_method = "${aws_api_gateway_method.get_zipcode.http_method}"
37
38    integration_http_method = "POST"
39    uri = "${aws_lambda_function.lookup.invoke_arn}"
40  }
41
42  resource "aws_api_gateway_deployment" "zipcode_api" {
43    depends_on = [
44      "aws_api_gateway_integration.zipcode_lookup"
45    ]
46
47    rest_api_id = "${aws_api_gateway_rest_api.rest_api.id}"
48    stage_name = "${var.stage}"
49  }
```

Figure C.1   Configuring an API Gateway function with the Serverless Framework vs. Terraform

built-in support for packaging your deployment artifact, nor is there any built-in support for running functions locally.

Whereas all the other tools in this list are built on top of CloudFormation, Terraform does its own thing and relies on AWS APIs to create resources. This means Terraform is not bound by CloudFormation limitations such as the aforementioned 500 resources per stack, but it also lacks the capabilities that CloudFormation offers.

For example, Terraform does not automatically rollback changes when a deployment fails halfway. Many HashiCorp fans would tell you that this is a feature, not a bug, but don't let them fool you. You don't want your application to be stuck in a halfway, broken state when a deployment fails.

There are also other problems to consider when using Terraform in serverless applications. For instance, because Terraform uses the AWS APIs to create resources, it often runs into throttling limits that CloudFormation does not. A common example is the `ResourceConflictException` due to the number of concurrent updates to a Lambda function. This can happen when you make certain changes to a Lambda function that requires multiple API calls to achieve. This has been a long-standing problem (see this issue from 2018 at http://mng.bz/RqJK), and the only viable workaround is to daily-chain changes with `depends_on` clauses.

Terraform keeps track of resource states and can persist them to data stores such as S3. However, it does not encrypt these state files, which means any sensitive information such as credentials and API keys are stored in plain text. It's up to you to ensure that the S3 bucket enables server-side encryption (SSE). To be even more secure, use customer-managed keys to ensure that only you can decrypt the data.

Overall, the severe lack of productivity alone makes Terraform a bad choice when it comes to building serverless applications. We strongly recommend against it. However, it's taken a strong hold in the DevOps culture and many infrastructure teams mandate the use of Terraform within their organizations. If you're struggling to convince your manager to let you use something other than Terraform in your serverless project, then consider doing the following:

- *Show them the difference in lines of code that you need to write for something as simple as a single API endpoint.* Translate this into development time and cost. For example, "It'll take a week to do with Terraform versus a couple of hours with Serverless Framework or SAM" is a convincing argument.
- *Explain to the infrastructure team (they might be incorrectly labeled the DevOps team in your organization) that there is an integration path between Terraform and the Serverless Framework or SAM.* They can still use Terraform to provision shared infrastructure resources such as VPCs; they just need to share the ARNs or names of these resources as SSM parameters. Both the Serverless Framework and SAM can reference these parameters. This way, both the infrastructure and feature teams can use the right tool for the job and everyone's happy.

C.4 *Cloud Development Kit*

The AWS Cloud Development Kit (CDK), available at https://aws.amazon.com/cdk, is a relatively new kid on the block but has received a lot of interest from the community. CDK differs from the aforementioned frameworks in that it does not use a markup language. Instead, CDK lets you describe the resources you want to provision using a general-purpose programming language such as TypeScript or Python.

It's easy to see the appeal of using a general-purpose programming language in an IaC tool. Developers can use their favorite programming language to write their application as well as how it should be deployed. There's no need to learn another language such as YAML or HCL (the JSON-based configuration language that Terraform uses). This doesn't necessarily mean that CDK is a better IaC tool because it gives developers what they want. After all, no matter how much we like eating cakes and candies, it doesn't change the fact that these sugary delights are bad for our health.

For anyone who proclaims that YAML or HCL is not code, just remember that not long ago, Java and .Net developers said the same thing about JavaScript and Python. This kind of gatekeeping and putting others down to raise one's standing happens in lots of places and have no place in our community. *Configuration files are code.* A CloudFormation template is a set of instructions to tell CloudFormation what resources to provision and that is the dictionary definitions of *code.* Now that we got the common misconceptions out of the way, let's talk about where CDK really shines and the challenges it faces.

C.4.1 *Where CDK shines*

General-purpose programming languages give you much more expressive power compared with configuration files like YAML. This makes CDK a fantastic choice when it comes to templating some complex AWS environments. CloudFormation offers a range of templating options with its intrinsic functions and conditionals, but these are limited and often require complex YAML code to achieve basic branching logic or mapping input values against a dictionary. CDK makes these child's play and can easily express them in a few lines of code in TypeScript or Python.

Being able to use general-purpose programming languages like TypeScript and Python also means having access to the package managers for those languages. This means you can take common architectural patterns and create reusable constructs and share them as packages. The CDK Patterns (https://cdkpatterns.com) project is a great example of this. Instead of everyone taking the same recipe and implementing these common patterns from scratch, you can download the relevant package from NPM and simply customize it. This is a great way to perpetuate and spread best practices within a large organization. It makes it easy for teams to discover and share constructs that have those best practices and organizational norms baked in.

C.4.2   *CDK challenges*

Single-page application (SPA) frameworks such as React and Vue.js have made a successful attempt at unifying HTML, CSS, and your application code into a cohesive and productive JavaScript framework. CDK is doing something similar for infrastructure code.

However, whereas JavaScript is ubiquitous in the frontend world, the choice and preference for programming languages for backend applications are fractured and contextualized around use case. One of the benefits of microservices is to allow teams to choose the best language for the job. For example, Node.js might be great for building REST APIs, but Python is better suited for machine learning (ML) workloads because most of the libraries are written in Python. The fact that different teams in the organization would prefer to use a different language can present a problem for CDK.

If everyone agrees on using one programming language, then CDK makes it easy to share reusable constructs. But if teams want to use different languages, then you have to maintain different versions of these constructs. You can even see this problem manifest in the patterns on https://cdkpatterns.com, where some patterns support TypeScript, Python, Java, and C#, but most don't support all four languages.

Our other concern about CDK is that, whereas everyone must write the same YAML if they want to provision resources with the same configurations, that's not the case with a general-purpose programming language. Personal preferences and idioms can come into play and suddenly it requires more cognitive energy to understand the infrastructure code. It's no longer configuration—the infrastructure code now contains business logic.

This is especially problematic for those infrastructure teams that need to oversee an organization's AWS environment and provide guidance and oversight for feature teams. Suddenly, they must work with infrastructure code that's written in multiple languages that they might not be familiar with. And because this infrastructure code can contain ample business logic, it makes it doubly hard for infrastructure teams to do their job. This is why we still prefer the declarative approach of YAML and think the fact that it's difficult to add complex logic into infrastructure code is actually a blessing.

C.5   *Amplify*

AWS Amplify (https://aws.amazon.com/amplify) is a set of tools and services that can be used together to build frontend web and mobile applications quickly. It consists of the following:

- *Amplify CLI*—A CLI tool that lets you configure AWS resources.
- *Amplify libraries*—A set of open source libraries that helps you consume AWS resources such as Cognito and AppSync.
- *Amplify UI components*—A collection of drop-in UI components that works with AWS resources to provide authentication, storage, and interactions.

- *Amplify console*—An AWS service that builds and hosts your single-page application (think AWS's version of Netlify: https://www.netlify.com).
- *Amplify Admin UI*—A visual UI that lets you provision and configure AWS resources as well as manage the data in your application.

You can use each of these Amplify tools independently. For example, many teams would use the Amplify libraries and UI components without using the Amplify CLI or Admin UI to manage AWS resources. For this comparison, we'll consider only the Amplify CLI.

Whereas the other frameworks we have discussed so far take a resource centric view of serverless applications, the Amplify CLI takes a utility-centric approach. Instead of configuring a Cognito User Pool as a resource, you would run the command `amplify add auth`. The Amplify CLI would then prompt you with a few questions about what you want to do. This would bootstrap a CloudFormation template and configure a Cognito User Pool and maybe a Cognito Identity Pool too, depending on how you answer the questions from the CLI.

Similarly, you can use a single command to bootstrap a brand-new AppSync API: `amplify add api`. You can then focus on defining the model of your API, and the Amplify CLI can generate a lot of the underlying AWS resources for you, including the relevant AppSync resolvers and even the DynamoDB tables.

As you can see, the Amplify CLI can make a lot of decisions for you and get things wired up quickly. As such, it's targeted at a slightly different demographic of developers. The other deployment frameworks in this list are typically used by backend teams who work with AWS daily. Amplify on the other hand, targets frontend–focused teams who are not as well versed with AWS and just want something that works.

It's a powerful tool and gives a lot of power to these frontend–focused teams to build something quickly, without having to spend many hours learning about each of the AWS services they need to use and configure. But there also lies the pitfall, that teams are not aware of and do not understand the decisions that Amplify CLI makes for them and are not able to debug problems when they arise. For example, the Amplify CLI defaults to using DynamoDB scans for list operations in a GraphQL schema. Although this works, it's not an optimal solution and can become problematic as the system scales because DynamoDB scans are expensive and should be used sparingly.

Amplify CLI automates a lot of things, and that's what makes it a productive tool. But it also limits your ability to customize how those AWS resources are configured. When you reach the limit of what you can achieve with Amplify CLI, there's currently no escape hatch to move away from it. Many teams have had to rewrite their entire application from scratch when they reached this point, which can be a struggle because many teams don't understand what Amplify CLI has done for them and have a hard time replicating the setup because they know only how to do things with Amplify.

In our opinion, the ideal users for tools like Amplify CLI are developers who understand AWS well and have experience working with and configuring those underlying resources. You shouldn't automate things that you don't understand, which puts you in a dangerous position of being over reliant on the tool and lets the tail wag the dog.

The Amplify team is working hard to address the problems that we have brought up here and are looking into building escape hatches so teams can transition away from it when they need to. And we are excited to see where it goes, but for the time being, we think Amplify CLI should be confined to building proof of concepts or very simple applications. For production applications that need to be maintained and iterated over time, the risk of running into blockers and not being able to easily transition away from it is too great. However, it shouldn't stop you from using other Amplify components such as the Amplify libraries in your frontend project or the Amplify console to build and host your SPA.

In this appendix, we looked at five of the most popular ways people are provisioning and deploying their serverless applications. We looked at the Serverless Framework and SAM, which provide a layer of abstraction over CloudFormation to make it easier to build serverless applications. Both support a set of value-add CLI commands, such as being able to invoke functions locally or run a local instance of API Gateway, that aid you in your development workflow.

The main difference between the two is that the Serverless Framework has a flexible plugin system and a rich ecosystem of existing plugins that can extend the framework's capabilities. Whereas with SAM, you're limited by what it supports, and there is also no easy way to change the framework's default behavior beyond the available configurations.

We also looked at Terraform, which is a popular IaC tool and used by many infrastructure teams. We explained the problems with using Terraform in serverless applications and why we strongly recommend against it. It's an unproductive tool when it comes to building serverless applications.

Both CDK and Amplify CLI are relative newcomers in this space, and both have gained a lot of momentum and are attracting many admirers. Whereas the Serverless Framework, SAM, and Terraform all use a markup language to describe the resources for your serverless application, CDK and Amplify CLI take different approaches.

CDK lets you use general-purpose programming languages to describe the resources you want to provision. It's a double-edged sword, which offers the full flexibility that a general-purpose programming language offers as well as the package management system that comes with that language. It lets developers use their favorite programming language for both their application code as well as their infrastructure code and can easily share reusable patterns as packages. However, it can also be problematic in organizations where teams use different programming languages in their application code. This limits the ability to share CDK constructs because the creators of these constructs have to support multiple languages. Letting developers add business logic to their infrastructure code opens the door for extensive customization for complex AWS environments, but it also makes infrastructure code harder to comprehend and govern by infrastructure teams.

Finally, with Amplify CLI, you're not configuring AWS resources so much as saying what capabilities you need in your application. Amplify CLI makes the magic happen and configures the necessary AWS resources with sensible defaults based on your input. It's a super-productive tool and can help you build a fully working application in no time. But it's also a black box and has no escape hatch that lets you transition away from it when you reach the limit of what it can do. This puts you in a precarious position, where you face the real possibility of having to rebuild the application from the ground up if you ever hit a snag with Amplify CLI.

Each of these tools has its strengths, but none is perfect. A good principle that will stand you in good stead, regardless of what tool you decide to use, is to understand how the AWS services you need to work with operate and how the deployment mechanism works before you try to automate it. Blindly automating what you don't understand is dangerous. But once you understand the underlying machineries, then you should look for tools that allow you to move up the abstraction levels and be more productive.

index

RELATED MANNING TITLES

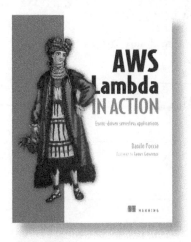

AWS Lambda in Action
by Danilo Poccia
Foreword by James Governor

ISBN 9781617293719
384 pages, $49.99
November 2016

AWS Security
by Dylan Shields

ISBN 9781617297335
425 pages (estimated), $49.99
Summer 2022 (estimated)

MLOps Engineering at Scale
by Carl Osipov

ISBN 9781617297762
344 pages, $49.99
February 2022

For ordering information go to www.manning.com